PAUL VERLAINE was born in Metz, eastern France, in 1844, the only son of an army captain; his mother came from a well-to-do family. In 1851 they moved to Paris, where Verlaine received a formal education. His father died in 1865. At first Verlaine was destined for a career as a civil servant, but his literary talents and ambitions brought him into the artistic milieux of Paris. His first poems were published in his early twenties. In 1870 he married the very young Mathilde Mauté. But Verlaine's erratic and drunken behaviour was unacceptable to her respectable family. Matters became worse when, in 1871, Verlaine invited to his in-laws' home the precocious and ill-behaved 16-year-old Rimbaud. Soon the two poets left to roam France, Belgium, and England together. Their scandalous liaison spelled the ruin of Verlaine's marriage. In 1873 he shot and wounded Rimbaud, for which he served eighteen months in prison. By then he already had four collections of poetry to his name: *Poèmes saturniens* (1866), *Fêtes galantes* (1869), *La Bonne Chanson* (1870), and *Romances sans paroles* (1874). For a while, intermittently buttressed by religious faith, he held his life together with brief spells of farming and teaching. The collection *Sagesse* appeared in 1880. But after the death of his over-indulgent mother in 1886, Verlaine's life drifted into disease and destitution. Nevertheless, he continued to write and publish substantial amounts of poetry. *Jadis et Naguère* (1884), *Amour* (1888), *Parallèlement* (1889), *Dédicaces* (1890), *Bonheur* (1891), *Chansons pour Elle* (1891), *Liturgies intimes* (1892), *Odes en son honneur* (1893), *Dans les limbes* (1894), *Épigrammes* (1894). *Chair* and *Invectives* were published posthumously. Verlaine also wrote a number of prose works, including criticism and an autobiography. He was elected Prince of Poets in 1894. Destitute, he died in Paris in 1896.

MARTIN SORRELL is Reader in French and Translation Studies at the University of Exeter. His monograph *Francis Ponge* was published by Twayne in 1980; his bilingual anthology *Modern French Poetry* by Forest Books in 1992; *Elles: A Bilingual Anthology of Modern French Poetry by Women* by University of Exeter Press in 1995. Many other translations of French poetry have appeared in various journals. In addition, Sorrell has translated plays for the stage and radio. Two original plays and three stories have been broadcast on BBC Radio.

OXFORD WORLD'S CLASSICS

*For over 100 years Oxford World's Classics have brought
readers closer to the world's great literature. Now with over 700
titles—from the 4,000-year-old myths of Mesopotamia to the
twentieth century's greatest novels—the series makes available
lesser-known as well as celebrated writing.*

*The pocket-sized hardbacks of the early years contained
introductions by Virginia Woolf, T. S. Eliot, Graham Greene,
and other literary figures which enriched the experience of reading.
Today the series is recognized for its fine scholarship and
reliability in texts that span world literature, drama and poetry,
religion, philosophy and politics. Each edition includes perceptive
commentary and essential background information to meet the
changing needs of readers.*

OXFORD WORLD'S CLASSICS

====

PAUL VERLAINE

Selected Poems

====

Translated with an Introduction and Notes by
MARTIN SORRELL

OXFORD
UNIVERSITY PRESS

OXFORD

UNIVERSITY PRESS

Great Clarendon Street, Oxford OX2 6DP

Oxford University Press is a department of the University of Oxford.
It furthers the University's objective of excellence in research, scholarship,
and education by publishing worldwide in

Oxford New York

Athens Auckland Bangkok Bogotá Buenos Aires Calcutta
Cape Town Chennai Dar es Salaam Delhi Florence Hong Kong Istanbul
Karachi Kuala Lumpur Madrid Melbourne Mexico City Mumbai
Nairobi Paris São Paulo Singapore Taipei Tokyo Toronto Warsaw

with associated companies in Berlin Ibadan

Oxford is a registered trade mark of Oxford University Press
in the UK and in certain other countries

Published in the United States
by Oxford University Press Inc., New York

British Library Cataloguing in Publication Data

Data available

Library of Congress Cataloging in Publication Data

Data available

ISBN 978-0-19-955401-0

12

Typeset by RefineCatch Limited, Bungay, Suffolk
Printed in Great Britain by
Clays Ltd, Elcograf S.p.A.

For Robert Niklaus

CONTENTS

From *La Bonne Chanson* (1870)

From *Romances sans paroles* (1874)

From *Sagesse* (1880)

From *Jadis et Naguère* (1884)

From *Amour* (1888)

From *Parallèlement* (1889)

From *Dédicaces* (1890)

From *Bonheur* (1891)

From *Chansons pour Elle* (1891)

From *Liturgies intimes* (1892)

From *Odes en son honneur* (1893)

From *Le Livre posthume* (1893)

From *Dans les limbes* (1894)

From *Épigrammes* (1894)

From *Chair* (1896)

From *Invectives* (1896)

From *Biblio-Sonnets* (1913)

From *Poèmes divers*

INTRODUCTION

Verlaine's Life and Career

As a man and as a poet, Verlaine spent his life facing in two directions at once, unable to choose one at the expense of the other. The emotional man who yearned for peaceful family life was also the drunken assailant of his mother and his wife; the humble believer in God was also a foul-mouthed blasphemer; the poet with the most delicate touch imaginable was also the author of the most aggressively pornographic verse. In fact, in an implied recognition of the watermark duality imprinted in him, Verlaine entitled one of his later collections *Parallèlement*, and the image of parallel lines is as appropriate as any to sum up both the poetry and the person.

Whether with regard to his personal life or to his poetic voice, Verlaine found himself in a constant succession of self-imposed crises of irresolution that, viewed a century or so later, appear to form a seamless continuity. However, whereas his inability to be decisive had disastrous consequences for his life and the lives of others, he made of indecision (or imprecision, or vagueness, terms favoured by many of Verlaine's commentators) a significant poetic virtue, so much so that it has become the quality most readily associated with the best of his prolific and diverse work. A deliberate imprecision is at the heart of such of his poetic techniques as are innovative. There is a close connection between Verlaine's techniques and the aesthetics of music and painting; this connection will be discussed later.

In terms of literary as well as of personal history, Verlaine stood at a crossroads. Born in 1844, while Romanticism was still dominant, he was 13 years old when Baudelaire's epoch-making *Flowers of Evil* was published (1857), heralding a decisive shift away from the Romantic movement, and indeed, the birth of the modern literary age. The adolescent Verlaine, reading widely, and already writing verse (which later he categorized as of 'the obscene-macabre genre'), fell for a while under the spell of the semi-demonic Baudelaire, whose dark masterpiece influenced the handful of his late-teens poems as much as did certain of the principal figures of the

Romantic movement, notably Victor Hugo, Théophile Gautier, and Marceline Desbordes-Valmore.

However, his first publication of significance seemed to suggest that, by his early twenties, when he was frequenting certain Parisian literary salons, Verlaine was allied not so much to Romanticism or to the modernizing Baudelaire as to a quite different literary movement. In 1866 there appeared a publication of some significance. *Le Parnasse contemporain*, an anthology of contemporary poems, which was followed by two further issues under the same title, contained seven poems by Verlaine, and thus constituted his first important publication. The Parnassian movement sought to counter Romanticism's cult of inspiration and subjectivity with an altogether more science-based aesthetic of dispassion and objectivity.[1] Yet Verlaine's contributions to *Le Parnasse contemporain* revealed a poet whose approach was altogether too personal and emotional to be truly Parnassian. And, if his first collection proper, *Poèmes saturniens*, also of 1866, showed some traces of Baudelaire, of Romanticism, and of Parnassianism, there were equally firm indications that he would not be long in finding his poetic individuality. Much of what would soon become recognized as uniquely Verlainian was evident in *Poèmes saturniens*: sensuality, a disposition to melancholy and to daydreaming, misty half-tones, and patterns of versification straining to break the stricter rules of French prosody.

If the distinctively Verlainian tones could already be seen and heard in *Poèmes saturniens*, this was nevertheless an untidy volume, a collection of disparate poems which did not seem to blend completely happily with one another. The contrast, therefore, with Verlaine's next book, *Fêtes galantes* (1869), was a marked one, for this volume was clearly held together by strong thematic ties. Figures taken from Italian *commedia dell'arte* flit in and out of pastoral scenes reminiscent of the paintings of Watteau, a century or so before. But Verlaine was not only reflecting a contemporary interest in eighteenth-century art; *Fêtes galantes* is more personal than that. There is a chilly feeling that all is not lightness and insouciance among the revellers in the graceful parklands. It is as if anxious dawn

---

[1] The Parnassian ideal dominated French poetry around the middle years of the 19th century. Leconte de Lisle was recognized as its leader. The movement yielded three influential volumes of verse, *Le Parnasse contemporain* (1866, 1871, and 1876), to which Verlaine and other emerging poets contributed.

must follow drunken night, and happiness were a house of cards built on foundations of melancholy.

Fêtes galantes appeared at the time when Verlaine's contradictory impulses, both personal and poetic, were becoming impossible to ignore. While he was preparing the refined poems of *Fêtes galantes*, a quite different collection—of lesbian poems, in fact—was being banned by a court of law; while he was getting drawn into the so-bourgeois Mauté family, and attracted to its young, upright daughter Mathilde, he was also indulging in unbridled orgies of drink and sex, and even violence. On one occasion, he attacked (and not for the last time) his long-suffering and over-indulgent mother. But whenever he went too far in one direction, Verlaine would either repent or rebel, as the circumstances demanded, and then see-saw the other way. So it was that, in 1870, engaged to Mathilde Mauté and in well-behaved mode, he published *La Bonne Chanson*, a paean to the domestic decencies of the married state. This is the most obviously autobiographical of Verlaine's collections. It expresses the hopes he had at that time of disciplining himself through well-ordered family life. The quality of *La Bonne Chanson*, however, does not match the behavioural ideals. The direct expression of fervent regard for a loved one, and of hopes for happiness, are not of themselves powerful poetry, and the collection represents that particular tendency which Verlaine would regularly indulge throughout his writing career, of purveying raw sentiment or religious urgency as if it were finished art.

However, his next volume, *Romances sans paroles* (1874), was as full of art and artistry as *La Bonne Chanson* had been flatly direct. The consensus is that this collection is Verlaine's best. Certainly, it contains exquisitely crafted, often short poems composed of short lines, and which have the effect of the most delicate and evanescent tone poems, haunted by copper skies, suns, mists, and sadnesses. Yet these gems were for the most part written during a period when Verlaine's life was at its most ambivalent, not to say chaotic. His marriage to Mathilde, which took place in August 1870, came under great strain from the very start. The Franco-Prussian War, the Siege of Paris, followed by the bloody weeks of the Paris Commune, all drew in Verlaine, to a lesser or greater extent, and had damaging effects on his employment prospects in a volatile and highly politicized Paris. But something even more momentous was to come, and that was Arthur Rimbaud. When Verlaine invited the extraordinarily precocious and un-house-trained Rimbaud to stay in the Mauté family flat in Paris, he set in train a series of events which would be as disastrous to his personal life as they were productive in his development as a poet. The liaison, at first ambiguous then overtly homosexual, between the two young poets soon resulted in their fleeing the various oppressions of family and of Paris. Their wanderings in Belgium and England, their separations and reunions, the growing impatience of the iron-willed Rimbaud with the vacillations of an ambivalent Verlaine, culminating in the latter's bungled attempt to shoot Rimbaud, are notorious, and have been extensively documented. So, too, have the effects on Verlaine's writing of Rimbaud's rigorous and unremitting search for absolute and objective truth, which led to a poetry incandescent with solar energy,[2] the likes of which had never been seen before in French poetry. Verlaine was as ambitious poetically during his association with Rimbaud as he ever was, although he was to continue producing adventurous and exciting poetry all through his life, albeit more spasmodically. The little volume *Romances sans paroles*, then, is Verlaine at his best. At the same time, though, it should be stressed that its major strengths—those indeterminate northern landscapes which stand as objective correlatives (to borrow T. S. Eliot's celebrated term, whereby aspects of the external, physical world are made symbolically to express the poet's moods and inner states), and a near-minimalism of language combined with echoes of street and popular utterance—are equally evident both in later poems and in certain earlier ones, notably some of the more sophisticated poems of *Poèmes saturniens*.

After *Romances sans paroles*, published when Verlaine was serving out his jail sentence in Belgium for the shooting of Rimbaud, the predictable see-saw effect produced a change both in his personal life and in the poems he next wrote. The Janus-like Verlaine, never able to decide whether he wanted to be bourgeois or bohemian; the bisexual, emotionally bifocused Verlaine, unable voluntarily to relinquish either Mathilde or Rimbaud, now found himself

[2] The solar image is apposite. Where Rimbaud's quest for a kind of cosmic revelation made him worship the sun's power to absorb and take him over, Verlaine's poems dating from the early 1870s reveal almost an equal fascination with the sun, but as a star whose force is shrouded, guarded, veiled, and intangible. In a fascinating way, the two poets' concern with the sun is the two sides of one coin, and can stand emblematically as their quest to make poetry an instrument of knowledge and even of change.

scorned by Rimbaud and on an irreversible path to divorce from Mathilde, despite some unconvincing steps on both sides to rescue the marriage. Alone in his prison cell, he turned to the comforts of religion, as he would do periodically throughout his life, when the need was pressing. If a somewhat saccharine conversion to Catholicism helped ease his long months of confinement, and produced a number of delicate and genuinely touching poems, regrettably it also engendered what the critic Albert-Marie Schmidt has dismissed as the bleating effusions of an anodyne spirituality. What are being described are those poems from prison which Verlaine intended for a collection entitled *Cellulairement*, which never appeared. However, they were retained as the nucleus of *Sagesse*, which was then expanded with more poems of a similar stamp. To be fair to *Sagesse*, there is a body of critical opinion which sees the volume as proof of Verlaine's stature as a great religious poet.

Sagesse appeared in 1880, some five years after Verlaine's release from Mons prison. In the intervening years, the crises of irresolution in his personal life continued unabated. Going to Stuttgart in 1875, to meet Rimbaud for what turned out to be the last time, the recent convert to Catholicism evidently was quickly seduced, as Rimbaud put it with searing brutality, into renouncing his God and causing the ninety-eight wounds of Our Saviour to bleed. If this was one of the lowest points in Verlaine's increasingly desperate life, at least there followed a period of some stability, in England, first alone, then later in the company of Lucien Létinois, the young man whom Verlaine took under his wing when for a brief time he was a teacher in northern France. Even their ill-fated adventure, trying to make a go of running a farm together, had a fresh idealism about it. By the time Létinois died, in 1883, and his personal fortunes dived once more, the desolate Verlaine had enough material for his next volume, *Jadis et Naguère*, published in 1884. Unfortunately, this was an uneven collection, mainly because there were assembled in it not only some of his most recent compositions, but also others which dated back some fifteen years, and which appear to have been pressed into service somewhat opportunistically. One poem in particular has always been singled out, 'The art of poetry'. Written in fact some ten years before, it is often taken—wrongly—as the definitive statement of Verlaine's poetic credo, his way forward from that point, and as a manifesto of sorts for the emergent Symbolist movement, which was getting itself established in the decade of the 1880s. Definitions of Symbolism are notoriously difficult, but, broadly, what was meant in late nineteenth-century France was a movement in the arts away from realist modes and towards idealism, a search for the Absolute. As it was claimed that the Absolute could not be expressed directly, an allusive, symbolic way of reaching the mysteries behind appearance was sought, and, to that end, poetry of suggestion was considered the key instrument to map out the symbolic. Verlaine's poem 'The art of poetry' has at its heart the belief that poetry is all suggestion, and that suggestion is best achieved through musical effects.

For some critics, Verlaine's poetry deteriorated rapidly after *Jadis et Naguère*. For others, it was even earlier. Few have disputed that *Amour* (1888) is disappointing. Yet, in the cycle of twenty-five poems devoted to sad recollections of Létinois, some have a poignancy, a naked grief expressed with enough verbal power to make them work as poetry. Much of *Amour*, though, is an over-sentimental apologia for Catholicism, and falls into the old trap of *Sagesse*, that strong sentiment does not of itself make art. On the other hand, *Parallèlement* (1889), too easily dismissed by the critical consensus, celebrates what Verlaine knows best and captures best in verse, the honest joys of physical pleasure. However morally troublesome or downright shocking the types of love displayed, the vibrant note of authenticity which Verlaine conveys is what breathes life into much, though certainly not all, of *Parallèlement*.

A similar claim could be made for at least some of the patchy and hastily turned-out volumes which followed, and which mark the final abject years of Verlaine's life. By the early 1890s, with his devoted and regularly abused mother dead, his ex-wife and his son seemingly estranged for good, his modest fortune recklessly squandered or given away, his health failing fast, his squalid life divided between certain shady ladies and a variety of charitable Parisian hospitals, Verlaine was still able to write and get his work published. The quality of his output was as unreliable as ever it had been, but it is unfair to dismiss out of hand everything from his final period. *Bonheur* (1891) overall is weak, but parts of *Chansons pour Elle* (1891 also) and *Odes en son honneur* (1893) have an acerbic wit about them, a knowing, wry tone which is also present in *Liturgies intimes* (1892), as well as *Dans les limbes* and *Épigrammes* (both of 1894). The posthumous *Chair* and *Invectives*, too, have an acid sharpness, even if, as a whole, these volumes are relatively lightweight. It would be foolish to make too extravagant claims for each and every one of the collections after *Parallèlement*, but the consensus that there is a 'good' first phase in Verlaine's poetic life, and a 'bad' second, is altogether too peremptory.[3] The position is more subtle. Clearly, the sheer number of poems Verlaine produced suggests that quality control was not his strongest suit; and, undoubtedly, a considerable amount of what was published should have been sifted out before it reached the printer. But then, Verlaine always had money problems, and writing was the only trade he could ever sustain. His poetic skills never entirely deserted him, and a proportion at least of his final poems repay attention. Certainly, that must have been the opinion of those cognoscenti who invited him, in his final years, to deliver lectures in Holland, Belgium, and England. It must have been the opinion, too, of his peers, who, in 1894, on the death of the Parnassian Leconte de Lisle, elected Verlaine Prince of Poets.

Verlaine's Poetic Form (i) Musicality

The greatness and uniqueness of Verlaine's poetry is often said to inhere in a number of distinctive and fairly precise features. Among them, there are two which particularly repay close attention—music, or musicality; and literary impressionism.

For many readers and critics, Verlaine tends to mean music, or perhaps more precisely, musicality. He was the poet who, more than any other of his time, loosened the conventional metres of French prosody and helped them shed excess weight. Undoubtedly this is the achievement of several early poems, most notably those in *Romances sans paroles*, but many in other collections as well. A note of caution, though; the fact is that short, light, and elusive poems are in a minority. Over-extravagant claims should not be made for Verlaine's innovations. All in all, he was a reasonably cautious technician, capable of remarkable things, but mostly content not to wander too far off the established highways.

Music, then, and musicality. The two should be distinguished one

---

[3] At least one critic, Antoine Adam, has attempted to rehabilitate Verlaine's most readily dismissed collections. The spirited defence he puts up for the religious verse, though, seems largely unconvincing. See Select Bibliography.

from the other, the more so as, in the final decades of the nineteenth century, Symbolism saw in music the supreme art form, to the condition of which, borrowing from one of the most influential English critics of the day, Walter Pater, all art constantly aspired.[4] In poetry, this meant not so much an ambition to sound fluent and melodious as an aspiration to make organized words act non-representationally. That is, the ambition was to detach words as far as possible from the flux of banal and contingent meaning, and to place them instead in collocations far removed from the approximations of daily usage. Thus, poetic language would be as disconnected from the 'real' world as, say, a piano sonata or a string quartet. Crucial in this ambition was the perception that 'pure' music, such as the sonata and quartet, while redolent with meaning about human life, was 'about' nothing other than itself. A sonata's content might be said to be the possibilities of its own form. What Symbolist writers and theoreticians so valued was that music, by virtue of this autonomy and purity, seemed to speak as deeply and perfectly to and about the heart and spirit as was humanly possible. It yielded profound truths about the human condition in the most allusive (symbolic) way, and without the need for mimesis, that is, without having to imitate or represent the world directly. The greatest French exponent of poetry-as-music was undoubtedly Mallarmé. Indeed, his pronouncements on the art of suggestion—the essence of music, surely—as well as his astonishing and often difficult poems can be considered the cornerstone of Symbolism, in whose orbit Verlaine moved.

But another aspect of Symbolism was musicality, as opposed to music. If words finally could not be freed from their day-to-day meanings, as Mallarmé's glorious but doomed enterprise seemed to betoken, at least they could be made to sing. This, of course, is an age-old ambition of poetry. An essential quality of good poetry always has been its capacity to resonate, to sound more musical than prose (or, at least, than most prose). French verse produces melodies quite unlike those of English. Without going into the detailed issues of accent and stress,[5] the French line of poetry conventionally has

[4] Walter Pater, *The Renaissance*, 'The School of Giorgione', ed. Donald Hill (Berkeley and Los Angeles: University of California Press, 1980).

[5] Much has been written on this subject, both in English and French. In English, C. Scott, *French Verse-Art: A Study* (Cambridge: CUP, 1980) and R. Lewis, *On Reading*

been organized by length. That is, the exact number of syllables per line has determined metre, rather than the number of stresses or beats, as generally happens in English metres. Over the centuries, line-lengths of eight, ten, and twelve syllables have prevailed in French prosody. Of these, the twelve-syllable line, the alexandrine, probably has had the most application. And, equally conventionally, certain patterns of end-rhyme have dominated. Crafted by great writers, such seemingly rigid measures have produced the most subtle and varied verse. Deployed by lesser talents, however, the same measures too often have produced leaden-footed results. Until Verlaine, the greatest French poets were technically conservative, even if they allowed themselves a modicum of adventure within formality. The patterns of fixed-syllable lines, weighted with rhyme, continued unbroken. The parisyllabic (even-numbered) line predominated, even in the poetry of such a modernizing spirit as Baudelaire.

What Verlaine did was to challenge the hegemony of established metres, more especially of the longer, parisyllabic line. So, when commentators speak of his music, generally they mean the musicality of lines of five, seven, nine syllables, and sometimes of fewer, sometimes more.

As already mentioned, in 'The art of poetry' of 1874 Verlaine appears to set out his poetic manifesto. This is only an appearance, however, because this poem is in truth less the declaration of a consolidated position or of future intent than a recapitulation of what he had been doing at an earlier stage of his career. In the much-quoted opening lines, Verlaine calls for music above all else, to be produced by the use of imparisyllabic lines. The relationship between musical verse and imparisyllables is a subtle one. As Verlaine amplifies it in the next lines of the poem, an odd number of syllables in a line produces something more vague, more evanescent, lighter, and airier. The point, of course, is that, given that a parisyllabic line can be divided and subdivided into equal fractions, given the French tendency to prescription in matters of language, all too easily the caesura (that lightest of pauses which comes at some point within the line) in the alexandrine tended to fall exactly midway, so that a long

French Verse: A Study of Poetic Form (Oxford: Clarendon Press, 1982) are advanced and absorbing studies. An easier introduction to the subject might be Peter Broome and Graham Chesters, *The Appreciation of Modern French Poetry, 1850–1950*.

poem routinely divided six by six could and did become excessively
monotonous. In 'The art of poetry' Verlaine is saying in so many
words that such regularity has had its day. At least, in imparisyllabic
metres, the caesura will have to fall somewhere off-centre. Note that
'The art of poetry' itself is written entirely in nine-syllable lines, and
that the caesura generally falls after the fourth syllable. Thus:

> De la musiqu/(e) avant toute chose,
> Et pour cela/ préfère l'Impair . . .

The ear attuned to the sounds of French will appreciate the uneven
pattern of this rhythm. It represents a greater departure from the
norm than anglophone readers sometimes think.

When Verlaine uses shorter imparisyllabic metres, the effect is
even more distinctive. In *Sagesse*, a little, untitled poem has the
following opening line (again, which must be given in French):
'L'échelonnement des haies' and the poem continues to use this
seven-syllable length. Then, in *Romances sans paroles*, the poem
whose opening line is 'Dans l'interminable' has lines consistently of
five syllables each. The length, in such a case, is so restricted that it
scarcely allows for a caesura.

The section of *Romances sans paroles* entitled 'Ariettes oubliées'
has been much praised and much anthologized, commentators
commending its dexterous lightness of touch. But, interestingly,
while it contains several imparisyllabic metres, the 'Ariettes' section
has a solid representation of even-numbered ones too, and the poems
written parisyllabically dance every bit as gracefully as the others. It
is justified, therefore, to downplay a little the importance of the
imparisyllabic measure. It is one among several aspects which com-
bine to create that unique Verlainian music. The poem which, argu-
ably, has been more anthologized than any other, 'Autumn song',
from *Poèmes saturniens*, is as fine an example as exists of the poet's
sure touch with fragile metres (p. 24). But one notes that the pre-
dominant line-length is of four syllables, substantially outnumbering
those of three. Much of the musical pleasure of this poem derives
from the off-set pattern of $4 + 4 + 3$, from the carefully controlled
nasal vowels, often rhyming, and from the frequent carry-over of
meaning from one line to the next (so-called *enjambement*). The dif-
ficult achievement in this remarkable little poem, so slight as almost
to evaporate, is to have created the most perfect tension between a

severely restricted form and a content always in expansion. The shape is constantly under threat while wholly maintained.

Overall, what Verlaine did of such lasting value was to unshackle French versification by creating what has come to be known as the 'vers libéré', or liberated verse, thereby setting French poetry on the road towards the 'vers libre', or free verse, a road taken by some of his contemporaries, though most of them lesser poets. Ever since Verlaine, the gates have been wide open for innovation, experiment, and new definitions.

That other crucial building-block of orthodox French prosody, rhyme, also comes in for Verlaine's criticism in 'The art of poetry'. Wrongly used, he claims, rhyme is a flashy and cheap trinket which rings false and hollow. Yet, virtually nowhere does Verlaine himself truly abjure it. Admittedly, he uses assonance from time to time. However, what he is really saying in 'The art of poetry' is that rhyme needs to be not so much abandoned as tamed. And, by and large, his own rhymes have a lightness, and sometimes a freedom bordering on the approximate, and they ring more mellifluously for that.

One final observation regarding musicality in Verlaine. He had an excellent ear for the sounds and strains of popular language, as heard in the streets or in ballads, songs, and refrains. For the critic Jacques Robichez, this was a manifestation of Verlaine's taste for popular-populist ways, part of his constant drift towards 'low life', a drift which put him so often in prisons, hospitals, and slums. For another critic, Gaëtan Picon, rather more positively, Verlaine was masterly in his 'poetization' of the spoken language. Among the best examples of poetry which deploys the popular language of street ballads are 'False impression', 'Another', and 'Reversibilities' (all in *Parallèlement*), to name but three. Note, too, the decidedly casual, spoken syntax Verlaine uses in a line such as the first in 'Landscape': 'Vers Saint-Denis c'est bête et sale la campagne'.

Verlaine's Poetic Form (ii) Literary Impressionism

The second of the two Verlainian features which repay close attention might be called literary impressionism. Verlaine's career, spanning as it did the second half of the nineteenth century, ran simultaneously with the Impressionist movement in painting. The revolutionary work of its great masters—Monet, Pissarro, Manet,

Sisley, Degas, and others, at work roughly between 1860 and 1890—was almost bound to have some effect on a rising poet of the period. In an era of redefinition in all the arts, it was quite predictable that a poet such as Verlaine would respond as much to remarkable developments in painting as to musical techniques.

Many established ideas about painting were under scrutiny, among them, the perennial and thorny issue of 'objectivity', that is, the imitation of what was understood as reality. So, the techniques used to paint 'objectively'—perspective, balance, pattern, shape, the different values attached to tones, the principles of chiaroscuro—all were under examination and were subject to redefinition. So, too, was the important assumption that painting was to be done in the artist's studio, not outdoors, and that, concomitantly, light would be even and flat.

With the advent of Impressionism—generally considered to have started in 1863, when Manet's *Déjeuner sur l'herbe* was exhibited at the Salon des Refusés—different principles were in the ascendancy. Most importantly, perhaps, painters began to emphasize colour for its own sake, so that it appeared more obviously to be the picture's subject-matter than did the objects and shapes it was filling. If the idea of representation, of mimesis, was not lost, certainly it was radically rethought. As changing ideas about the composition of light and of colour evolved, the interest was transferred, in a new phenomenology of painting, from the 'reality' of the external world to the ways in which that world was mediated by light. The 'truth' of things depicted lay in the intercession of light and colour. That most celebrated of techniques elaborated by the Impressionists, pointillism, the breaking-down of an apparently unified colour into its constituent parts, tiny individual points of vibrating light, gave a much greater degree of autonomy to colour, which seemingly became as much the 'subject' of a painting as was a field, a sunset, or a street. The primacy of sensation—the blue of the sea, the yellow of a flower, the black of an article of clothing as, above all else, a blue, a yellow, a black—indicates a refusal to see art as predominantly cerebral and intellectual. And, in the same way that Impressionism moved some distance away from the anecdotal, from narrative, refusing as a consequence the mythological and the allegorical, so Verlaine, in some of his poetry at least, and arguably in the best, turned to subjects and techniques favoured by the Impressionists.

That is, open-air scenes, urban decors, suburban scenarios, railway stations, sunsets, fairgrounds, fountains, town squares... And, more than that, some of his poems puzzled contemporary readers by the strangeness of the sensations presented, the tones and colours used. What Verlaine did in a certain kind of poem was to put on paper a sensation, and in that he was not far from one of Impressionism's aims.

What is meant by sensation? How does poetry of sensation differ from other kinds in its use of language? It is a subtle issue, and has to do with a movement away from predominantly intellectual and rational explanation, representation, and narrative. Instead, words are made to appeal as directly as possible to the reader's senses. Verlaine's poems of sensation tend to reject a story-line; rather, they are more static. Such poems are to be found principally in *Romances sans paroles*. However, there are examples also in the earlier *Poèmes saturniens*, although, in these, experimentation with sensory impression is perhaps less subtle than in the later volume. But in both, Verlaine makes his language abrupt and immediate, bypassing much of the syntactical apparatus of connection and explanation. An excellent example of such immediacy is 'Walcourt', from *Romances sans paroles* (p. 76). It is striking in its enumeration and juxtaposition of nouns; also, in its lack of verbs (verbs generally giving a forward and organizing impetus), and of articles and conjunctions. Sensation is conveyed instead with immediacy and without explanatory links. Things are set out unexplained. The effect is to remove objects from expected contexts, and to bring them directly to our senses without the agency of a rationalizing intellect. Similarly, in 'Right time for lovers' (*Poèmes saturniens*), redness becomes a subject in the first stanza. A landscape is evoked by means of colour, but also by blurred tones ('haze-shrouded', 'mists', 'cloudy'). Perhaps no poet has captured better the vagueness of landscape or the imprecision of associated feelings than has Verlaine.[6] Unlike, for example, Baudelaire, he does not explore metaphysical dimensions in poems of this kind.

So long as Verlaine confines himself to the task of registering a

---

[6] The matter of Verlaine's 'vagueness', seen as a way of apprehending and conveying the world, and which thereby is an organizing principle of his poetry, is discussed in one of the most illuminating pieces on Verlaine, J.-P. Richard's essay 'Fadeur de Verlaine', in his *Poésie et profondeur*. See Select Bibliography.

sensation, of snatching fleeting frissons of feeling, then he is truly remarkable. The extraordinary little eighth poem of the 'Ariettes oubliées' section of *Romances sans paroles*, which starts 'Endless sameness', exemplifies his skill in evoking a scene and a corresponding mood, both of them embedded in mists (p. 74). This is a poem very close to the principles of Impressionism. Its point of departure is a sensation and an emotional state of 'ennui', a word best left untranslated, as English equivalents do not fully capture the spiritual desolation which, from Baudelaire onwards, it has come to connote. The poem's construction is repetitive—the first stanza becomes the last, the second the fourth. The sense is that 'ennui' is a given, which, by its very nature, is immobile. Beyond this, the poem vouchsafes little information. It is made up of the slightest variations on a theme. The immobility is bathed in a diffuse light; the colour quality of the snow is 'uncertain', causing it to be confused with sand. The very verb 'gleams' suggests a light without particular definition. Similarly, the colour of the sky is impossible to determine. And is the moon shining or is it not? The trees have a ghostly, unreal aspect. What Verlaine is doing is to blur contour and to create imprecision by precise means, in a way which corresponds in some measure to Impressionist painting. Time, place, narrative scarcely exist, if at all. By contrast, a certain impression reaches directly to the senses, especially sight. Furthermore, there is a fusion of the exterior world with the poet's inner places. The first two lines give the sensory impression of a bleak plain and the emotional category of 'ennui'. As the poem unfolds, so the plain *becomes* the 'ennui'. To speak of one is to speak of the other. Verlaine does not tell us what causes the 'ennui'; the rationale of cause and effect is not his business. The effects themselves, the sensation, the impression, these are his poetic truths.

In other poems, such as 'The piano kissed ...' (also from *Romances sans paroles*), equally there is a nebulous, diaphanous quality, a delicacy, achieved not only by the means so far discussed, but also perhaps by certain ambiguities of language and grammar which convey the intangible, even fractile aspects of experience, aspects which are not reducible simply to the intellect. The excellent 'Setting suns' (*Poèmes saturniens*), for example, is a model of restraint, of movement within stillness. This undivided poem of sixteen lines unfolds without apparently going anywhere; if divided up into groups of four lines each, it is apparent that they mirror one another, that they present the scene—sunset over a shore—and the emotion—melancholy—face to face, the two reflecting and complementing each other until, finally, through the delicately shifting but unchanging vocabulary, they become one. Here we have an admirable example of Verlaine's great gift for conflating pictorial effects, the world of the senses and the life of the emotions. Language, far removed from the conventions of narrative and intellectual apprehension, is being used in a way virtually unparalleled at the time.

The concept of literary impressionism in Verlaine thus has a real and forceful application. Nevertheless, its use is relatively limited. It could not be claimed with much justice that every poem he wrote is essentially like 'Setting suns' or 'Endless sameness'. But the concept can provide a fuller appreciation of, say, 'Home' (*La Bonne Chanson*) or 'Marine' (*Poèmes saturniens*), or even 'Night effect' (also *Poèmes saturniens*). However, this last poem equally could be seen as under the control of Parnassian ideals, as indicated perhaps by the title of the section from which it is taken: 'Eaux-fortes', or Aqua Fortis. The reference is to the engraver's precise technique, and to black-and-white results. Of course, at the time of the *Poèmes saturniens*, Verlaine was writing to a certain extent, at least, in the Parnassian way; celebrating the ideals of impassivity, as in, for example, the poem 'Savitri', in which he sought to give precise and accurate detail in as dispassionate a fashion as possible. None the less, a distinctly un-Parnassian judder of emotion runs through 'Night effect', bringing it closer than might at first appear to those crowning achievements of Verlaine's impressionist poetry, the 'Ariettes oubliées' and 'Paysages belges' sections of *Romances sans paroles*.

Verlaine's Achievements

How, finally, should we understand and judge Verlaine?

No one will disagree that, at his supreme best, he is the master of the art of suggestion. In his copious work are to be found surely the best examples in French of allusive poetry. Short in length and made up of short lines, some of his greatest poems see the world as diaphanous evanescence (to use vocabulary much favoured by the Symbolist movement). Reality is almost what is not. Verlaine creates vanishing topographies in a way no other French poet can. And, with consummate skill, he links indeterminate place to unfocused mood. The pathetic fallacy, that trick of making nature appear to feel the same way as humans, is superbly woven into the texture of many of his lines. Indeed, often it is a key element in holding together poems which are as translucent and elusive as what Gaëtan Picon, borrowing from Verlaine himself, has called 'the thing in flight'.

Verlaine's sheer endurance in the face of adversities, self-inflicted or not, has to be respected. The English poet Ted Walker has said that, whatever the deficiencies in the results, whatever the setbacks in his circumstances, it is wholly admirable that Verlaine 'kept going'. The remark is particularly pertinent, coming as it does from a fine poet and translator of Verlaine who has suffered the curse every writer dreads—drying up. When Verlaine died, worn out by disease and excess, and looking decades older than his 51 years, he was still writing. Indeed, his very last poem was written a mere matter of weeks before his death. So prolific was he that, although most of his work, both poetry and prose, was published in his life-time, a considerable quantity of uncollected writing had to wait for publication until much later.

Yet it must be said that Verlaine's ability to produce work has a debit as well as a credit side. While other poets—including, interestingly, two of those with whom he is most often associated, Rimbaud and Mallarmé—allowed relatively little through, Verlaine seemed inspired or compelled to commit himself to paper as much as he could. If he was hoping for financial gain, he was out of luck, for such payment as he received did not get him out of the holes he dug for himself, and anyway, he was famously careless with money.

It may be that Verlaine was one of those poets (Apollinaire, later, would be another) whose lives of week-by-week turbulence nourish their art, and vice versa. A shambles of a man, he needed to tell all. He was constantly sorting his life out aloud, taxing friends, lovers, wife, and especially mother. His personality leached into his poetry when it did not positively flood into it. The risk, of course, for any fluent poet is that fluency can become logorrhoea. Poetry can die from an excess of words as much as from a paucity. No one knew this better than Mallarmé, the High Priest of refinement, the sculptor of language, whose poems were pared down to absolute essentials. No poet was more disillusioned by the poetic word than Rimbaud, who turned his back not only on Verlaine but also on all aspirations to make poetry significant. The tendency of both these great contemporaries of Verlaine was always towards reduction, even at the risk of silence. Verlaine, however, went on, and it is undeniable that in many poems there is too much mortar and too few bricks. When this is so, the frisson of poetry does not happen. There is not that wonderful hovering between sound and sense, as the last, great French Symbolist, Paul Valéry, put it.

Finally, to return to the first image of parallel lines, Verlaine was both a good and a bad poet, but at one and the same time, in tandem. At his best, he was sublime, unique. At his worst, pedestrian, not to say lame. For a variety of possible reasons, he did not suppress the bad. It might even be claimed that the crises of irresolution, the divisions in his life and work, somehow sustained him. Had it been possible to resolve them, quite conceivably his creativity would have dried up, and he might have become the unremarkable bourgeois which one critic at least (Jean Richer) thinks was a crucial aspect of his essential self.[7]

Instead, Verlaine's conflicts and contradictions, apparent from an early age, were never resolved, and the fundamentally Romantic icon of the untamed poet of genius was created. Bourgeois and bohemian, tender and brutal, coarse and refined, sentimental and hard-edged, religious and sacrilegious, Verlaine was all of these, at one and the same time. So was his poetry. In the last analysis, the best elements in Verlaine's poetry have to be those multiple and durable threads which celebrate sensation, whether robustly or with gossamer fragility. One such thread is those masterpieces of verbal painting or verbal musicality, those moods-in-landscape, landscapes-in-mood. Others would include the joyous and sunlit pleasures of the human body, the darker secrets of the riskiest eroticism, and the suspect affection for an unofficially adopted son, an attachment doing its best to stay on the acceptable side of morality. These are the strands, sometimes thin but always strong as cables, which run through all of Verlaine's poetry, from beginning to end. When he is not attempting—and failing—to make good art out of good morals, when, to gloss his own, dismissive final line of 'The art of poetry', he is not merely purveying the tired banalities of routine literature, Verlaine is a great and splendid poet, whose singing voice can be confused with no other.

---

[7] While he is well disposed to Verlaine's poetry, Richer's view of Verlaine the man is less positive. See Select Bibliography.

NOTE ON THE TEXT AND TRANSLATION

The principal editions of Verlaine's complete work are:

Œuvres complètes, 5 vols., published by Albert Messein (successor to Léon Vanier, Verlaine's first publisher) in 1923, and *Œuvres posthumes*, 3 vols., also published by Messein, between 1922 and 1929.

Œuvres poétiques complètes, Éditions Gallimard, Bibliothèque de la Pléiade, ed. Yves-Gérard Le Dantec, 1st pub. 1938, revised, completed, and presented by Jacques Borel in 1962.

Œuvres complètes, published by Le Club du meilleur livre in 2 vols., 1959–60, ed. Henry de Bouillane de Lacoste and Jacques Borel, with a preface by Octave Nadal.

The Messein edition is unannotated and contains a considerable number of inaccuracies. Since the time of its publication, and especially since the Second World War, Verlaine scholarship has moved substantially forward, and the benefits are visible in the Pléiade and the Club du meilleur livre editions, whose editors have been able to work from the Verlaine autograph manuscripts and papers in the archives of the Fonds Doucet in Paris. The dating of poems thereby has been made accurate. Furthermore, each edition gives comprehensive lists of variants. Both editions are accompanied by substantial, evaluative essays.

In preparing this edition, I have consulted all the editions mentioned, but have used the text of the 1962 Pléiade edition. One of the Pléiade edition's virtues is that it places Verlaine's uncollected poems in two sections, 'Premiers vers' and 'Poèmes divers'. This represents a more accurate distribution than do the rather provisional *Œuvres posthumes* of the Messein edition.

Jacques Robichez's annotations to his *Verlaine: œuvres poétiques* (Classiques Garnier), the updated edition of which appeared in 1995, are full and interesting. They constitute one of the best commentaries available. It should be noted that this edition does not seek to be complete, in that it contains Verlaine's poetry up to and including *Parallèlement* only.

The history of Verlaine in English translation reveals at least three significant features. First, many translators have taken on Verlaine. The catalogues of the principal copyright libraries reveal (on my last count) some thirty-five of them, and this number surely must be only a minimum. Secondly, no translator seems to have taken on the *whole* of Verlaine's poetry—admittedly a daunting task, and perhaps one without clear profit. By pointed contrast, however, the complete works of other major French poets of his time, such as Mallarmé, Rimbaud, Laforgue, and Corbière, have been done, in some cases more than once. At best, not even a substantial proportion of Verlaine's output has been attempted. C. F. MacIntyre and Joanna Richardson, two leading Verlaine translators, have done around eighty poems each, which, in percentage terms, is a modest amount. Thirdly, the choice of poems made by virtually all the translators reveals considerable adherence to the notion that only the early Verlaine is worth attention.

All in all, then, there seems to have existed, perhaps still to exist, in the English-speaking literary world a climate of hesitation around Verlaine. Of the French Symbolists, he has fared the worst at the hands of translators. Part of the explanation for this, I believe, must be that Verlaine's 'music', that exquisite delicacy of the early poems, has acted as a barrier. How to achieve in any other language the evanescence of those fine, gossamer lines? A fascination with this problem has manifested itself in one way particularly: translators return again and again to the same poems, poems of great technical skill, as if the challenge resided almost exclusively in getting those, and only those, just 'right'. So, there are numerous English versions of 'My recurring dream', 'Autumn song', 'Exchange of feelings', 'Falling tears', 'The sky above the roof', and, of course, 'The art of poetry'. Some of the translations are fine indeed; others, in my view, suffer from an over-reverence for the original. By that, I mean that too high a regard for exact metre, for solid and indeed insistent rhyme, and, most damagingly, for a kind of late-Victorian register and out-of-date syntactical structures have produced translations which read stiffly, even archaically. Thus, while the 1895 translations of William Robertson, those published in 1900 by Ernest Dowson, and Arthur Symons's well-known versions of 1924 are, to my mind, acceptable in that they belong firmly to their times, later translations work less well because they have refused to acknowledge the changes and developments in poetic codes of practice. In short, they seem stuck in the past and suggest that Verlaine can speak only to the past.

In preparing this book, my own principles have been rather different. First, I have chosen a greater number of poems than has any other edition of which I am aware. There are some 170 here. Secondly, I have moved away from the consensus by selecting a substantial number of poems from *Parallèlement* onwards, often considered the cut-off point between the best and the worst in Verlaine. As part of this approach, I have included relatively few of the religiously inspired poems. Despite the arguments of some critics, I cannot warm to them nor do I feel that more are required to give a balanced view of Verlaine's output. Thirdly, I have endeavoured to find ways of translating which chime with the English-language poetic practices of our own time. I felt, with echoes of 'The art of poetry' ringing in my ears, that the worst tyranny for any translator of Verlaine was rhyme. In many of the translations published over the last few decades, it does seem indeed that rhyme is the tail which wags the dog. The impression is strong that the translator somehow has first created a rhyme, and then has worked backwards from it, buckling syntax in order to accommodate it. Of course, it would be gratifying to make rhyme work in English as easily as Verlaine seems to in French. But perhaps that kind of success can occur consistently only when poets are composing original poetry in their own language. I wanted, then, on the whole to eschew rhyme, or at least not to be ruled by it, the more so as it does not anyway have such a strong place in modern English prosody. However, in certain poems, usually ones with a playful or humorous content, and in which the full force of meaning depended on rhyme, I judged it essential to keep full rhyme patterns.

I felt, too, that the syllabic metres of French could not and should not be transferred directly into English. Generally, syllabics are something of an oddity in English practice, and can yield quite mechanical and unmusical lines. As I saw it, a more appropriate way to try to capture Verlaine's musicality was to get away from the strictness of his metres and to use some considerably less constrained patterns, as the English tradition allows. As an example, where Verlaine uses a long line, sometimes I will go for a short one, and vice versa.

My translations, then, will often appear free, sometimes moderately so, sometimes considerably. I hope, nevertheless, that this appearance is just that, an appearance which does not mask the truth of the originals. As I think there is great diversity within Verlaine's poems, I have tried to vary style, tone, and register. My translations are not universally of one 'type'. Two small examples of what I mean: sometimes I will use 'it is', at others, 'it's'; some of my versions are carefully punctuated, with grammatically correct commas, semicolons etc., but others, more free and needing swifter rhythms, deliberately have a more casual punctuation. My aim, though this might not seem to square with the translator's licence I have allowed myself, has been honesty. Honesty to Verlaine's essential *poetry*, lying just below the surface of the lines, and perhaps a touch obscured by their formalities; and honesty to English poetic diction, constructed on different principles from those governing French. I have tried to preserve the essence of Verlaine in my English pieces, which, I hope, have at least some claim to be called poems—poems appropriate to the climate of late twentieth-century English-language writing. Through them, I hope that Verlaine's voice, more diverse in its tonalities than is sometimes thought, will be heard for what it is.

I would like to extend my thanks to Pierre Brunel, of the Sorbonne, Paris. The invitation he made me to speak at his institution on 'Verlaine in Translation' started me in earnest on this book. I would like to acknowledge the admirable initiative of Edith McMorran and Jane Taylor, both of Oxford University, in setting up and sustaining Translation Research in Oxford. It has always been a pleasure and a privilege to participate in TRIO's stimulating debates. Similarly, the two colloquia 'Translating French Literature and Film' organized by Professor Geoffrey Harris of the European Studies Research Institute, University of Salford, were stimulating, and gave me a welcome opportunity to try out some ideas about Verlaine. My thanks go also to Harry Guest, whose expert suggestions of ways to translate one particularly elusive poem pushed me to reconsider several others. Reading the work of my Exeter colleagues Michael Pakenham and James Kearns was a stimulus, as was talking with them both. They provided me with valuable information from an unrivalled storehouse of knowledge of Verlaine and his times. Other colleagues kept

Note on the Text and Translation

up their encouragement, none more so than Keith Cameron. Andrea Williams unravelled many typographical tangles. To all, my thanks. But first and last, my deepest thanks go to Claire. She has kept this show firmly on the road with loving discretion and patience, as always.

SELECT BIBLIOGRAPHY

Editions

Œuvres complètes de Paul Verlaine, 5 vols. (Paris: Messein, 1923).

Œuvres posthumes de Paul Verlaine, 3 vols. (Paris: Messein, 1922–9).

Paul Verlaine: œuvres complètes, 2 vols. (Paris: Le Club du meilleur livre, 1959–60).

Paul Verlaine: œuvres poétiques complètes (Paris: Gallimard, Bibliothèque de la Pléiade, 1st pub. 1938, rev. edn. 1962).

Paul Verlaine: œuvres en prose complètes (Paris: Gallimard, Bibliothèque de la Pléiade, 1972).

Paul Verlaine: œuvres poétiques complètes (Paris: Laffont, Collection 'Bouquins', 1992).

Paul Verlaine: œuvres poétiques (Paris: Garnier, rev. edn. 1995). Verlaine's poetry up to and including *Parallèlement*.

Biography

Lepelletier, Edmond, *Paul Verlaine: sa vie, son œuvre* (Paris: Mercure de France, 1907). Biography by the man who was one of Verlaine's closest friends. Published in English as *Paul Verlaine: His Life – His Work*, trans. E. M. Lang (London: T. Werner Laurie, 1909).

Petitfils, Pierre, *Verlaine* (Paris: Julliard, 1981). A biographical and critical study.

Richardson, Joanna, *Verlaine* (London: Weidenfeld & Nicolson, 1971). A detailed, critical biography.

Roberts, Bechhofer, *Paul Verlaine* (London: Jarrolds, 1937). A general study.

Verlaine, Ex-Madame Paul, *Mémoires de ma vie* (Seyssel: Champ Vallon, Collection 'Dix-neuvième', 1992). This new edition of the memoirs of Verlaine's wife Mathilde supersedes that of 1935; it contains a valuable preface and notes by Michael Pakenham.

Critical Studies

Adam, Antoine, *Verlaine*, trans. as *The Art of Paul Verlaine* (New York: New York University Press, 1963). Adam is the principal apologist of Verlaine, making a positive case for even his indifferent poems.

Bornecque, J. H., *Verlaine par lui-même* (Paris: Seuil, Collection 'Écrivains de toujours', 1966). Short, lively, illustrated study containing many poems given in full.

Select Bibliography

Buisine, Alain, *Verlaine: Histoire d'un corps* (Paris: Tallandier, 'Figures de proue' series, 1995). Looks at ways in which Verlaine's writing manifests a connection between the body and literary creation.

Chadwick, Charles, *Verlaine* (London: The Athlone Press, 'Athlone French Poets' series, 1973). A useful monograph.

—— *Paul Verlaine: 'Sagesse'* (London: The Athlone Press, 'Athlone French Poets' series, 1973). Detailed commentary on one collection; companion volume to Chadwick's monograph.

Hillery, David, *Paul Verlaine: 'Romances sans paroles'* (London: The Athlone Press, 'Athlone French Poets' series, 1976). Detailed commentary; a further and very valuable volume in this excellent series.

Martino, Pierre, *Verlaine* (Paris: Boivin, 1st pub. 1924). Focuses on the poetry more than the man.

Mourot, Jean, *Verlaine* (Nancy: Presses Universitaires de Nancy, Collection 'Phares', 1988). Critical study of earlier poetry, with a chapter on Verlaine's psychological make-up.

Nadal, Octave, *Paul Verlaine* (Paris: Mercure de France, 1961). A shrewd and absorbing critical study. Devotes much space to Verlaine's musical and pictorial impressionism.

Pakenham, Michael, *Paul Verlaine: nos murailles littéraires* (Paris: L'Échoppe, 1997). Writing by Verlaine, both poetry and prose, recently discovered by Pakenham, and edited and annotated by him.

Richard, Jean-Pierre, *Poésie et profondeur* (Paris: Seuil, 1955). Contains an absorbing essay, 'Fadeur de Verlaine'. The so-called vagueness in Verlaine's poetry is seen as his distinguishing and creative quality.

Richer, Jean, *Paul Verlaine* (Paris: Seghers, Collection 'Poètes d'aujourd'hui', 1st pub. 1953). A short, lively, and often psycho-analytical account, with a selection of poems.

Taylor-Horrex, S., *Verlaine: 'Fêtes galantes' and 'Romances sans paroles'* (London: Grant & Cutler, 'Critical Guides to French Texts', 1988). A short study of two of Verlaine's collections in this helpful series.

Underwood, V. P., *Verlaine et l'Angleterre* (Paris: Nizet, 1956). A detailed examination of Verlaine's time in England.

Zimmerman, Eléonore, *Magies de Verlaine* (Paris: Corti, 1967). A study of the ways in which Verlaine's poetry developed.

Background

Balakian, Anna, *The Symbolist Movement: A Critical Appraisal* (New York: Random House, 1967). A wide-ranging study.

Carter, A. E., *The Idea of Decadence in French Literature, 1830–1900* (Toronto: Toronto University Press, 1958). A study of a movement to which Verlaine belonged, at least to an extent.

Chadwick, Charles, *Symbolism* (London: Methuen, 'The Critical Idiom' series, 1971). In this short and useful book, there is a section on Verlaine.

Cornell, Kenneth, *The Symbolist Movement* (New Haven: Yale University Press, 1951). A detailed account of the years 1885–1900 in France.

Huret, Jules, *Enquête sur l'évolution littéraire* (Paris: Charpentier, 1891). The celebrated results of Huret's questionnaires to leading writers of Verlaine's time about the state of literature. Many poets responded.

Lehmann, Andrew, *The Symbolist Aesthetic in France 1885–1895* (Oxford: Blackwell, 1st pub. 1950). A wide-ranging and detailed study.

Porter, Laurence M., *The Crisis of French Symbolism* (Ithaca, NY: Cornell University Press, 1990). Symbolism revisited in a careful and challenging study. Contains a chapter on Verlaine's subversion of language.

Raitt, Alan, *Villiers de l'Isle-Adam et le mouvement symboliste* (Paris: Corti, 1965). Considers Verlaine, among many others.

Schmidt, Albert-Marie, *La Littérature Symboliste* (Paris: Presses Universitaires de France, 1st edn. 1942). Puts forward stimulating and decided views of what is good and what is bad in the poet's work.

Starkie, Enid, *Rimbaud* (London: Faber & Faber, 1st pub. 1938). This major biography of Rimbaud has many pages on Verlaine.

Stephan, Philip, *Paul Verlaine and the Decadence, 1882–90* (Manchester: Manchester University Press, 1974). A study of the relationship between Verlaine and the Decadent movement.

Symons, Arthur, *The Symbolist Movement in Literature* (London: Heinemann, 1899). This book by one of Symbolism's first champions contains a study of Verlaine.

Wilson, Edmund, *Axel's Castle: A Study in the Imaginative Literature of 1870–1930* (New York: Scribner's, 1931). This celebrated and influential book contains a few pages on Verlaine.

Zayed, Georges, *La Formation littéraire de Verlaine* (2nd edn. Paris: Nizet, 1970). Detailed study of Verlaine's literary background and antecedents.

A journal devoted to the study of Verlaine, *Cahiers des amis de Paul Verlaine*, was inaugurated in 1993, and is published by the Musée-Bibliothèque de Charleville-Mézières, France.

Many articles have been published on Verlaine, too numerous to list, and scattered in various scholarly journals.

Further Reading in Oxford World's Classics

Baudelaire, Charles, *The Flowers of Evil*, trans. James McGowan, with an introduction by Jonathan Culler.

—— *The Prose Poems and La Fanfarlo*, trans. and ed. Rosemary Lloyd.

A CHRONOLOGY OF PAUL VERLAINE

1844 Birth of Paul-Marie Verlaine on 30 March in Metz, eastern France. His father is an army captain; his mother is from a prosperous middle-class family.

1851 Verlaine's father resigns his army commission. The family moves to Paris.

1853 Birth of Mathilde Mauté, Verlaine's future wife.

1853–62 School years, including the Lycée Bonaparte (Condorcet).

1854 Birth of Arthur Rimbaud.

1858 Verlaine sends his first poem ('Death') to Victor Hugo.

1860 Meets Edmond Lepelletier, who will become his lifelong friend and biographer.

1862 Obtains baccalaureate.

1863 First published poem ('Mr Pomp and Circumstance') appears in *La Revue du progrès moral*, under the name of Pablo. Starts to frequent the Parnassian literary milieu of Paris.

1864 Works for an insurance company; then as a clerk in the Hôtel de Ville of Paris.

1865 Death of Verlaine's father. He contributes to the reviews *Le Hanneton* and *L'Art*.

1866 Publication of *Poèmes saturniens*.

1869 Engagement to Mathilde Mauté. Publication of *Fêtes galantes*.

1870 Publication of *La Bonne Chanson*. Verlaine marries Mathilde on 11 August. He joins the National Guard. The Franco-Prussian War begins.

1871 Siege of Paris and the Commune. Verlaine works as a press officer; briefly flees to the family home at Fampoux, north-eastern France, at the end of the war. Invites Rimbaud to Paris. Rimbaud stays in the Mauté household. Verlaine is increasingly violent towards his wife. Birth of his son Georges.

1872 Verlaine tries to strangle Mathilde. He sends Rimbaud away, but after a reconciliation they go to Belgium. Verlaine is briefly reconciled with Mathilde, but returns to Rimbaud. The two go to live in London. Rimbaud leaves but soon returns. Verlaine falls ill; his mother comes to London to look after him.

1873 Verlaine abandons Rimbaud in London. The two are later reunited in Brussels. When Rimbaud says he is leaving, Verlaine shoots and slightly wounds him. Verlaine sentenced to two years in prison, but serves only eighteen months, mostly in Mons.

1873–4 From prison, Verlaine writes poems for *Cellulairement*; this volume is never published. The poems later appear in other collections.

1874 Publication of *Romances sans paroles*. Mathilde obtains a legal separation. Verlaine announces his conversion to Catholicism.

1875 Leaves prison in January and makes vain attempts at reconciliation with Mathilde. Goes to Stuttgart in a failed attempt at reconciliation with Rimbaud. Takes up a teaching position in Stickney, England.

1876 From September, teacher in Bournemouth, England, until autumn 1877.

1877–9 Teacher at Rethel, north-eastern France; start of friendship with a pupil, Lucien Létinois.

1879 Goes to England with Létinois. Létinois teaches in Stickney, Verlaine in Lymington, Hampshire. They return to France at Christmas.

1880 Verlaine and Létinois in Coulommes. Verlaine buys a farm at Juniville, near Rethel, where he settles with Létinois. Publication of *Sagesse*.

1881–2 The experiment with rural life and farming fails. The farm is sold.

1882 Spends summer in Paris, near his mother and Létinois.

1883 Létinois dies on 7 April. Verlaine returns to his mother's house at Coulommes. Start of bohemian existence. Publication of *Jadis et Naguère*.

1885 Legal separation from Mathilde becomes divorce. Sentenced to one month in prison for attacking his mother. He later goes to Paris with her. A diseased knee leads to hospitalization.

1886 Verlaine's mother dies. Further stays in hospital.

1887 Several stays in hospital. Contemplates suicide.

1888 Publication of *Amour*.

1889 Publication of *Parallèlement*. Another stay in hospital, then a course of treatment at Aix-les-Bains.

1890 Publication of *Dédicaces*.

1891   Publication of *Bonheur, Chansons pour Elle*. Rimbaud dies. From this time, when not in hospital, Verlaine lives alternately with Philomène Boudin and Eugénie Krantz.

1892   Publication of *Liturgies intimes*. Series of lectures in Holland.

1893   Lectures in Belgium. Unsuccessfully seeks election to Académie française. Publication of *Odes en son honneur*. Lectures in England.

1894   Publication of *Dans les limbes*. Elected Prince of Poets. Publication of *Épigrammes*.

1895   Writes preface for *Poésies complètes* of Rimbaud. By December, declining health confines him permanently to bed.

1896   Dies on 8 January. Funeral on 10 January. Gabriel Fauré is organist at the service. Among hundreds of mourners, the most distinguished are Mallarmé, Heredia, Sully-Prudhomme, Moréas, Mendès, Coppée, Barrès, Richepin, Fort, Vanier, Lepelletier. Publication later in the year of *Chair* and *Invectives*.

SELECTED POEMS

Premiers vers

Aspiration

Des ailes! Des ailes!
(Rückert)

Cette vallée est triste et grise: un froid brouillard
    Pèse sur elle;
L'horizon est ridé comme un front de vieillard;
    Oiseau, gazelle,
Prêtez-moi votre vol; éclair, emporte-moi!
    Vite, bien vite,
Vers ces plaines du ciel où le printemps est roi,
    Et nous invite
A la fête éternelle, au concert éclatant
    Qui toujours vibre,
Et dont l'écho lointain, de mon cœur palpitant
    Trouble la fibre.
Là, rayonnent, sous l'œil de Dieu qui les bénit,
    Des fleurs étranges,
Là, sont des arbres où gazouillent comme un nid
    Des milliers d'anges;
Là, tous les sons rêvés, là, toutes les splendeurs
    Inabordables
Forment, par un hymen miraculeux, des chœurs
    Inénarrables!
Là, des vaisseaux sans nombre, aux cordages de feu,
    Fendent les ondes
D'un lac de diamant où se peint le ciel bleu
    Avec les mondes;
Là, dans les airs charmés, volètent des odeurs
    Enchanteresses,
Enivrant à la fois les cerveaux et les cœurs
    De leurs caresses.
Des vierges, à la chair phosphorescente, aux yeux
    Dont l'orbe austère
Contient l'immensité sidérale des cieux
    Et du mystère,

Aspiration

Wings! Wings!

(Rückert)*

This valley's sad, grey. Hanging mist
    Chills the air.
The sky-rim's like a pensioner's brow.
    Bird, gazelle,
Teach me to fly. Take me, lightning
    Flash,
High into blue fields where the Lord of Spring
    Invites us
To endless fêtes, bursting
    Symphonies
Whose long echoes move my dancing heart
    Deeply.
There: a watchful God blesses
    Strange flowers,
Trees like nests sing clouded
    With angels.
Every sound ever dreamt, every out-of-reach
    Splendour
Bring together fine choirs in miraculous
    Marriage!
Lines of fire-rigged boats cut
    Through waves
On a diamond lake beneath blue
    Cluttered skies.
In charmed air, scented enchantments
    Flutter,
Caress hearts and minds to limits
    Of delirium.
Pure girls with luminous skin
    And grave eyes
Welled with the sky's starred magnitude,
    Welled with mystery,

Y baisent chastement, comme il sied aux péris,
    Le saint poète,
Qui voit tourbillonner des légions d'esprits
    Dessus sa tête.

L'âme, dans cet Éden, boit à flots l'idéal,
    Torrent splendide,
Qui tombe des hauts lieux et roule son cristal
    Sans une ride.

Ah! pour me transporter dans ce septième ciel,
    Moi, pauvre hère,
Moi, frêle fils d'Adam, cœur tout matériel,
    Loin de la terre,

Loin de ce monde impur où le fait chaque jour
    Détruit le rêve,
Où l'or remplace tout, la beauté, l'art, l'amour,
    Où ne se lève

Aucune gloire un peu pure que les siffleurs
    Ne la déflorent,
Où les artistes pour désarmer les railleurs
    Se déshonorent,

Loin de ce bagne où, hors le débauché qui dort,
    Tous sont infâmes,
Loin de tout ce qui vit, loin des hommes, encor
    Plus loin des femmes,

Aigle, au rêveur hardi, pour l'enlever du sol,
    Ouvre ton aile!
Éclair, emporte-moi! Prêtez-moi votre vol,
    Oiseau, gazelle!

10 mai 1861

A don Quichotte

Ô don Quichotte, vieux paladin, grand Bohème,
En vain la foule absurde et vile rit de toi:
Ta mort fut un martyre et ta vie un poème,
Et les moulins à vent avaient tort, ô mon roi!

Kiss chastely as in fairy-tales
　　The poet-saint
Who sees a thousand spirits whirl around
　　His head.
In this Eden, the soul drinks the Ideal,
　　A splendour
Cascading from heights, spreading
　　Pristine crystal.
Take me to this heaven of heavens, me,
　　Nothing,
Adam's feeble son, mere flesh and blood.
　　Take me far
From this tainted world where statistics
　　Murder dreams,
Where art, beauty, love, everything's money,
　　Where anything
Worthwhile's booed off the stage
　　By vulgar claques,
Where true artists sell themselves cheap
　　To silence critics.
Take me far from this prison where all's vile save
　　The sleeping debauchee,
Far from all that lives, far from men, farther still
　　From women—
Eagle, take the daring dreamer up, wing him
　　Far away!
Take me, lightning flash. Teach me to fly,
　　Bird, gazelle!

10 May 1861

To Don Quixote

Don Quixote, old errant knight, grand bohemian,
The vile crass crowd pokes pointless fun at you;
Your death was pure martyrdom, your whole life poetry,
And the windmills, good my King, were well and truly wrong.

Va toujours, va toujours, protégé par ta foi,
Monté sur ton coursier fantastique que j'aime.
Glaneur sublime, va!—les oublis de la loi
Sont plus nombreux, plus grands qu'au temps jadis
    lui-même.

Hurrah! nous te suivons, nous, les poètes saints
Aux cheveux de folie et de verveine ceints.
Conduis-nous à l'assaut des hautes fantaisies,

Et bientôt, en dépit de toute trahison,
Flottera l'étendard ailé des Poésies
Sur le crâne chenu de l'inepte raison!

Mars 1861

Un soir d'octobre

L'automne et le soleil couchant! Je suis heureux!
    Du sang sur de la pourriture!
L'incendie au zénith! La mort dans la nature!
    L'eau stagnante, l'homme fiévreux!

Oh! c'est bien là ton heure et ta saison, poète
    Au cœur vide d'illusions,
Et que rongent les dents de rats des passions,
    Quel bon miroir, et quelle fête!

Que d'autres, des pédants, des niais ou des fous,
    Admirent le printemps et l'aube,
Ces deux pucelles-là, plus roses que leur robe;

Moi, je t'aime, âpre automne, et te préfère à tous
    Les minois d'innocentes, d'anges,
Courtisane cruelle aux prunelles étranges.

10 octobre 1862

Keep the armour of your faith, keep riding
That unreal charger I adore.
Keep at it, harvester sublime! Now the law's
Shortcomings are worse than once they were.

We cheer you on and follow in your steps,
We, the mad-haired poet-saints fragrant with verbena.
Help us take the high walls of fantasy,
So that soon, flying in the face of treachery,

The winged standard of Poetry must
Flutter over feeble Reason's dust.

March 1861

October evening

Autumn and the setting sun. I'm happy.
  Blood on corruption,
Zenith of fire, death in nature,
  Stagnant water, feverish man.

It's indeed your hour, your season, poet
  Of illusion-emptied heart,
Poet ripped by the rat-teeth of passion,
  What mirror, what fête!

So many others, pedants, madmen, imbeciles,
  Admire the Spring and dawn,
That pair of virgins, more rosy than their frocks.

Stinging autumn, you I love, more than
  Any little angel face,
You, cruel and strange-eyed courtesan.

10 October 1862

L'Apollon de Pont-Audemer

Un solide gaillard! dix-huit ans: larges bras;
Mains à vous arracher la tête de l'épaule;
Sur un front bas et dur, cheveux roux, coupés ras.
Puis, à la danse, il a, ma foi, crâne air, le drôle!

Les enfants poussent drus aux filles qu'il enjôle,
Dans la puberté fière et fauve, le beau gas
Va, comme dans sa pourpre un roi qui sait son rôle
Et parle à voix hautaine, et marche à vastes pas.

Plus tard, soit que le sort l'épargne ou le désigne,
On le verra, bon vieux, barbe blanche, œil terni,
S'éteindre doucement, comme un jour qui finit,

Ou bien, humble héros, martyr de la consigne,
Au fond d'une tranchée obscure ou d'un talus
Rouler, le crâne ouvert par quelque éclat d'obus.

                                        9 septembre 1864

Vers dorés

L'art ne veut point de pleurs et ne transige pas,
Voilà ma poétique en deux mots: elle est faite
De beaucoup de mépris pour l'homme et de combats
Contre l'amour criard et contre l'ennui bête.

Je sais qu'il faut souffrir pour monter à ce faîte
Et que la côte est rude à regarder d'en bas.
Je le sais, et je sais aussi que maint poète
A trop étroits les reins ou les poumons trop gras.

Aussi ceux-là sont grands, en dépit de l'envie,
Qui, dans l'âpre bataille ayant vaincu la vie
Et s'étant affranchis du joug des passions,

The Apollo of Pont-Audemer

Strapping eighteen-year-old with arms like trees,
Hands to tear your head off just like that,
And on a low hard brow, close-cropped ginger hair.
But at the dance this clown is gallantry itself.

Children swarm around the girls he's out to impress.
Proudly, savagely pubescent, the handsome lad
Parades like a purple-robed king who knows his role
And speaks in lofty tones and walks like a giant.

Later—will Fate spare or pick him out?—
The old boy he'll become—white beard, dim eyes—
Will quietly die like dying day,

Or else, humble hero and martyr to duty,
He'll topple down some bank into a trench,
His head split open by a bursting shell.

9 September 1864

Golden lines

Art wants no tears and takes no prisoners—
That's my creed summed up. Poetry's composed
Of huge contempt for man, of combats
Against loud love and mindless boredom.

I know we must suffer to reach these heights,
I know the road looks rough, seen from below.
I know. I know too that many a poet
Has neither lungs nor stomach for it.

But greatness lies in ignoring desire,
In fighting pitched battles with life
And winning. Passion must be conquered.

Tandis que le rêveur végète comme un arbre
Et que s'agitent,—tas plaintif,—les nations,
Se recueillent dans un égoïsme de marbre.

[1866]

Dreamers do nothing, like trees,
Nations rise and fall in moaning heaps,
Greatness is a granite self-sufficiency.

[1866]

Poèmes saturniens

Nevermore

Souvenir, souvenir, que me veux-tu? L'automne
Faisait voler la grive à travers l'air atone,
Et le soleil dardait un rayon monotone
Sur le bois jaunissant où la bise détone.

Nous étions seul à seule et marchions en rêvant,
Elle et moi, les cheveux et la pensée au vent.
Soudain, tournant vers moi son regard émouvant:
'Quel fut ton plus beau jour?' fit sa voix d'or vivant,

Sa voix douce et sonore, au frais timbre angélique.
Un sourire discret lui donna la réplique,
Et je baisai sa main blanche, dévotement.

—Ah! les premières fleurs, qu'elles son parfumées!
Et qu'il bruit avec un murmure charmant
Le premier *oui* qui sort de lèvres bien-aimées!

Mon rêve familier

Je fais souvent ce rêve étrange et pénétrant
D'une femme inconnue, et que j'aime, et qui m'aime
Et qui n'est, chaque fois, ni tout à fait la même
Ni tout à fait une autre, et m'aime et me comprend.

Car elle me comprend, et mon cœur, transparent
Pour elle seule, hélas! cesse d'être un problème
Pour elle seule, et les moiteurs de mon front blême,
Elle seule les sait rafraîchir, en pleurant.

Est-elle brune, blonde ou rousse?—Je l'ignore.
Son nom? Je me souviens qu'il est doux et sonore
Comme ceux des aimés que la Vie exila.

Nevermore

Memories, memories, what do you want of me?
Autumn sent the thrush winging through bland air.
The sun darted monochrome light
Into ochre woodlands where winds howl.

We were alone, walking as in a dream,
She, I, hair, thoughts blown by the wind.
Suddenly her haunting look was on me:
'Which day was most beautiful for you?'

Asked that voice of living gold, soft, fresh, an angel's
Cadence. I smiled discreetly in reply,
And kissed her white hand with deep reverence.

Ah, the first flowers, how full their perfume is,
What spell the whisper-sound
Of the first *yes* murmured by beloved lips.

My recurring dream

I often have a strange and searing dream
About an unknown woman whom I love
And who loves me. Never quite the same
Nor someone else, she loves, she understands me.

Yes, she understands; the pity is
For her alone my heart is obvious,
Simple for her alone who brings to life
My dead face running with her tears.

Is she dark, auburn, blond? I don't know.
Her name? It echoes
Soft as names of loved ones gone for good.

Son regard est pareil au regard des statues,
Et, pour sa voix, lointaine, et calme, et grave, elle a
L'inflexion des voix chères qui se sont tues.

L'Angoisse

Nature, rien de toi ne m'émeut, ni les champs
Nourriciers, ni l'écho vermeil des pastorales
Siciliennes, ni les pompes aurorales,
Ni la solennité dolente des couchants.

Je ris de l'Art, je ris de l'Homme aussi, des chants,
Des vers, des temples grecs et des tours en spirales
Qu'étirent dans le ciel vide les cathédrales,
Et je vois du même œil les bons et les méchants.

Je ne crois pas en Dieu, j'abjure et je renie
Toute pensée, et quant à la vieille ironie,
L'Amour, je voudrais bien qu'on ne m'en parlât plus.

Lasse de vivre, ayant peur de mourir, pareille
Au brick perdu jouet du flux et du reflux,
Mon âme pour d'affreux naufrages appareille.

Croquis parisien

La lune plaquait ses teintes de zinc
    Par angles obtus.
Des bouts de fumée en forme de cinq
Sortaient drus et noirs des hauts toits pointus.

Le ciel était gris. La bise pleurait
    Ainsi qu'un basson.
Au loin, un matou frileux et discret
Miaulait d'étrange et grêle façon.

Her gaze is like a statue's gaze,
And in her calm and grave and distant voice
Are modulations of loved voices gone to earth.

Anguish

Nature, you don't move me, not at all, not your
Rich fields, not your rose-touched country scenes
In Sicily, not your dawn pomp,
And not the solemn grandeur of your setting suns.

I laugh at Art, I laugh at Mankind too, at songs,
At verse, Greek temples and the spiral towers
Cathedrals push up into empty skies;
Good folk and bad are all the same to me.

I don't believe in God, I turn my back
On thought, and as for that old irony
Called Love, I want to hear no more of that again.

Too tired to live, too scared to die,
Unmasted boat loosed on the sea,
My soul prepares itself for grim catastrophe.

Sketch of Paris

The moon put down metallic tints
     Angling the light.
Smoke-smears in stacks of five lifted
Straight and black from pointed roofs.

The sky was grey. The wind growled low
     As a bassoon.
A distant cat cold and alone
Miaowed its strange and high-pitched note.

Moi, j'allais, rêvant du divin Platon
    Et de Phidias,
Et de Salamine et de Marathon,
Sous l'œil clignotant des bleus becs de gaz.

Cauchemar

J'ai vu passer dans mon rêve
    —Tel l'ouragan sur la grève,—
D'une main tenant un glaive
Et de l'autre un sablier,
        Ce cavalier

Des ballades d'Allemagne
Qu'à travers ville et campagne,
Et du fleuve à la montagne,
Et des forêts au vallon,
        Un étalon

Rouge-flamme et noir d'ébène,
Sans bride, ni mors, ni rêne,
Ni hop! ni cravache, entraîne
Parmi des râlements sourds
        Toujours! toujours!

Un grand feutre à longue plume
Ombrait son œil qui s'allume
Et s'éteint. Tel, dans la brume,
Éclate et meurt l'éclair bleu
        D'une arme à feu.

Comme l'aile d'une orfraie
Qu'un subit orage effraie,
Par l'air que la neige raie,
Son manteau se soulevant
        Claquait au vent,

I walked, my thoughts on great Plato*
   And Phidias,*
On Salamis* and Marathon,*
Under the gas-lamps' flicker of blue.

Nightmare

I saw go by in my dream
Like a storm over sand
A great sword in one hand
An hourglass in the other
   That horseman

Of German ballads*
Whom across country through towns
Over rivers up mountains
Through forests down valleys
   A stallion

Flame-red ebony-dark
No bridle no bit no reins
No giddy-up no whip
On and on through mute death
   Carries

A long-feathered broad felt hat
Over his eyes now bright
Now dull like the brilliant blue
Then dead flash of firearms
   Seen in the mist

As an osprey's wing
Feathers rising full
Of fear in a snow-flecked
Sudden storm
   Clacked in the wind

Et montrait d'un air de gloire
Un torse d'ombre et d'ivoire,
Tandis que dans la nuit noire
Luisaient en des cris stridents
   Trente-deux dents.

Marine

L'océan sonore
Palpite sous l'œil
De la lune en deuil
Et palpite encore,

Tandis qu'un éclair
Brutal et sinistre
Fend le ciel de bistre
D'un long zigzag clair,

Et que chaque lame
En bonds convulsifs
Le long des récifs
Va, vient, luit et clame,

Et qu'au firmament,
Où l'ouragan erre,
Rugit le tonnerre
Formidablement.

Effet de nuit

La nuit. La pluie. Un ciel blafard que déchiquette
De flèches et de tours à jour la silhouette
D'une ville gothique éteinte au lointain gris.
La plaine. Un gibet plein de pendus rabougris
Secoués par le bec avide des corneilles
Et dansant dans l'air noir des gigues nonpareilles,
Tandis que leurs pieds sont la pâture des loups.

And in triumph disclosed
A shadow-and-ivory torso
While in the black night
Amid screeching gleamed
Two-and-thirty teeth.

Marine

Sonorous seas
Beat beneath the
Moon's grieving eye
And beat again.

A lightning flash
Brute sinister
Splits brown skies with
Long zigzag light

And breaking waves
Come go shine shout
In bursts and spurts
All down the rocks

And in tall skies
Where great storms cry
The thunder roars
Formidably.

Night effect

Night. Rain. An off-white sky ripped open by
The spires and glowing towers of a silhouetted
Gothic town lost in distant grey.
The plain. A gallows-crop of stunted bodies
Pushed and shoved by beaks of greedy crows
Dancing mad jigs in darkened air,
Their feet the feeding-ground of wolves.

Quelques buissons d'épine épars, et quelques houx
Dressant l'horreur de leur feuillage à droite, à gauche,
Sur le fuligineux fouillis d'un fond d'ébauche.
Et puis, autour de trois livides prisonniers
Qui vont pieds nus, un gros de hauts pertuisaniers
En marche, et leurs fers droits, comme des fers de herse,
Luisent à contre-sens des lances de l'averse.

Soleils couchants

Une aube affaiblie
Verse par les champs
La mélancolie
Des soleils couchants.
La mélancolie
Berce de doux chants
Mon cœur qui s'oublie
Aux soleils couchants.
Et d'étranges rêves,
Comme des soleils
Couchants sur les grèves,
Fantômes vermeils,
Défilent sans trêves,
Défilent, pareils
A des grands soleils
Couchants sur les grèves.

Promenade sentimentale

Le couchant dardait ses rayons suprêmes
Et le vent berçait les nénuphars blêmes;
Les grands nénuphars entre les roseaux
Tristement luisaient sur les calmes eaux.
Moi j'errais tout seul, promenant ma plaie
Au long de l'étang, parmi la saulaie
Où la brume vague évoquait un grand
Fantôme laiteux se désespérant

Scattered thorn-bushes, holly-trees
Raising frightful foliage to left and right
Against the smoke-smudged smears of a background sketch.
And then, hustling three barefoot blood-drained
Prisoners, a party of tall partisans
Marching, their straight portcullis pikes
Gleaming upwards as the shower rains down its blades.

Setting suns

A sickly dawn
Spreads over fields
The sadnesses
Of setting suns.
The sadnesses
Lull with soft songs
My heart lost in
The setting suns.
And then strange dreams
Which seem like suns
That set on shores
Vermilion ghosts
Drift endlessly
Reminding me
Of mighty suns
That set on shores.

Sentimental walk

The sunset glinted supreme rays.
Pale lilies swayed in the wind
Great lilies among reeds
Shining sadly on calm water.
I wandered lonely and wounded
The length of the pond among willows
Where vague mists stirred echoes
Of a great clouded phantom in despair

Et pleurant avec la voix des sarcelles
Qui se rappelaient en battant des ailes
Parmi la saulaie où j'errais tout seul
Promenant ma plaie; et l'épais linceul
Des ténèbres vint noyer les suprêmes
Rayons du couchant dans ses ondes blêmes
Et les nénuphars, parmi les roseaux,
Les grands nénuphars sur les calmes eaux.

Nuit du Walpurgis classique

C'est plutôt le sabbat du second Faust que l'autre.
Un rhythmique sabbat, rhythmique, extrêmement
Rhythmique.—Imaginez un jardin de Lenôtre,
    Correct, ridicule et charmant.

Des ronds-points; au milieu, des jets d'eau; des allées
Toutes droites; sylvains de marbre; dieux marins
De bronze; çà et là, des Vénus étalées;
    Des quinconces, des boulingrins;

Des châtaigniers; des plants de fleurs formant la dune;
Ici, des rosiers nains qu'un goût docte affila;
Plus loin, des ifs taillés en triangles. La lune
    D'un soir d'été sur tout cela.

Minuit sonne, et réveille au fond du parc aulique
Un air mélancolique, un sourd, lent et doux air
De chasse: tel, doux, lent, sourd et mélancolique,
    L'air de chasse de *Tannhäsuser*.

Des chants voilés de cors lointains où la tendresse
Des sens étreint l'effroi de l'âme en des accords
Harmonieusement dissonants dans l'ivresse;
    Et voici qu'à l'appel des cors

Crying its teal-duck call,
Remembering in time with the beat of its wings
In among willows where I wandered lonely
And wounded. And the thick shroud
Of darkness came and drowned the supreme
Sunset rays in bloodless folds
And lilies among reeds,
Great lilies on calm water.

Classic Walpurgis Night

Sabbath of the second Faust and not the first.
A rhythmic Sabbath, rhythmic, very full of
Rhythm—think of a garden by Lenôtre,*
    Tidy, ridiculous, charming.

Circular set-pieces; in the middle, fountains;
Straight-line alleys; marble wood-nymphs; bronze
Poseidons; here and there, Venuses sprawl;
    Trees in rows, formal lawns.

Chestnut trees; a mound planted with flowers;
Here, dwarf roses pruned by expert hands;
There, triangles of trimmed yews. And on it all
    A summer evening moon.

Chiming midnight conjures from the aulic deep
A melancholy air, a dull, slow, soft
Hunting-song; like the soft, slow, dull, melancholy
    Song in *Tannhäuser*.*

Elusive sounds of distant horns, where tender
Feelings hug the frightened soul lost
In music heady with dissonant harmonies.
    Now as the horns sound

S'entrelacent soudain des formes toutes blanches,
Diaphanes, et que le clair de lune fait
Opalines parmi l'ombre verte des branches,
   —Un Watteau rêvé par Raffet!—

S'entrelacent parmi l'ombre verte des arbres
D'un geste alangui, plein d'un désespoir profond,
Puis, autour des massifs, des bronzes et des marbres,
   Très lentement dansent en rond.

—Ces spectres agités, sont-ce donc la pensée
Du poëte ivre, ou son regret, ou son remords,
Ces spectres agités en tourbe cadencée,
   Ou bien tout simplement des morts?

Sont-ce donc ton remords, ô rêvasseur qu'invite
L'horreur, ou ton regret, ou ta pensée,—hein?—tous
Ces spectres qu'un vertige irrésistible agite,
   Ou bien des morts qui seraient fous?—

N'importe! ils vont toujours, les fébriles fantômes,
Menant leur ronde vaste et morne et tressautant
Comme dans un rayon de soleil des atomes,
   Et s'évaporant à l'instant

Humide et blême où l'aube éteint l'un après l'autre
Les cors, en sorte qu'il ne reste absolument
Plus rien—absolument—qu'un jardin de Lenôtre,
   Correct, ridicule et charmant.

Chanson d'automne

     Les sanglots longs
     Des violons
      De l'automne
     Blessent mon cœur
     D'une langueur
      Monotone.

Diaphanous white forms suddenly entwine.
Moonlight makes them opalescent
Among green shadows cast by branches
  —Watteau* dreamt by Raffet!*—

Among the trees' green shadows they entwine
Deep with languid misery. Then around
The hillocks bronze and marble figures slowly
  Start their circle-dance.

These agitated ghosts, are they the poet's
Drunken thoughts, or his regret, his remorse,
Ghosts spinning to the cadence of chaos,
  Or are they just dead?

Could they be your own remorse, you horror-haunted
Dreamer, or your regrets, your thoughts, eh?, all
These ghosts restless with delirium,
  Or have they died mad?

No matter. On they go, these feverish ghosts
Circling in their huge dark awkward dance
Like atoms swirling in a sunray then
  Etherizing just when

Damp colourless dawn stifles one by one
The horns, leaving absolutely nothing—
Absolutely—other than a garden by Lenôtre,
  Tidy, ridiculous, charming.

Autumn song

The long sobs of
The violins
  Of autumn
Lay waste my heart
With monotones
  Of boredom.

Tout suffocant
Et blême, quand
   Sonne l'heure,
Je me souviens
Des jours anciens
   Et je pleure;

Et je m'en vais
Au vent mauvais
   Qui m'emporte
Deçà, delà,
Pareil à la
   Feuille morte.

L'Heure du berger

La lune est rouge au brumeux horizon;
Dans un brouillard qui danse la prairie
S'endort fumeuse, et la grenouille crie
Par les joncs verts où circule un frisson;

Les fleurs des eaux referment leurs corolles;
Des peupliers profilent aux lointains,
Droits et serrés, leurs spectres incertains;
Vers les buissons errent les lucioles;

Les chats-huants s'éveillent, et sans bruit
Rament l'air noir avec leurs ailes lourdes,
Et le zénith s'emplit de lueurs sourdes.
Blanche, Vénus émerge, et c'est la Nuit.

Femme et chatte

Elle jouait avec sa chatte,
Et c'était merveille de voir
La main blanche et la blanche patte
S'ébattre dans l'ombre du soir.

Quite colourless
And choking when
   The hour strikes
I think again
Of vanished days
   And cry.

And so I leave
On cruel winds
   Squalling
And gusting me
Like a dead leaf
   Falling.

Right time for lovers

Red moon on haze-shrouded horizon.
In swirling mists the meadow lies
Cloudy with sleep, and frogs call
From green bulrushes shimmering.

Water-lilies close their corollas.
Tight ranks of poplar-trees stand out
Like ghosts in the distance.
Around bushes, fireflies dance and glance.

Screech-owls wake then silently
They row dark air with heavy wings.
Matt lustres fill tall skies.
White Venus shows, and it is Night.

Woman and cat

She was playing with her cat, and
It was marvellous to see
The white paw and the white hand
Fencing with the evening shade.

Elle cachait—la scélérate!—
Sous ses mitaines de fil noir
Ses meurtriers ongles d'agate,
Coupants et clairs comme un rasoir.

L'autre aussi faisait la sucrée
Et rentrait sa griffe acérée,
Mais le diable n'y perdait rien...

Et dans le boudoir où, sonore,
Tintait son rire aérien,
Brillaient quatre points de phosphore.

Monsieur Prudhomme

Il est grave: il est maire et père de famille.
Son faux col engloutit son oreille. Ses yeux
Dans un rêve sans fin flottent insoucieux,
Et le printemps en fleur sur ses pantoufles brille.

Que lui fait l'astre d'or, que lui fait la charmille
Où l'oiseau chante à l'ombre, et que lui font les cieux,
Et les prés verts et les gazons silencieux?
Monsieur Prudhomme songe à marier sa fille

Avec monsieur Machin, un jeune homme cossu.
Il est juste-milieu, botaniste et pansu.
Quant aux faiseurs de vers, ces vauriens, ces maroufles,

Ces fainéants barbus, mal peignés, il les a
Plus en horreur que son éternel coryza,
Et le printemps en fleur brille sur ses pantoufles.

She was hiding (sheer wickedness)
Under black-thread mittens
Murderous agate nails
As clear and cutting as razors.

The other one was at the same
Sweet game, razor claws
Hypocritically drawn in...

And in the bedroom where her laugh was bright
As a bell,
Four points of phosphorus were alight.

Mr Pomp and Circumstance

He's the mother of all fathers. Gravitas,
Mayor* to boot, false collar high as a neck-brace,
Untroubled eyes on journeys into space.
Radiant Spring makes his carpet-slippers shine.

What use to him the Golden Orb, the pergola
Where dawn birds chorus in the shade, what use
The sky, green meadows, silent lawns? Mr
Pomp and Circumstance has got it planned:

His daughter will wed Mr Whatsit,
Young man of means, pot-bellied, middle-of-the-road
And fond of Nature. As for Po-wets, verse-

Mongering, unwashed letter-louts, he finds them worse
Than the head-cold he's a martyr to.
And radiant Spring shines on his carpet-slippers.

Çavitrî

(Maha-baratta)

Pour sauver son époux, Çavitrî fit le vœu
De se tenir trois jours entiers, trois nuits entières,
Debout, sans remuer jambes, buste ou paupières:
Rigide, ainsi que dit Vyaça, comme un pieu.

Ni, Çurya, tes rais cruels, ni la langueur
Que Tchandra vient épandre à minuit sur les cimes
Ne firent défaillir, dans leurs efforts sublimes,
La pensée et la chair de la femme au grand cœur.

—Que nous cerne l'Oubli, noir et morne assassin,
Ou que l'Envie aux traits amers nous ait pour cibles,
Ainsi que Çavitrî faisons-nous impassibles,
Mais, comme elle, dans l'âme ayons un haut dessein.

Marco

Quand Marco passait, tous les jeunes hommes
Se penchaient pour voir ses yeux, des Sodomes
Où les feux d'Amour brûlaient sans pitié
Ta pauvre cahute, ô froide Amitié;
Tout autour dansaient des parfums mystiques
Où l'âme en pleurant s'anéantissait;
Sur ses cheveux roux un charme glissait;
Sa robe rendait d'étranges musiques
    Quand Marco passait.

Quand Marco chantait, ses mains sur l'ivoire
Évoquaient souvent la profondeur noire
Des airs primitifs que nul n'a redits,
Et sa voix montait dans les paradis
De la symphonie immense des rêves,

Savitri

(Mahabharata)

To save her husband Savitri vowed
To stand stock-still for three full days and nights,
Not twitching the smallest muscle, not blinking
Even once, still as a stake, as Vyasa said.

Neither Curya's burning rays not Chandra's
Midnight languor drifting over mountain-tops
Could break the mind or flesh
Of this great and loyal woman.

That dark and dull assassin Forgetfulness
Or sour-faced Envy may target us;
Like Savitri, we should make ourselves impassive,
Like her, our soul should be the loftiest.

Marco

When Marco passed, the young men
Shifted round to see her eyes, those Sodoms
Where Love's fires consumed the pitiful
Frozen shack called Friendship.
All around, mystic perfumes danced
And drowned the weeping soul.
Spells flitted through her auburn hair,
Her dress made strange, strange music
    When Marco passed.

When Marco sang, her hands on ivory
Teased out deep and dark and secret airs,
Those ancient airs which nobody now sings.
Her soaring voice was paradise,
A vast symphonic score of dreams.

Et l'enthousiasme alors transportait
Vers des cieux *connus* quiconque écoutait
Ce timbre d'argent qui vibrait sans trêves,
   Quand Marco chantait.

Quand Marco pleurait, ses terribles larmes
Défiaient l'éclat des plus belles armes;
Ses lèvres de sang fonçaient leur carmin
Et son désespoir n'avait rien d'humain;
Pareil au foyer que l'huile exaspère,
Son courroux croissait, rouge, et l'on aurait
Dit d'une lionne à l'âpre forêt
Communiquant sa terrible colère,
   Quand Marco pleurait.

Quand Marco dansait, sa jupe moirée
Allait et venait comme une marée,
Et, tel qu'un bambou flexible, son flanc
Se tordait, faisant saillir son sein blanc:
Un éclair partait. Sa jambe de marbre,
Emphatiquement cynique, haussait
Ses mates splendeurs, et cela faisait
Le bruit du vent de la nuit dans un arbre,
   Quand Marco dansait.

Quand Marco dormait, oh! quels parfums d'ambre
Et de chairs mêlés opprimaient la chambre!
Sous les draps la ligne exquise du dos
Ondulait, et dans l'ombre des rideaux
L'haleine montait, rhythmique et légère;
Un sommeil heureux et calme fermait
Ses yeux, et ce doux mystère charmait
Les vagues objets parmi l'étagère,
   Quand Marco dormait.

Mais quand elle aimait, des flots de luxure
Débordaient, ainsi que d'une blessure
Sort un sang vermeil qui fume et qui bout,
De ce corps cruel que son crime absout;

And anyone who heard the endless play
Of silver notes was taken up
To heavens already known,
 When Marco sang.

When Marco wept, alarming tears
Blunted the keenest weapons' sharp attack.
Her blood-red lips went darker red,
Her despair seemed hardly human.
Like a fire raging with new fuel
Her red-hot anger grew. She was
The lioness shouting her fury
To an unbending forest,
 When Marco wept.

When Marco danced, her shimmering skirt
Swished back and forth like tides,
And like bamboo her waist
Twisted, lifting white breasts high.
A lightning flash, calculating
Glorious marble thighs heightened
Understated splendours; all this made
A whisper-wind of trees by night,
 When Marco danced.

When Marco slept, oh then such amber scent
Mixed with her own and filled the room!
Beneath the sheet the line of her exquisite back
Curved and in the curtains' shadows
Her breathing rose and fell on breaths of air.
Calm untroubled sleep lay on her eyes
And sweet mystery lent charm
To vague things scattered on the shelves,
 When Marco slept.

But when she loved, then waves of pleasure
Like boiling smoking crimson blood
Spilling from a wound burst the banks
Of that cruel body absolved by its crime.*

Le torrent rompait les digues de l'âme,
Noyait la pensée, et bouleversait
Tout sur son passage, et rebondissait
Souple et dévorant comme de la flamme,
     Et puis se glaçait.

Épilogue

I

Le soleil, moins ardent, luit clair au ciel moins dense.
Balancés par un vent automnal et berceur,
Les rosiers du jardin s'inclinent en cadence.
L'atmosphère ambiante a des baisers de sœur.

La Nature a quitté pour cette fois son trône
De splendeur, d'ironie et de sérénité:
Clémente, elle descend, par l'ampleur de l'air jaune,
Vers l'homme, son sujet pervers et révolté.

Du pan de son manteau que l'abîme constelle,
Elle daigne essuyer les moiteurs de nos fronts,
Et son âme éternelle et sa forme immortelle
Donnent calme et vigueur à nos cœurs mous et prompts.

Le frais balancement des ramures chenues,
L'horizon élargi plein de vagues chansons,
Tout, jusqu'au vol joyeux des oiseaux et des nues,
Tout, aujourd'hui, console et délivre.—Pensons.

II

Donc, c'en est fait. Ce livre est clos. Chères Idées
Qui rayiez mon ciel gris de vos ailes de feu
Dont le vent caressait mes tempes obsédées,
Vous pouvez revoler devers l'Infini bleu!

Torrents breached the soul's defences,
Drowned thought and shattered everything
In their path, then sprang up again
Agile and voracious as flames
  Before they froze.

Epilogue

I

A weakened sun brightens a thinner sky.
Moved by autumn's lullaby of air
Garden-roses bend their stems together.
All around, the air is like a chaste girl's kiss.

This time Nature's stepped down from its throne
Of serenity, irony, splendour.
In gentle mode she descends yellow space to meet
Her human subjects, rebellious and wild.

With star-sown folds of her vast cloak
She deigns to dry our beads of sweat.
Her deathless soul, her timeless form
Calmly strengthen our rash and foolish hearts.

Consider the cooling sway of large old branches,
The wide horizon filled with wisps of song,
The joyful fly-past of birds and clouds—
All today is freedom, everything consoles.

II

So that's that. The book's closed. Much-loved ideas
Which scored my sombre skies with flights of fire
Where soothing eddies stroked my manic head—
Go find your place again in the Beyond.

Et toi, Vers qui tintais, et toi, Rime sonore,
Et vous, Rhythmes chanteurs, et vous, délicieux
Ressouvenirs, et vous, Rêves, et vous encore,
Images qu'évoquaient mes désirs anxieux,

Il faut nous séparer. Jusqu'aux jours plus propices
Où nous réunira l'Art, notre maître, adieu,
Adieu, doux compagnons, adieu, charmants complices!
Vous pouvez revoler devers l'Infini bleu.

Aussi bien, nous avons fourni notre carrière
Et le jeune étalon de notre bon plaisir,
Tout affolé qu'il est de sa course première,
A besoin d'un peu d'ombre et de quelque loisir.

—Car toujours nous t'avons fixée, ô Poésie,
Notre astre unique et notre unique passion,
T'ayant seule pour guide et compagne choisie,
Mère, et nous méfiant de l'Inspiration.

III

Ah! l'Inspiration superbe et souveraine,
L'Égérie aux regards lumineux et profonds,
Le Genium commode et l'Erato soudaine,
L'Ange des vieux tableaux avec des ors au fond,

La Muse, dont la voix est puissante sans doute,
Puisqu'elle fait d'un coup dans les premiers cerveaux,
Comme ces pissenlits dont s'émaille la route,
Pousser tout un jardin de poëmes nouveaux,

La Colombe, le Saint-Esprit, le saint Délire,
Les Troubles opportuns, les Transports complaisants,
Gabriel et son luth, Apollon et sa lyre,
Ah! l'Inspiration, on l'invoque à seize ans!

And you, ringing line of verse, sonorous rhyme,
Singing rhythms, and you, delicious
Memories, dreams, and then again you,
Pictures conjured up by disturbed desires,

We must say our goodbyes. Until those happier days
When we'll be rejoined by our Great Master, Art,
Farewell, my good companions, sweet accomplices!
Spread your wings, find the Blue Unknown.

Besides, it's been a lengthy course to stay
For the stallion at full stretch.
Panic-stricken after its first race,
It needs a shady place to rest.

—For we've always taken our bearings, Poetry,
On you, our lode-star, our one passion,
Our only guide and chosen companion,
Our mother steering us away from Inspiration.

III

Superb, superlative Inspiration,
Egeria* of the luminous deep gaze,
Biddable Genius,* impulsive Erato,*
The Angel in old paintings on a background of gold,

The Muse with the power in her voice
To create out of nothing on fresh ground
(Like dandelions which fleck a path)
Whole gardens planted with new poetry.

Saintly Delirium, the Dove, the Holy Ghost,
Timely Anxieties, easy Excitements,
Gabriel* and his harp, Apollo* and his lyre—
Ah, Inspiration, the door we try when we're sixteen.

Ce qu'il nous faut à nous, les Suprêmes Poëtes
Qui vénérons les Dieux et qui n'y croyons pas,
A nous dont nul rayon n'auréola les têtes,
Dont nulle Béatrix n'a dirigé les pas,

A nous qui ciselons les mots comme des coupes
Et qui faisons des vers émus très froidement,
A nous qu'on ne voit point les soirs aller par groupes
Harmonieux au bords des *lacs* et nous pâmant,

Ce qu'il nous faut, à nous, c'est, aux lueurs des lampes,
La science conquise et le sommeil dompté,
C'est le front dans les mains du vieux Faust des estampes,
C'est l'Obstination et c'est la Volonté!

C'est la Volonté sainte, absolue, éternelle,
Cramponnée au projet comme un noble condor
Aux flancs fumants de peur d'un buffle, et d'un coup d'aile
Emportant son trophée à travers les cieux d'or!

Ce qu'il nous faut à nous, c'est l'étude sans trêve,
C'est l'effort inouï, le combat nonpareil,
C'est la nuit, l'âpre nuit du travail, d'où se lève
Lentement, lentement, l'Œuvre, ainsi qu'un soleil!

Libre à nos Inspirés, cœurs qu'une œillade enflamme,
D'abandonner leur être aux vents comme un bouleau;
Pauvres gens! l'Art n'est pas d'éparpiller son âme:
Est-elle en marbre, ou non, la Vénus de Milo?

Nous donc, sculptons avec le ciseau des Pensées
Le bloc vierge du Beau, Paros immaculé,
Et faisons-en surgir sous nos mains empressées
Quelque pure statue au péplos étoilé,

Afin qu'un jour, frappant de rayons gris et roses
Le chef-d'œuvre serein, comme un nouveau Memnon,
L'Aube-Postérité, fille des Temps moroses,
Fasse dans l'air futur retentir notre nom!

What we need, Supreme Poets, worshippers
Of gods we don't believe in,
We whose brows were never ringed with light,
Whose steps were guided by no Beatrice,*

We who fashion words like silversmiths
And sculpt confessions with cool detachment,
We who never stroll accompanied by friends
Along the shores of lakes, dizzy with emotion—

What our kind wants is to conquer heights
Of knowledge on open-eyed lamp-lit nights,
That old image of Faust,* head in hands;
In two words, Obstinacy and Will.

Sacred, eternal, absolute Will
Which grabs its prey the way a noble condor
Grips the sweating flanks of terrified beasts,
And takes its trophy high into golden skies.

What we ask is unremitting study,
Colossal effort, unequalled fight.
We need night, the raw night of work, from which
The Magnum Opus slowly rises like a sun!

As for those they call Inspired, too easily charmed
By a smile, let them blow in the wind like a tree.
Pity them; wills-of-the-wisp can't make true Art.
The Venus de Milo:* is she marble or not?

So, with the chisel of Thought we must work
Fresh-quarried Beauty, virgin Paros* marble.
Our busy hands must reveal
The pure and perfect statue draped in stars.

So that soon the dawn of Posterity, daughter
Of dismal Times, touching with greys and pinks
The sublime chef-d'œuvre, may make your name sing
On future winds, like a Memnon* of our times.

Fêtes galantes

Sur l'herbe

L'abbé divague.—Et toi, marquis,
Tu mets de travers ta perruque.
—Ce vieux vin de Chypre est exquis
Moins, Camargo, que votre nuque.

—Ma flamme...—Do, mi, sol, la, si.
L'abbé, ta noirceur se dévoile!
—Que je meure, Mesdames, si
Je ne vous décroche une étoile!

—Je voudrais être petit chien!
—Embrassons nos bergères l'une
Après l'autre.—Messieurs, eh bien?
—Do, mi, sol.—Hé! bonsoir, la Lune!

Les Ingénus

Les hauts talons luttaient avec les longues jupes,
En sorte que, selon le terrain et le vent,
Parfois luisaient des bas de jambes, trop souvent
Interceptés!—et nous aimions ce jeu de dupes.

Parfois aussi le dard d'un insecte jaloux
Inquiétait le col des belles sous les branches,
Et c'étaient des éclairs soudains de nuques blanches,
Et ce régal comblait nos jeunes yeux de fous.

Le soir tombait, un soir équivoque d'automne:
Les belles, se pendant rêveuses à nos bras,
Dirent alors des mots si spécieux, tout bas,
Que notre âme, depuis ce temps, tremble et s'étonne.

On the grass

The abbé rambles—Marquis, I think you'll find
You've put your wig on all askew.
—This Cyprus wine's not so divine,
Camargo of the lovely neck, as you.

—I burn...—Do re mi fa sol la.
—Your black soul's showing under your black cloak,
Abbé.—Sweet ladies, may I choke
If I don't reach you down a star!

—I'd love to be your little doggie!
—Let's kiss these shepherdesses, one by
One, good gentleman. So, who's with me?
—Do re mi.—Oh look, there's a moon in the sky!

Without guile

High heels fought a battle with long skirts
So that, subject to terrain and strength of wind,
An ankle sometimes was glimpsed, too often
Caught!—we loved to work out who was fooling whom.

And sometimes too a darting jealous insect swooped
And irritated lovely necks beneath the trees.
Flashing glimpses of pale napes were seen,
A sight for young besotted eyes.

Evening fell, autumnal, indeterminate.
The lovely girls in a dream on our arms
Murmured such empty words so low
That ever since we've trembled with delight.

Cortège

Un singe en veste de brocart
Trotte et gambade devant elle
Qui froisse un mouchoir de dentelle
Dans sa main gantée avec art,

Tandis qu'un négrillon tout rouge
Maintient à tour de bras les pans
De sa lourde robe en suspens,
Attentif à tout pli qui bouge;

Le singe ne perd pas des yeux
La gorge blanche de la dame,
Opulent trésor que réclame
Le torse nu de l'un des dieux;

Le négrillon parfois soulève
Plus haut qu'il ne faut, l'aigrefin,
Son fardeau somptueux, afin
De voir ce dont la nuit il rêve;

Elle va par les escaliers,
Et ne paraît pas davantage
Sensible à l'insolent suffrage
De ses animaux familiers.

Les Coquillages

Chaque coquillage incrusté
Dans la grotte où nous nous aimâmes
A sa particularité.

L'un a la pourpre de nos âmes
Dérobée au sang de nos cœurs
Quand je brûle et que tu t'enflammes;

Cortège

In its tiny brocade coat
A monkey twists and turns in front of her.
She holds a crumpled handkerchief
In a carefully gloved hand.

Her black page, a lad all dressed in red,
Holds high the lady's heavy train.
He moves the weight from arm to arm,
His eye on every shifting fold.

The monkey keeps its gaze fixed on
The lady's throat displaying wealth
And opulence just meant to grace
The naked splendour of a god.

Sometimes the scheming page lifts up
A good deal higher than he should
His rich responsibility
To spy what in his dreams he sees.

Then she climbs the flight of stairs
Quite ignorant, it seems,
Of how her too-familiar pets
Are full of disrespectful praise.

Shells

Each encrusted shell
In our grotto of love
Is unique.

One has the red of our two souls
Stolen from our hearts
When I burn and you're on fire.

Cet autre affecte tes langueurs
Et tes pâleurs alors que, lasse,
Tu m'en veux de mes yeux moqueurs;

Celui-ci contrefait la grâce
De ton oreille, et celui-là
Ta nuque rose, courte et grasse;

Mais un, entre autres, me troubla.

Fantoches

Scaramouche et Pulcinella
Qu'un mauvais dessein rassembla
Gesticulent, noirs sur la lune.

Cependant l'excellent docteur
Bolonais cueille avec lenteur
Des simples parmi l'herbe brune.

Lors sa fille, piquant minois,
Sous la charmille, en tapinois,
Se glisse, demi-nue, en quête

De son beau pirate espagnol,
Dont un langoureux rossignol
Clame la détresse à tue-tête.

En bateau

L'étoile du berger tremblote
Dans l'eau plus noire et le pilote
Cherche un briquet dans sa culotte.

C'est l'instant, Messieurs, ou jamais,
D'être audacieux, et je mets
Mes deux mains partout désormais!

One takes on your languor,
Your tired pallor,
Resentment of my mocking eyes.

This one mimics the grace
Of your ear, that one your pink
And chubby little neck.

But one among the rest has got to me.

Weird as puppets

Scaramouche* and Pulchinella*
Making evil plans together
Wave their arms, moon-silhouettes.

But the excellent Bolognese
Doctor's picking some of these
Special herbs among the grass.

His daughter with the pretty eyes,
In the arbour, on the sly's
Looking—semi-naked—for

Her handsome Spanish buccaneer
Whose sad affliction she can hear
Well noted by a nightingale.

Boating

Evening star bobbing
On black water; helmsman searching
Pocket for lighter.

Gentlemen, it's now or never.
Take your courage in both hands—
My two hands will go a-roaming.

Le chevalier Atys, qui gratte
Sa guitare, à Chloris l'ingrate
Lance une œillade scélérate.

L'abbé confesse bas Églé,
Et ce vicomte déréglé
Des champs donne à son cœur la clé.

Cependant la lune se lève
Et l'esquif en sa course brève
File gaîment sur l'eau qui rêve.

Le faune

Un vieux faune de terre cuite
Rit au centre des boulingrins,
Présageant sans doute une suite
Mauvaise à ces instants sereins

Que m'ont conduit et t'ont conduite,
—Mélancoliques pèlerins,—
Jusqu'à cette heure dont la fuite
Tournoie au son des tambourins.

A Clymène

Mystiques barcarolles,
Romances sans paroles,
Chère, puisque tes yeux,
Couleur des cieux,

Puisque ta voix, étrange
Vision qui dérange
Et trouble l'horizon
De ma raison,

Lord Atys* plucking strings
Makes eyes at Chloris.*
Result, why, not a thing.

The abbot hears Aglaia's*
Whispered confession; a mad Count
Lets his heart roam free.

Moon emerging;
Small boat on short journey,
Glide on water, dreaming.

The faun

An old terracotta faun
Laughs in the smooth grass
Foreseeing no doubt bad
Things after such

Serenity, which led me, led you
Like melancholy pilgrims
To this moment passing
In a dance of tambourins.

To Clymene*

Mystic barcarolles,
Songs without words...*
Sweet girl, your eyes
    Colour of skies,

Your voice, unsettling
And strange vision
Clouding my reason's
    Horizon,

Puisque l'arome insigne
De ta pâleur de cygne,
Et puisque la candeur
   De ton odeur,

Ah! puisque tout ton être,
Musique qui pénètre,
Nimbes d'anges défunts,
   Tons et parfums,

A, sur d'almes cadences,
En ses correspondances
Induit mon cœur subtil,
   Ainsi soit-il!

Colombine

Léandre le sot,
Pierrot qui d'un saut
   De puce
Franchit le buisson,
Cassandre sous son
   Capuce,

Arlequin aussi,
Cet aigrefin si
   Fantasque
Aux costumes fous,
Ses yeux luisant sous
   Son masque,

—Do, mi, sol, mi, fa,—
Tout ce monde va,
   Rit, chante
Et danse devant
Une belle enfant
   Méchante

Your scent, unique
And pale as swans,
The fresh candour
   Of your smell...

Since all that is you,
Deepest music,
Lost angels' haloes,
   Sweet scent, tones,

Has to pastoral
Cadences freed and
Charmed my subtle heart,
   Let it be so!

Colombine*

Stupid Leander,*
Pierrot* who with a
   Flea-hop
Clears the espalier,
Pantaloon* under
   His cloak,

Harlequin* also,
That reprobate so
   Bizarre
In his crazy clothes
With his glowing eyes
   Disguised,

—Do re mi fa sol,
Round and round they go,
   Laugh, sing
And dance before a
Sweet improper
   Young thing

Dont les yeux pervers
Comme les yeux verts
    Des chattes
Gardent ses appas
Et disent: 'A bas
    Les pattes!'

—Eux ils vont toujours!
Fatidique cours
    Des astres,
Oh! dis-moi vers quels
Mornes ou cruels
    Désastres

L'implacable enfant,
Preste et relevant
    Ses jupes,
La rose au chapeau,
Conduit son troupeau
    De dupes?

En sourdine

Calmes dans le demi-jour
Que les branches hautes font,
Pénétrons bien notre amour
De ce silence profond.

Fondons nos âmes, nos cœurs
Et nos sens extasiés,
Parmi les vagues langueurs
Des pins et des arbousiers.

Ferme tes yeux à demi,
Croise tes bras sur ton sein,
Et de ton cœur endormi
Chasse à jamais tout dessein.

Whose eyes say beware,
The way the green stare
  Of cats
Entices and draws
In and says: 'Keep your
  Hands off!'

The others dance on
Like fated astron-
  Omers...
Tell me, towards which
Ghastly or savage
  Wreckage

The determined child
With lifted hem, wild
  And loose,
A flower in her hat,
Is leading her lamb-
  Like fools?

Muted tones

Calm in the half-light
Cast by high branches
Let the deep quiet
Reach into our love.

Melt as one soul
One heart one charm
Of senses under soft swaying
Pines and arbuti.

Half-close your eyes
Fold your arms
Empty for good your sleeping heart
Of all its concerns.

Laissons-nous persuader
Au souffle berceur et doux
Qui vient à tes pieds rider
Les ondes de gazon roux.

Et quand, solennel, le soir
Des chênes noirs tombera,
Voix de notre désespoir,
Le rossignol chantera.

Colloque sentimental

Dans le vieux parc solitaire et glacé,
Deux formes ont tout à l'heure passé.

Leurs yeux sont morts et leurs lèvres sont molles,
Et l'on entend à peine leurs paroles.

Dans le vieux parc solitaire et glacé,
Deux spectres ont évoqué le passé.

—Te souvient-il de notre extase ancienne?
—Pourquoi voulez-vous donc qu'il m'en souvienne?

—Ton cœur bat-il toujours à mon seul nom?
Toujours vois-tu mon âme en rêve?—Non.

—Ah! les beaux jours de bonheur indicible
Où nous joignions nos bouches!—C'est possible.

—Qu'il était bleu, le ciel, et grand, l'espoir!
—L'espoir a fui, vaincu, vers le ciel noir.

Tel ils marchaient dans les avoines folles,
Et la nuit seule entendit leurs paroles.

Be captivated by
Air's lullaby
Whispering over
The russet lawn where you stand.

And when solemn evening
Falls dark with oak
That voice of our despair
The nightingale will start to sing.

Exchange of feelings

In the old park frozen and alone,
Two shapes passed by a while ago.

Their eyes were dead, their lips weak,
And the words they spoke were barely heard.

In the old park frozen and alone
Two ghosts recalled a vanished time.

'Do you recall how much we were in love?'
'Why should I want to think of that?'

'Does your heart still beat to my name alone?
When you dream, is it me you dream about?' 'No.'

'Sweet days of happiness beyond words,
Days that passed in a kiss!' 'And why not.'

'Such blue skies, then, such great hopes!'
'Hope's done for, a black hole in space.'

And so they went on among the rough grass
With only the night to hear what they said.

L'Enterrement

Je ne sais rien de gai comme un enterrement!
Le fossoyeur qui chante et sa pioche qui brille,
La cloche, au loin, dans l'air, lançant son svelte trille,
Le prêtre, en blanc surplis, qui prie allégrement,

L'enfant de chœur avec sa voix fraîche de fille,
Et quand, au fond du trou, bien chaud, douillettement,
S'installe le cercueil, le mol éboulement
De la terre, édredon du défunt, heureux drille,

Tout cela me paraît charmant, en vérité!
Et puis, tout rondelets sous leur frac écourté,
Les croque-morts au nez rougi par les pourboires,

Et puis les beaux discours concis, mais pleins de sens,
Et puis, cœurs élargis, fronts où flotte une gloire,
    Les héritiers resplendissants!

[1865?]

The burial

I know nothing that's more fun than a burial.
The sexton sings away, his pick-axe gleams,
The distant bell trills thinly in the air,
The white-frocked priest skips through the prayers.

The choirboy's treble flutes like a girl,
And when, nice and warm and snug, the coffin
Settles in its hole followed by the thud of earth
(The dear departed's eiderdown, the lucky man),

I have to say, the whole thing's quite charming.
Then there's the undertakers, plump in their short
Formal coats, their ruddy noses tipped with drink,

Then the eulogies, not long but full of sense,
And then, brows luminous, hearts bursting,
   The heirs.

[1865?]

La Bonne Chanson

'La lune blanche'

La lune blanche
Luit dans les bois;
De chaque branche
Part une voix
Sous la ramée...

Ô bien-aimée.

L'étang reflète,
Profond miroir,
La silhouette
Du saule noir
Où le vent pleure...

Rêvons, c'est l'heure.

Un vaste et tendre
Apaisement
Semble descendre
Du firmament
Que l'astre irise...

C'est l'heure exquise.

'Le paysage dans le cadre . . .'

Le paysage dans le cadre des portières
Court furieusement, et des plaines entières
Avec de l'eau, des blés, des arbres et du ciel
Vont s'engouffrant parmi le tourbillon cruel
Où tombent les poteaux minces du télégraphe
Dont les fils ont l'allure étrange d'un paraphe.

White moon . . .

White moon gleaming
Among trees,
From every branch
Sound rising into
Canopies...

Oh my love.

Mirror-pond
Giving back deep
Silhouettes
Of dark willow-trees
In the wind, weeping...

A time for dreams.

Vast tender calm
Seemingly
Descending
From colour-spectrum skies
Huge with stars...

Exquisite hour.

'The landscape framed . . .'

The landscape framed in the carriage window
Runs past at furious speed and whole plains
Of water wheat trees sky
Are swallowed in vortices
Felling one by one the slender telegraph poles
Whose wires make strange flourishes like a pen.

Une odeur de charbon qui brûle et d'eau qui bout,
Tout le bruit que feraient mille chaînes au bout
Desquelles hurleraient mille géants qu'on fouette;
Et tout à coup des cris prolongés de chouette.
—Que me fait tout cela, puisque j'ai dans les yeux
La blanche vision qui fait mon cœur joyeux,
Puisque la douce voix pour moi murmure encore,
Puisque le Nom si beau, si noble et si sonore
Se mêle, pur pivot de tout ce tournoiement,
Au rhythme du wagon brutal, suavement.

'Son bras droit . . .'

Son bras droit, dans un geste aimable de douceur,
Repose autour du cou de la petite sœur,
Et son bras gauche suit le rythme de la jupe.
A coup sûr une idée agréable l'occupe,
Car ses yeux si francs, car sa bouche qui sourit
Témoignent d'une joie intime avec esprit.
Oh! sa pensée exquise et fine, quelle est-elle?
Toute mignonne, tout aimable, et toute belle,
Pour ce portrait, son goût infaillible a choisi
La pose la plus simple et la meilleure aussi:
Debout, le regard droit, en cheveux; et sa robe
Est longue juste assez pour qu'elle ne dérobe
Qu'à moitié sous ses plis jaloux le bout charmant
D'un pied malicieux imperceptiblement.

'Quinze longs jours . . .'

Quinze longs jours encore et plus de six semaines
Déjà! Certes, parmi les angoisses humaines,
La plus dolente angoisse est celle d'être loin.

On s'écrit, on se dit que l'on s'aime; on a soin
D'évoquer chaque jour la voix, les yeux, le geste
De l'être en qui l'on met son bonheur, et l'on reste

A smell of burning coal and water on the boil
A huge noise like a chain-gang of a thousand
Giants in agony under the lash
Then suddenly the long call of an owl—
How can this touch me, since I have
Before my eyes that white uplifting vision
Since the sweet voice still speaks low to me
Since the beautiful sonorous noble Name
Pure fulcrum of this wild velocity
Merges with the metal rhythm easily.

'Her right arm . . .'

Her right arm, in a lovely movement full of warmth,
Settles on the little sister's shoulder;
Her left arm echoes the rhythm of her skirt.
Some pleasant thought's surely in her mind,
For those frank eyes, that smile on her lips
Are living witness of a private joy.
So what can be her fine exquisite thought?
Delicious, lovely and so beautiful,
She's chosen for this portrait, with her usual
Perfect taste, the simplest pose, the best.
She stands bare-headed, eyes straight ahead; her dress
Is of a length to half-reveal
Under jealous folds a wicked foot's
Delightful point, emerging imperceptibly.

'One long fortnight . . .'

One long fortnight still to go, and over six weeks
Gone already! One thing's sure; in the catalogue
Of human woes, the worst is separation.

We write each other affirmations of love; try
Each day to conjure up voice, gestures, eyes
Of the one we ask to make us happy; spend hours

Des heures à causer tout seul avec l'absent.
Mais tout ce que l'on pense et tout ce que l'on sent
Et tout ce dont on parle avec l'absent, persiste
A demeurer blafard et fidèlement triste.

Oh! l'absence! le moins clément de tous les maux!
Se consoler avec des phrases et des mots,
Puiser dans l'infini morose des pensées
De quoi vous rafraîchir, espérances lassées,
Et n'en rien remonter que de fade et d'amer!
Puis voici, pénétrant et froid comme le fer,
Plus rapide que les oiseaux et que les balles
Et que le vent du sud en mer et ses rafales
Et portant sur sa pointe aiguë un fin poison,
Voici venir, pareil aux flèches, le soupçon
Décoché par le Doute impur et lamentable.

Est-ce bien vrai? Tandis qu'accoudé sur ma table
Je lis sa lettre avec des larmes dans les yeux,
Sa lettre, où s'étale un aveu délicieux,
N'est-elle pas alors distraite en d'autres choses?
Qui sait? Pendant qu'ici pour moi lents et moroses
Coulent les jours, ainsi qu'un fleuve au bord flétri,
Peut-être que sa lèvre innocente a souri?
Peut-être qu'elle est très joyeuse et qu'elle oublie?

Et je relis sa lettre avec mélancolie.

'Va, chanson . . .'

Va, chanson, à tire-d'aile
Au-devant d'elle, et dis-lui
Bien que dans mon cœur fidèle
Un rayon joyeux a lui,

One-sidedly conversing with the absentee.
But everything we think, we feel,
Everything we talk about stays bleak
Stubbornly, and resolutely sad.

Absence, the least forgiving pain!
Phrases and words may console,
But dig deep in the dark pit of thought,
Look for something to bolster fading hope,
And you dredge up only ash and bile.
Here, colder and more piercing than swords,
Swifter than birds, quicker than gunfire
Or sea-winds gusting from the south,
Tipped with sharp points of subtle poison,
Here, like showers of arrows, comes suspicion
Unleashed by unworthy, impure doubt.

Can it be true? I prop my elbows on my table
To read with tearful eyes her letter
Of delicious revelations—
But surely her mind's full now of other things?
Who knows? While for me the days here trickle by
Morose and slow as a river through barrenness,
Perhaps her blameless mouth's granting someone
Smiles? Is she joyful, starting to forget?

And I reread her words in melancholy mode.

'Go on song . . .'

Go on song, up and away,
Find her, be sure to tell
Her joy illuminates
My devoted heart

Dissipant, lumière sainte,
Ces ténèbres de l'amour:
Méfiance, doute, crainte,
Et que voici le grand jour!

Longtemps craintive et muette,
Entendez-vous? la gaîté,
Comme une vive alouette,
Dans le ciel clair a chanté.

Va donc, chanson ingénue,
Et que, sans nul regret vain,
Elle soit la bienvenue
Celle qui revient enfin.

'Le foyer, la lueur . . .'

Le foyer, la lueur étroite de la lampe;
La rêverie avec le doigt contre la tempe
Et les yeux se perdant parmi les yeux aimés;
L'heure du thé fumant et des livres fermés;
La douceur de sentir la fin de la soirée;
La fatigue charmante et l'attente adorée
De l'ombre nuptiale et de la douce nuit,
Oh! tout cela, mon rêve attendri le poursuit
Sans relâche, à travers toutes remises vaines,
Impatient des mois, furieux des semaines!

'J'ai presque peur . . .'

J'ai presque peur, en vérité,
Tant je sens ma vie enlacée
A la radieuse pensée
Qui m'a pris l'âme l'autre été,

La Bonne Chanson

Like holy light dispelling
Shadows clouding love;
Suspicion, fear, and doubt.
Tell her it's broad daylight now.

For too long shy and quiet,
Can you hear the joy, bright
As a lark on the wing
Starting to sing in clear skies?

Go then, simple artless song,
Set her free of vain regrets,
Bid her welcome,
She who's coming back at last.

'Home . . .'

Home; the snug glow of lamps;
Daydreams; a finger to the temple;
Eyes lost in loved ones' eyes;
The hour of fresh-made tea; of closed books;
Sweet sensation of evening ending;
Enchantment of sleep closing in; rapture
Of shadow-union coming in night's sweetness;
All this my melting dream pursues
And pursues, impatient with postponement,
Counting the months, furious with the weeks.

'I'm almost scared . . .'

I'm almost scared, if truth be told.
My life seems so meshed
With that most radiant thought
Which last summer blinded me,

Tant votre image, à jamais chère,
Habite en ce cœur tout à vous,
Mon cœur uniquement jaloux
De vous aimer et de vous plaire;

Et je tremble, pardonnez-moi
D'aussi franchement vous le dire,
A penser qu'un mot, un sourire
De vous est désormais ma loi,

Et qu'il vous suffirait d'un geste,
D'une parole ou d'un clin d'œil,
Pour mettre tout mon être en deuil
De son illusion céleste.

Mais plutôt je ne veux vous voir,
L'avenir dût-il m'être sombre
Et fécond en peines sans nombre,
Qu'à travers un immense espoir,

Plongé dans ce bonheur suprême
De me dire encore et toujours,
En dépit des mornes retours,
Que je vous aime, que je t'aime!

'Le bruit des cabarets . . .'

Le bruit des cabarets, la fange du trottoir,
Les platanes déchus s'effeuillant dans l'air noir,
L'omnibus, ouragan de ferraille et de boues,
Qui grince, mal assis entre ses quatre roues,
Et roule ses yeux verts et rouges lentement,
Les ouvriers allant au club, tout en fumant
Leur brûle-gueule au nez des agents de police,
Toits qui dégouttent, murs suintants, pavé qui glisse,
Bitume défoncé, ruisseaux comblant l'égout,
Voilà ma route—avec le paradis au bout.

So firmly is my image of you lodged
In this heart which beats for you alone,
Jealous guardian of its right
To love and give you pleasure.

Forgive me, then, if I tell you this,
As sincerely as I can:
I tremble knowing that a word,
A smile from you undo me,

That all it needs is a sign,
A word or a look in your eyes,
To plunge me into distress,
Grieving for my paradise.

No, I'd rather see you only
(However dark my life might be,
However bottomless the mineshaft
Of pain) through the glass of great hope,

Bathed in that great happiness,
Whatever sad vicissitudes,
Of knowing always I love the
All, the everything of you.*

'The noise of bars . . .'

The noise of bars, the filth in the streets,
The plane-trees shedding leaves in the dark,
The passing bus, thunder of scrap-iron and mud
Squealing with pain astride its four wheels,
Slowly rolling its green and red eyes;
Workers heading to their social club, puffing
Pipe-smoke in policemen's faces,
Water dripping from roofs, oozing walls, slippery roads,
Broken asphalt, overflowing drains;
Such is my route—paradise lies at the end.

L'Écolière

Je t'apprendrai, chère petite,
Ce qu'il te fallait savoir peu
Jusqu'à ce présent où palpite
Ton beau corps dans mes bras de dieu.

Ta chair, si délicate, est blanche,
Telle la neige et tel le lys,
Ton sein aux veines de pervenche
Se dresse en deux arcs accomplis;

Quant à ta bouche, rose exquise,
Elle appelle mon baiser fier;
Mais sous le pli de ta chemise
Rit un baiser encore plus cher...

Tu passeras, d'humble écolière,
J'en suis sûr et je t'en réponds,
Bien vite au rang de bachelière
Dans l'art d'aimer les instants bons.

A propos d'un mot naïf d'elle

Tu parles d'avoir un enfant
Et n'as qu'à moitié la recette.
Nous baiser sur la bouche, avant,
Est utile, certes, à cette
Besogne d'avoir un enfant.

Mais, dût s'en voir à tort marri
L'idéal pur qui te réclame,
En ce monde mal équarri,
Il te faut être en sus ma femme
Et moi me prouver ton mari.

[1869–70]

Schoolgirl

I'll teach you things, my little girl,
You didn't need to know before,
Since now the beauty that you are
Is trembling in my god-like arms.

Your skin—so delicate—is white,
Like lilies, like snow.
Your breasts like blue-veined flowers
Curve high in perfect symmetry.

As for your mouth, exquisite rose,
It seems to call for my proud lips;
But in a fold of your chemise
There smiles a kiss more precious still...

From humble schoolgirl you'll soon pass
(You have my written guarantee)
To somewhere you can take degrees
In 'Fun and Games', BA, First Class.

On a naïve word from her

You say you want to have a child,
But give just half the recipe.
Two mouths which first exchange a kiss
Can doubtless help in getting this
Babegetting underway.

But even though your high ideal
Might sadly start to crash to earth,
Here in this topsy-turvy world
Above all you must be a wife
Who makes her husband spring to life.

[1869–70]

Romances sans paroles

'C'est l'extase langoureuse'

Le vent dans la plaine
Suspend son haleine.

(Favart)

C'est l'extase langoureuse,
C'est la fatigue amoureuse,
C'est tous les frissons des bois
Parmi l'étreinte des brises,
C'est, vers les ramures grises,
Le chœur des petites voix.

Ô le frêle et frais murmure!
Cela gazouille et susurre,
Cela ressemble au cri doux
Que l'herbe agitée expire...
Tu dirais, sous l'eau qui vire,
Le roulis sourd des cailloux.

Cette âme qui se lamente
En cette plainte dormante
C'est la nôtre, n'est-ce pas?
La mienne, dis, et la tienne,
Dont s'exhale l'humble antienne
Par ce tiède soir, tout bas?

'Il pleure dans mon cœur'

Il pleut doucement sur la ville.

(Arthur Rimbaud)

Il pleure dans mon cœur
Comme il pleut sur la ville;
Quelle est cette langueur
Qui pénètre mon cœur?

'It's languor and ecstasy'

> The wind on the plain
> Ceases its flight.
>
> (Favart)*

It's languor and ecstasy,
It's the sleep of love,
Woods trembling
In the bite of the wind,
It's small voices chorusing
Over by the trees.

Fresh, frail murmur!
Whispers and warbles
Like the sigh
Of grass disturbed...
Like the muffled roll
Of pebbles under moving water.

This soul lost
In sleep-filled lamentation
Surely is ours?
Mine, surely, and yours,
Softly breathing
Low anthems on a warm evening?

'Falling tears . . .'

> Soft rain falling on the town.
>
> (Rimbaud)*

Falling tears in my heart,
Falling rain on the town.
Why this long ache,
A knife in my heart?

Ô bruit doux de la pluie
Par terre et sur les toits!
Pour un cœur qui s'ennuie
Ô le chant de la pluie!

Il pleure sans raison
Dans ce cœur qui s'écœure.
Quoi! nulle trahison?...
Ce deuil est sans raison.

C'est bien la pire peine
De ne savoir pourquoi
Sans amour et sans haine
Mon cœur a tant de peine!

'Il faut, voyez-vous . . .'

De la douceur, de la douceur, de la douceur.

(Inconnu)

Il faut, voyez-vous, nous pardonner les choses:
De cette façon nous serons bien heureuses
Et si notre vie a des instants moroses,
Du moins nous serons, n'est-ce pas? deux pleureuses.

Ô que nous mêlions, âmes sœurs que nous sommes,
A nos vœux confus la douceur puérile
De cheminer loin des femmes et des hommes,
Dans le frais oubli de ce qui nous exile!

Soyons deux enfants, soyons deux jeunes filles
Éprises de rien et de tout étonnées
Qui s'en vont pâlir sous les chastes charmilles
Sans même savoir qu'elles sont pardonnées.

Oh, soft sound of rain
On ground and roof!
For hearts full of ennui*
The song of the rain!

Tearfall without reason
In my sickened heart.
Really, no treason?
This grief has no reason.

By far the worst pain
Is not to understand
Why without love or hate
My heart's full of pain.

'You see, we have to be forgiven . . .'

Sweetness, sweetness, sweetness.
(Anonymous)

You see, we have to be forgiven things;
This way happiness lies,
And if our life goes through gloomy times,
Why then, we'll be a pair of snivellers.

How good if our twin souls could blend
Vague desires with the infantile joy
Of walking free of women and men,
Backs turned on persecutors.

Let's be children, let's be two young girls
Free as air and full of wonder,
Who grow pale in simple groves of trees,
Not knowing even that they've been forgiven.

'Le piano que baise . . .'

Son joyeux, importun, d'un clavecin sonore.

(Pétrus Borel)

Le piano que baise une main frêle
Luit dans le soir rose et gris vaguement,
Tandis qu'avec un très léger bruit d'aile
Un air bien vieux, bien faible et bien charmant
Rôde discret, épeuré quasiment,
Par le boudoir longtemps parfumé d'Elle.

Qu'est-ce que c'est que ce berceau soudain
Qui lentement dorlote mon pauvre être?
Que voudrais-tu de moi, doux Chant badin?
Qu'as-tu voulu, fin refrain incertain
Qui vas tantôt mourir vers la fenêtre
Ouverte un peu sur le petit jardin?

'Ô triste, triste . . .'

Ô triste, triste était mon âme
A cause, à cause d'une femme.

Je ne me suis pas consolé
Bien que mon cœur s'en soit allé,

Bien que mon cœur, bien que mon âme
Eussent fui loin de cette femme.

Je ne me suis pas consolé,
Bien que mon cœur s'en soit allé.

Et mon cœur, mon cœur trop sensible
Dit à mon âme: Est-il possible,

Est-il possible,—le fût-il,—
Ce fier exil, ce triste exil?

Mon âme dit à mon cœur: Sais-je
Moi même que nous veut ce piège

'The piano kissed . . .'

Unbidden, happy sound of a melodious harpsichord.

(Pétrus Borel)*

The piano kissed by a slender hand
Has vague sheens in the grey-pink light
Of evening, while on almost silent wings
A slight and very old and charming air
Roams discreetly as if scared
Of that inner sanctum full of Her.

Tell me, why suddenly this cradle
Rocking my poor bones to gentle rhythms?
Why this soft song playing games with me?
What did you want, you fine wisps
Of music dying at the window
Half-opened on the little garden?

'How sad I was . . .'

How sad I was, how sad,
Because of a woman, because.

The suffering endures
Although I've gone,

Heart, body and soul,
A world away from her.

No consolation,
Though in my heart I've gone.

My heart's long pain asks:
How can this be so,

How can it be? — Is this proud,
Sad exile just a dream?

I answer: I don't know
Why we're caught in this web,

D'être présents bien qu'exilés,
Encore que loin en allés?

'Dans l'interminable'

Dans l'interminable
Ennui de la plaine
La neige incertaine
Luit comme du sable.

Le ciel est de cuivre
Sans lueur aucune.
On croirait voir vivre
Et mourir la lune.

Comme des nuées
Flottent gris les chênes
Des forêts prochaines
Parmi les buées.

Le ciel est de cuivre
Sans lueur aucune.
On croirait voir vivre
Et mourir la lune.

Corneille poussive
Et vous, les loups maigres,
Par ces bises aigres
Quoi donc vous arrive?

Dans l'interminable
Ennui de la plaine
La neige incertaine
Luit comme du sable.

This warp of time and place,
This here and now and there and then?

'Endless sameness'

Endless sameness
Of the plain.
Uncertain snow
Gleams like sand.

A dull matt
Copper sky where
The moon appears
To live and die.

Like large clouds
Mist-shrouded
Oaks in woods
Nearby float grey.

A dull matt
Copper sky where
The moon appears
To live and die.

Asthmatic crow
Famished wolves
What's happening to you
In these sharp winds?

Endless sameness
Of the plain.
Uncertain snow
Gleams like sand.

'L'ombre des arbres . . .'

Le rossignol qui du haut d'une branche se regarde dedans, croit être tombé dans la rivière. Il est au sommet d'un chêne et toutefois il a peur de se noyer.

(Cyrano de Bergerac)

L'ombre des arbres dans la rivière embrumée
 Meurt comme de la fumée
Tandis qu'en l'air, parmi les ramures réelles,
 Se plaignent les tourterelles.

Combien, ô voyageur, ce paysage blême
 Te mira blême toi-même,
Et que tristes pleuraient dans les hautes feuillées
 Tes espérances noyées!

Mai, juin 72

Walcourt

Briques et tuiles,
Ô les charmants
Petits asiles
Pour les amants!

Houblons et vignes,
Feuilles et fleurs,
Tentes insignes
Des francs buveurs!

Guinguettes claires,
Bières, clameurs,
Servantes chères
A tous fumeurs!

Gares prochaines,
Gais chemins grands...

'Tree-shadows . . .'

The nightingale which, from the top of its branch, looks down into the river thinks it's fallen in. It's perched at the top of an oak-tree, and yet is scared it's going to drown.

(Cyrano de Bergerac)*

Tree-shadows in river-mists
   Die like smoke.
High in the air on real branches
   Doves lament.

Traveller, how often has this faded land
   Watched you fade,
How poignant your abandoned hopes
   High in trees!

May, June 1872

Walcourt*

Bricks, tiles,
Such charming
Small shelters
For lovers!

Vines, hops,
Flowers, leaves,
Known lairs of
Hard drinkers!

Beer gardens,
Ale, chatter,
Dear servants
Of smokers!

Nearby trains,
Living streets...

Quelles aubaines,
Bons juifs-errants!

Juillet 72

Bruxelles

Simples fresques I

La fuite est verdâtre et rose
Des collinés et des rampes
Dans un demi-jour de lampes
Qui vient brouiller toute chose.

L'or, sur les humbles abîmes,
Tout doucement s'ensanglante.
Des petits arbres sans cimes
Où quelque oiseau faible chante.

Triste à peine tant s'effacent
Ces apparences d'automne,
Toutes mes langueurs rêvassent,
Que berce l'air monotone.

Bruxelles

Simples fresques II

L'allée est sans fin
Sous le ciel, divin
D'être pâle ainsi:
Sais-tu qu'on serait
Bien sous le secret
De ces arbres-ci?

Des messieurs bien mis,
Sans nul doute amis
Des Royers-Collards,
Vont vers le château:

Good luck, all
Wanderers!

Brussels

Simple frescos I

Green-tinged pink tones fade
Up slopes and away up hills
In the half-light of lamps which casts
Question marks on everything.

In simple hollows gold
Gently turns blood-red.
In unseen tops of trees, somewhere
A bird sings a faint song.

I drift in a languor of dreams,
Becalmed in monotone air
And hardly even sad, so much
Does this early autumn picture fade.

Brussels

Simple frescos II

The path goes on and on
Beneath the sky, sacred
Because pallid.
You know, we'd feel so good
Here beneath the secret
Of these trees.

Some well-groomed gentlemen,
Friends surely
Of the Royers-Collards,*
Head towards the chateau.

J'estimerais beau
D'être ces vieillards.

Le château, tout blanc
Avec, à son flanc,
Le soleil couché,
Les champs à l'entour:
Oh! que notre amour
N'est-il là niché!

Estaminet du Jeune Renard, août 72

Bruxelles

Chevaux de bois

Par saint-Gille,
Viens-nous-en,
Mon agile
Alezan.

(V. Hugo)

Tournez, tournez, bons chevaux de bois,
Tournez cent tours, tournez mille tours,
Tournez souvent et tournez toujours,
Tournez, tournez au son des hautbois.

Le gros soldat, la plus grosse bonne
Sont sur vos dos comme dans leur chambre,
Car en ce jour au bois de la Cambre
Les maîtres sont tous deux en personne.

Tournez, tournez, chevaux de leur cœur,
Tandis qu'autour de tous vos tournois
Clignote l'œil du filou sournois,
Tournez au son du piston vainqueur.

C'est ravissant comme ça vous soûle
D'aller ainsi dans ce cirque bête:

I'd find it good
To be these old men.

On the white chateau
Ending sun declines
Down one elevation;
Fields on every side.
Why can't our love hide
In there somewhere?

The Jeune Renard estaminet, August 1872

Brussels

Wooden horses

> By St Giles,
> Bound over here,
> My agile
> Sorrel.
>
>   (V. Hugo)*

Go round and round, good wooden horses,
Turn a hundred times, a thousand,
Turn and turn and turn forever,
Round and round to fluting sounds.

The large soldier, the larger parlourmaid
Are as free on your backs as in their rooms,
For today master and mistress have gone
To be alone in Cambre woods.*

Round and round, horses of their hearts,
While all around your jousting-rings
The cutpurse trains his gimlet eye—
Round and round to deafening brass.

The delight of getting drunk just going
Round and round this silly circus!

Bien dans le ventre et mal dans la tête,
Du mal en masse et du bien en foule.

Tournez, tournez sans qu'il soit besoin
D'user jamais de nuls éperons
Pour commander à vos galops ronds,
Tournez, tournez, sans espoir de foin.

Et dépêchez, chevaux de leur âme:
Déjà voici que la nuit qui tombe
Va réunir pigeon et colombe
Loin de la foire et loin de madame.

Tournez, tournez! le ciel en velours
D'astres en or se vêt lentement.
Voici partir l'amante et l'amant.
Tournez au son joyeux des tambours!

Champ de foire de Saint-Gilles, août 72

Malines

Vers les prés le vent cherche noise
Aux girouettes, détail fin
Du château de quelque échevin,
Rouge de brique et bleu d'ardoise,
Vers les prés clairs, les prés sans fin...

Comme les arbres des féeries,
Des frênes, vagues frondaisons,
Échelonnent mille horizons
A ce Sahara de prairies,
Trèfle, luzerne et blancs gazons.

Les wagons filent en silence
Parmi ces sites apaisés.
Dormez, les vaches! Reposez,
Doux taureaux de la plaine immense,
Sous vos cieux à peine irisés!

Your stomach's fine, your head is not;
Feeling bad en masse, good in a crowd.

Round and round and never needing
Any spur to dig harder
And get a proper gallop going.
Round and round, no hope of hay.

Hurry, you horses of their souls.
Night is on its way
To unite pigeon and dove,
Far from the fair, far from madame.

Round and round! Slowly velvet sky
Pins golden stars to its dress.
Lover leaves the scene with lover.
Round and round to happy drums!

St Giles fairground, August 1872

Malines*

Over in the fields the wind provokes
The weathervanes, refinements
On some worthy burgher's country house,
Red of brick and blue of tile,
In the bright and endless fields...

In a kind of make-believe,
Vague leaf-sprouting ashes stand
In line around the thousand
Edges of this desert meadowland,
Clover, lucerne, white lawns.

Silently the train moves
Through a landscape deep in peace.
Sleep, cows! Lie down and rest,
Sweet bulls of this immensity
Below the sky's dull uniformity.

Le train glisse sans un murmure,
Chaque wagon est un salon
Où l'on cause bas et d'où l'on
Aime à loisir cette nature
Faite à souhait pour Fénelon.

Août 72

Birds in the night

Vous n'avez pas eu toute patience:
Cela se comprend par malheur, de reste
Vous êtes si jeune! Et l'insouciance,
C'est le lot amer de l'âge céleste!

Vous n'avez pas eu toute la douceur.
Cela par malheur d'ailleurs se comprend;
Vous êtes si jeune, ô ma froide sœur,
Que votre cœur doit être indifférent!

Aussi, me voici plein de pardons chastes,
Non, certes! joyeux, mais très calme en somme
Bien que je déplore en ces mois néfastes
D'être, grâce à vous, le moins heureux homme.

Et vous voyez bien que j'avais raison
Quand je vous disais, dans mes moments noirs,
Que vos yeux, foyers de mes vieux espoirs,
Ne couvaient plus rien que la trahison.

Vous juriez alors que c'était mensonge
Et votre regard qui mentait lui-même
Flambait comme un feu mourant qu'on prolonge,
Et de votre voix vous disiez: 'Je t'aime!'

Hélas! on se prend toujours au désir
Qu'on a d'être heureux malgré la saison...
Mais ce fut un jour plein d'amer plaisir
Quand je m'aperçus que j'avais raison!

The train slides without a sound,
Each coach a saloon
Full of quiet talk, easy vantage-point
To admire this Nature
Tailor-made for Fénelon.*

August 1872

Birds in the night

Of what's called patience you weren't exactly full.
Understandable, agreed, and anyway
You're young and the don't-give-a-damn approach
Is the older generation's bitter pill.

Of what's called sweetness neither were you full.
Understandable as well, regrettably.
You're young, milady of the ice-cold heart,
Indifference is your middle name.

So here I am, brimming with forgiveness.
Joyful, no, that's not the word, but let's say... calm,
Though I won't claim I've enjoyed these sad months
Of my reign as the World's Least Lucky Man.

And you can see how right I was
When I told you in my darkest moods
That your eyes, those foci of my oldest hopes,
Burned only with the fires of treachery.

You swore blind I'd made the whole thing up.
Your face, that catalogue of lies,
Flared like a dying fire's last hope—
And then: 'I love you!', in that voice of yours.

You see how we're caught by the need,
Come rain or shine, for happiness?...
But what a day it was, how bitter-sweet,
When I discovered just how right I'd been.

Aussi bien pourquoi me mettrais-je à geindre?
Vous ne m'aimiez pas, l'affaire est conclue,
Et, ne voulant pas qu'on ose me plaindre,
Je souffrirai d'une âme résolue.

Oui! je souffrirai, car je vous aimais!
Mais je souffrirai comme un bon soldat
Blessé qui s'en va dormir à jamais
Plein d'amour pour quelque pays ingrat.

Vous qui fûtes ma Belle, ma Chérie,
Encor que de vous vienne ma souffrance,
N'êtes-vous donc pas toujours ma Patrie,
Aussi jeune, aussi folle que la France?

Or, je ne veux pas—le puis-je d'abord?—
Plonger dans ceci mes regards mouillés.
Pourtant mon amour que vous croyez mort
A peut-être enfin les yeux dessillés.

Mon amour qui n'est plus que souvenance,
Quoique sous vos coups il saigne et qu'il pleure
Encore et qu'il doive, à ce que je pense,
Souffrir longtemps jusqu'à ce qu'il en meure,

Peut-être a raison de croire entrevoir
En vous un remords (qui n'est pas banal)
Et d'entendre dire, en son désespoir,
A votre mémoire: 'Ah! fi! que c'est mal!'

Je vous vois encor. J'entr'ouvris la porte.
Vous étiez au lit comme fatiguée.
Mais, ô corps léger que l'amour emporte,
Vous bondîtes nue, éplorée et gaie.

Ô quels baisers, quels enlacements fous!
J'en riais moi-même à travers mes pleurs.
Certes, ces instants seront, entre tous,
Mes plus tristes, mais aussi mes meilleurs.

Je ne veux revoir de votre sourire
Et de vos bons yeux en cette occurrence
Et de vous enfin, qu'il faudrait maudire,
Et du piège exquis, rien que l'apparence.

But there it is, no self-pity now.
You weren't in love with me, and that is that.
I shan't go seeking people's sympathy.
I'll plump for silent suffering instead.

Oh yes, I'll feel the pangs of love all right.
But: I'll be like the valiant soldier
Full of love for his ungrateful country,
As he lies dying.

You may have been the cause of my distress,
My love, my darling, my princess,
But still I think of you as my Motherland,
Young and mad, like France itself.

Now, one thing I don't want
Is to wallow in great floods of tears.
But my love for you (which you thought dead)
Sees things at last for what they are.

My love which now is memory,
But still bleeds from the shelling
It's endured, weeps and must, I think,
Go on in pain until it dies.

I may be right to think I glimpse remorse
In you (rare, to say the very least),
To think I hear your memory say
In its despair: 'No, this is wrong, no, this is bad.'

I still picture it, how I eased open
The door, and there you were in bed,
Tired, so I thought. But, full of love and light
As air, up you jumped, naked, tearful, glad.

Then what kisses, what gymnastics!
Even I was laughing through my tears.
Of all moments this will no doubt be
The saddest but the best for me.

All I want to keep of your smile and your eyes'
Goodness and your tender traps, in short
—And against my better judgement—of simply you
Is the appearance of you.

Je vous vois encore! En robe d'été
Blanche et jaune avec des fleurs de rideaux.
Mais vous n'aviez plus l'humide gaîté
Du plus délirant de tous nos tantôts.

La petite épouse et la fille aînée
Était reparue avec la toilette
Et c'était déjà notre destinée
Qui me regardait sous votre voilette.

Soyez pardonnée! Et c'est pour cela
Que je garde, hélas! avec quelque orgueil,
En mon souvenir, qui vous cajola,
L'éclair de côté que coulait votre œil.

Par instants je suis le Pauvre Navire
Qui court démâté parmi la tempête
Et, ne voyant pas Notre-Dame luire,
Pour l'engouffrement en priant s'apprête.

Par instants je meurs la mort du Pécheur
Qui se sait damné s'il n'est confessé
Et, perdant l'espoir de nul confesseur,
Se tord dans l'Enfer, qu'il a devancé.

Ô mais! par instants, j'ai l'extase rouge
Du premier chrétien sous la dent rapace,
Qui rit à Jésus témoin, sans que bouge
Un poil de sa chair, un nerf de sa face!

Bruxelles, Londres, septembre–octobre 72

Green

Voici des fruits, des fleurs, des feuilles et des branches
Et puis voici mon cœur qui ne bat que pour vous.
Ne le déchirez pas avec vos deux mains blanches
Et qu'à vos yeux si beaux l'humble présent soit doux.

I still picture you in a white and yellow
Summer dress with curtain-print flowers,
But without that moist abandon
Of the most abandoned time we knew.

The little wife, the eldest daughter
Had come back in that dress,
And straight away I knew our fate
Was watching me beneath your veil.

May you be forgiven. It's for this reason
My eloquent memory of you
Hangs on with still some pride
To that flashing sidelong glance you gave.

Sometimes I'm the Stricken Ship
Which lurches unmasted through storms,
Deprived of guiding lights, but
Deep in prayer as it goes down.

Sometimes I die the Sinner's Death
Who knows he's damned without a priest.
Gone all hope of absolution,
He writhes in self-inflicted Hell.

But sometimes I know the first Christian's
Blood-red joy in the lions' den,
Smiling up at Jesus looking down,
His face and flesh the model of calm.

Brussels–London.—September–October 1872

Green

There's fruit, flowers, branches and leaves,*
Then there's my heart, which beats only for you.
Don't tear it apart with those two white hands;
It's my humble gift to your lovely eyes.

J'arrive tout couvert encore de rosée
Que le vent du matin vient glacer à mon front.
Souffrez que ma fatigue à vos pieds reposée
Rêve des chers instants qui la délasseront.

Sur votre jeune sein laissez rouler ma tête
Toute sonore encor de vos derniers baisers;
Laissez-la s'apaiser de la bonne tempête,
Et que je dorme un peu puisque vous reposez.

Spleen

Les roses étaient toutes rouges
Et les lierres étaient tout noirs.

Chère, pour peu que tu te bouges,
Renaissent tous mes désespoirs.

Le ciel était trop bleu, trop tendre,
La mer trop verte et l'air trop doux.

Je crains toujours,—ce qu'est d'attendre!—
Quelque fuite atroce de vous.

Du houx à la feuille vernie
Et du luisant buis je suis las,

Et de la campagne infinie
Et de tout, fors de vous, hélas!

Streets I

Dansons la gigue!

J'aimais surtout ses jolis yeux,
Plus clairs que l'étoile des cieux,
J'aimais ses yeux malicieux.

I stand before you, my face still frozen
By the sharpness of the morning dew.
Let me recover at your feet
And dream the perfect moments of new life.

Let me rest my head on your young breast,
My head still swirling with your last embrace;
Let it find refuge from the storm
And let me sleep since now you've found some rest.

Spleen*

The roses were bright red
The ivy deepest black.

My love, your slightest movement
Rekindles my despair.

Too blue, the sky, too soft,
The sea too green, too sweet the air.

And still I fear you'll vanish—
Such torture, waiting!

I'm tired of waxy-leaf holly,
Of gleaming box-tree,

I'm tired of endless countryside,
Of all, in fact, save you.

Streets I

A jig! Let's dance!

What I loved most were her fine eyes
Firmament-bright.
Those eyes, malice personified.

Dansons la gigue!

Elle avait des façons vraiment
De désoler un pauvre amant,
Que c'en était vraiment charmant!

Dansons la gigue!

Mais je trouve encore meilleur
Le baiser de sa bouche en fleur
Depuis qu'elle est morte à mon cœur.

Dansons la gigue!

Je me souviens, je me souviens
Des heures et des entretiens,
Et c'est le meilleur de mes biens.

Dansons la gigue!

Soho

Streets II

Ô la rivière dans la rue!
Fantastiquement apparue
Derrière un mur haut de cinq pieds,
Elle roule sans un murmure
Son onde opaque et pourtant pure
Par les faubourgs pacifiés.

La chaussée est très large, en sorte
Que l'eau jaune comme une morte
Dévale ample et sans nuls espoirs
De rien refléter que la brume,
Même alors que l'aurore allume
Les cottages jaunes et noirs.

Paddington

A jig! Let's dance!

She had such charming ways and means
Of ruining her men
She'd be forgiven anything.

A jig! Let's dance!

But now that I no longer care
What I much prefer's
The brush of her lovely lips.

A jig! Let's dance!

I remember—oh and how—
Those times those conversations
My greatest consolations.

A jig! Let's dance!

Soho

Streets II

A river in the street!*
Dream apparition
Flowing soundless
Behind a five-foot wall.
Dark yet still pure tide
Threading the quiet town.

The road's so wide
That death-yellow water spreads
Unable to reflect
More than fog
Though dawn lights
Black and yellow houses up.

Paddington

Child wife

Vous n'avez rien compris à ma simplicité,
    Rien, ô ma pauvre enfant!
Et c'est avec un front éventé, dépité,
    Que vous fuyez devant.

Vos yeux qui ne devaient refléter que douceur,
    Pauvre cher bleu miroir,
Ont pris un ton de fiel, ô lamentable sœur,
    Qui nous fait mal à voir.

Et vous gesticulez avec vos petits bras
    Comme un héros méchant,
En poussant d'aigres cris poitrinaires, hélas!
    Vous qui n'étiez que chant!

Car vous avez eu peur de l'orage et du cœur
    Qui grondait et sifflait,
Et vous bêlâtes vers votre mère—ô douleur!—
    Comme un triste agnelet.

Et vous n'aurez pas su la lumière et l'honneur
    D'un amour brave et fort,
Joyeux dans le malheur, grave dans le bonheur,
    Jeune jusqu'à la mort!

Londres, 2 avril 1873

Beams

Elle voulut aller sur les flots de la mer,
Et comme un vent bénin soufflait une embellie,
Nous nous prêtâmes tous à sa belle folie,
Et nous voilà marchant par le chemin amer.

Child wife

You've grasped nothing of my simplicity,
  Not a thing, poor child.
You're running on ahead, annoyed,
  Nose in the air.

Your eyes, which should be sweetness itself,
  Poor blue mirrors,
Are deeply tainted, wretched girl,
  And painful to behold.

So you wave those little arms about
  Like some vicious hero,
And utter sharp bronchitic cries,
  You who used to be all song.

So, the storms, the fuss, this turbulent heart
  Frightened you away?
Back to mummy, then—the pain of it!—
  Bleating like a little lamb.

You won't know the luminous honour
  Of strong, bold love,
Joyful in misfortune, grave in happiness,
  And young unto death!

London, 2 April 1873

Beams

She wanted to tread the surge of the sea,
And as pleasant breezes cleared the skies
We fell in with her little whim
And started on the tricky walk.

Le soleil luisait haut dans le ciel calme et lisse,
Et dans ses cheveux blonds c'étaient des rayons d'or,
Si bien que nous suivions son pas plus calme encor
Que le déroulement des vagues, ô délice!

Des oiseaux blancs volaient alentour mollement
Et des voiles au loin s'inclinaient toutes blanches.
Parfois de grands varechs filaient en longues branches,
Nos pieds glissaient d'un pur et large mouvement.

Elle se retourna, doucement inquiète
De ne nous croire pas pleinement rassurés,
Mais nous voyant joyeux d'être ses préférés,
Elle reprit sa route et portait haut la tête.

Douvres–Ostende, à bord de la 'Comtesse-de-Flandre', 4 avril 1873

The sun stood tall in a quiet smooth sky;
Her light hair was touched with gold.
Enchanted, we followed her calm steps,
Calmer than the sigh of waves.

White sea-birds circled aimlessly.
In the distance clean white sails were leaning.
Great hanks of seaweed drifted past.
Bravely, our feet slithered on.

She turned around, sweetly anxious
To reassure us.
But seeing we were thrilled to be her chosen ones,
Off she went again, her head held high.

Dover–Ostend, aboard the *Countess of Flanders*, 4 April 1873

Sagesse

'Beauté des femmes . . .'

Beauté des femmes, leur faiblesse, et ces mains pâles
Qui font souvent le bien et peuvent tout le mal,
Et ces yeux, où plus rien ne reste d'animal
Que juste assez pour dire: 'assez' aux fureurs mâles!

Et toujours, maternelle endormeuse des râles,
Même quand elle ment, cette voix! Matinal
Appel, ou chant bien doux à vêpre, ou frais signal,
Ou beau sanglot qui va mourir au pli des châles!...

Hommes durs! Vie atroce et laide d'ici-bas!
Ah! que du moins, loin des baisers et des combats,
Quelque chose demeure un peu sur la montagne,

Quelque chose du cœur enfantin et subtil,
Bonté, respect! Car, qu'est-ce qui nous accompagne,
Et vraiment, quand la mort viendra, que reste-t-il?

'La vie humble aux travaux . . .'

La vie humble aux travaux ennuyeux et faciles
Est une œuvre de choix qui veut beaucoup d'amour.
Rester gai quand le jour, triste, succède au jour,
Être fort, et s'user en circonstances viles,

N'entendre, n'écouter aux bruits des grandes villes
Que l'appel, ô mon Dieu, des cloches dans la tour,
Et faire un de ces bruits soi-même, cela pour
L'accomplissement vil de tâches puériles,

'Beauty of women . . .'

Beauty of women, their weakness, those pale hands
Which often do good and can do every harm,
And those eyes, just animal enough
To say 'Enough!' to the rampant male.

Always that voice, rage-calming lullaby,
Even when it's lying. Morning call
Or soft sunset song or bright sign
Or beautiful sob lost in the folds of a shawl...

Hard men! Ugly, awful life on this earth!
Far from fights and caresses,
Let something at least remain on the mountain,

Something of the subtle childlike heart,
Goodness, respect. For what accompanies us,
And when death comes, what is left which lasts?

'The humble life . . .'

The humble life of dull and easy work
Is choice labour requiring great love.
Lifting spirits day after dismal day,
Keeping us strong, worn down by vile conditions,

Hearing, listening only in the city's noise,
Great God, to the church-tower's ring of bells,
Joining in the noise oneself
To put an awful end to childish tasks,

Dormir chez les pêcheurs étant un pénitent,
N'aimer que le silence et converser pourtant;
Le temps si long dans la patience si grande,

Le scrupule naïf aux repentirs têtus,
Et tous ces soins autour de ces pauvres vertus!
—Fi, dit l'Ange gardien, de l'orgueil qui marchande!

'Écoutez la chanson . . .'

Écoutez la chanson bien douce
Qui ne pleure que pour vous plaire.
Elle est discrète, elle est légère:
Un frisson d'eau sur de la mousse!

La voix vous fut connue (et chère?),
Mais à présent elle est voilée
Comme une veuve désolée,
Pourtant comme elle encore fière,

Et dans les longs plis de son voile
Qui palpite aux brises d'automne,
Cache et montre au cœur qui s'étonne
La vérité comme une étoile.

Elle dit, la voix reconnue,
Que la bonté c'est notre vie,
Que de la haine et de l'envie
Rien ne reste, la mort venue.

Elle parle aussi de la gloire
D'être simple sans plus attendre,
Et de noces d'or et du tendre
Bonheur d'une paix sans victoire.

Accueillez la voix qui persiste
Dans son naïf épithalame.
Allez, rien n'est meilleur à l'âme
Que de faire une âme moins triste!

Asleep, a penitent among sinners,
Liking only silence but chattering still...
Time stretching out in fields of patience,

Naïve scruples with their stubborn remorse
And all that fuss about feeble virtues!
—Don't accept, my angel says, deals proposed by pride.

'Hear the soft . . .'

Hear the soft and dulcet song
Plangent only for your pleasure.
Discreet and light, a floating song,
A tremble of water on moss.

The voice was known (and dear?) to you
But today it's veiled
Like a widow dark with grief.
Yet like her still it has its pride,

And in the long folds of the veil,
A flutter in autumn air,
Hidden truth astounds the heart,
A truth like stars.

She says in her familiar voice
That goodness is our life,
That when death arrives,
Nothing of hate or of envy remains.

She speaks as well of great
Simplicity devoid of hope,
Golden marriage, tender, happy
Unvictorious peace.

Welcome this voice which persists
In its artless wedding-song.
Go on, nothing better suits the soul
Than to make someone less sad.

Elle est *en peine* et *de passage*,
L'âme qui souffre sans colère,
Et comme sa morale est claire!...
Écoutez la chanson bien sage.

'Les chères mains . . .'

Les chères mains qui furent miennes,
Toutes petites, toutes belles,
Après ces méprises mortelles
Et toutes ces choses païennes,

Après les rades et les grèves,
Et les pays et les provinces,
Royales mieux qu'au temps des princes,
Les chères mains m'ouvrent les rêves.

Mains en songe, mains sur mon âme,
Sais-je, moi, ce que vous daignâtes,
Parmi ces rumeurs scélérates,
Dire à cette âme qui se pâme?

Ment-elle, ma vision chaste
D'affinité spirituelle,
De complicité maternelle,
D'affection étroite et vaste?

Remords si cher, peine très bonne,
Rêves bénis, mains consacrées,
Ô ces mains, ces mains vénérées,
Faites le geste qui pardonne!

'Voix de l'Orgueil . . .'

Voix de l'Orgueil: un cri puissant comme d'un cor,
Des étoiles de sang sur des cuirasses d'or.
On trébuche à travers des chaleurs d'incendie...
Mais en somme la voix s'en va, comme d'un cor.

The person who suffers in silence
Is *in distress, not here for long*,
And the message is all too clear...
Hear the wise and prudent song.

'Dear hands . . .'

Dear hands which once were mine,
Small hands, such pretty hands,
After such human mistakes
And pagan things,

After my banishment,
Laid up, stranded, I have
Your courtly hands
Disclosing dreams for me.

Hands in dreams, hands on my soul,
What can I know of what,
Among scabrous whispers, you deigned tell
This poor, this swooning soul?

A lie, my chaste vision
Of spiritual unison,
A mother's complicity,
A narrow, vast affection?

Such dear remorse, such good suffering,
Blessed dreams, consecrated hands.
Oh you venerated hands,
Make me the sign that forgives!

'Voice of Pride . . .'

Voice of Pride: shout of blaring trumpets,
Stars of blood on golden breast-plates,
A stumble through heat as intense as fire...
But then the sound's dispelled like trumpets.

Voix de la Haine: cloche en mer, fausse, assourdie
De neige lente. Il fait si froid! Lourde, affadie,
La vie a peur et court follement sur le quai
Loin de la cloche qui devient plus assourdie.

Voix de la Chair: un gros tapage fatigué.
Des gens ont bu. L'endroit fait semblant d'être gai.
Des yeux, des noms, et l'air plein de parfums atroces
Où vient mourir le gros tapage fatigué.

Voix d'Autrui: des lointains dans des brouillards. Des
    noces
Vont et viennent. Des tas d'embarras. Des négoces,
Et tout le cirque des civilisations
Au son trotte-menu du violon des noces.

Colères, soupirs noirs, regrets, tentations
Qu'il a fallu pourtant que nous entendissions
Pour l'assourdissement des silences honnêtes,
Colères, soupirs noirs, regrets, tentations,

Ah, les Voix, mourez donc, mourantes que vous êtes,
Sentences, mots en vain, métaphores mal faites,
Toute la rhétorique en fuite des péchés,
Ah, les Voix, mourez donc, mourantes que vous êtes!

Nous ne sommes plus ceux que vous auriez cherchés.
Mourez à nous, mourez aux humbles vœux cachés
Que nourrit la douceur de la Parole forte,
Car notre cœur n'est plus de ceux que vous cherchez!

Mourez parmi la voix que la Prière emporte
Au ciel, dont elle seule ouvre et ferme la porte
Et dont elle tiendra les sceaux au dernier jour,
Mourez parmi la voix que la Prière apporte,

Mourez parmi la voix terrible de l'Amour!

Voice of Hate: bell on the sea, flat note muffled
By dogged snow. Such cold! Drab and heavy,
Life takes fright and flees down quays
Away from the bell, getting more muffled.

Voice of Flesh: huge, weary commotion,
The tipsy and drunk, a pretence of fun.
Eyes, names, air heavy with awful scent
Smothering the huge and weary commotion.

Voice of Others: space in mist, wedding-parties
Leaving, arriving. Difficulties, dealings,
The whole circus of civilizations
To the skipping violins of wedding-parties.

Anger, black sighs, regrets, temptations
Which we had to hear so that mute-damped
Honest silence might be heard,
Anger, black sighs, regrets, temptations,

Voices, die then, since you're dying
Away, maxims, vain words, ill-turned metaphors,
Rhetoric of sin in flight,
Die then, Voices, since you're dying.

We're no longer those you'd want to find.
Be dead to us, dead to humble hidden prayers
Nourished by the strong Word's gentleness,
Because our heart's no longer what you'd want to find.

Die in the voice which Prayer
Lifts to Heaven, whose gate it alone can work,
Whose seal it will set on Judgement Day,
Die in the voice brought by Prayer,

Die in the awesome voice of Love!

'L'ennemi se déguise . . .'

L'ennemi se déguise en l'Ennui
Et me dit: 'A quoi bon, pauvre dupe?'
Moi je passe et me moque de lui.
L'ennemi se déguise en la Chair
Et me dit: 'Bah, retrousse une jupe!'
Moi j'écarte le conseil amer.

L'ennemi se transforme en un Ange
De lumière et dit: 'Qu'est ton effort
A côté des tributs de louange
Et de Foi dus au Père céleste?
Ton amour va-t-il jusqu'à la mort?'
Je réponds: 'L'Espérance me reste.'

Comme c'est le vieux logicien,
Il a fait bientôt de me réduire
A ne plus *vouloir* répliquer rien.
Mais sachant *qui c'est*, épouvanté
De ne plus sentir les mondes luire,
Je prierai pour de l'humilité.

'L'espoir luit . . .'

L'espoir luit comme un brin de paille dans l'étable.
Que crains-tu de la guêpe ivre de son vol fou?
Vois, le soleil toujours poudroie à quelque trou.
Que ne t'endormais-tu, le coude sur la table?

Pauvre âme pâle, au moins cette eau du puits glacé,
Bois-la. Puis dors après. Allons, tu vois, je reste,
Et je dorloterai les rêves de ta sieste,
Et tu chantonneras comme un enfant bercé.

Midi sonne. De grâce, éloignez-vous, madame.
Il dort. C'est étonnant comme les pas de femme
Résonnent au cerveau des pauvres malheureux.

'The enemy . . .'

The enemy takes on the disguise of Ennui
And says to me, 'Why bother, poor fool.'
For my part, I pass by and laugh.
The enemy becomes Flesh and says to me,
'Put your hand up a skirt.'
For my part, I ignore the cynical advice.

The enemy becomes an Angel of Light
And says, 'Your efforts aren't worth
A jot compared to the praise and Faith
Due to our Father in Heaven.
Is your love a Love-Unto-Death?'
I reply, 'Hope is what I have left.'

As he's the old logician,
Soon he's reduced me
To not *wanting* at all to reply.
But knowing *who he is*, appalled
That light's fading in every world,
I'll seek humility through prayer.

'Hope like a wisp of straw . . .'

Hope like a wisp of straw shines in the stable.
Why do you fear the crazed flight of the drunken wasp?
See, still the powdered sunlight shows in some recess.
Why didn't you sleep, your elbow on the table?

Poor soul, drink at least this freezing water
From the well. Then sleep. There, see, I'll stay
And cradle the dreams in your sleep,
And you'll coo like a cradled child.

Midday strikes. I beg of you madame, go.
He's asleep. It's startling how women's feet
Send echoes through the heads of poor unhappy men.

Midi sonne. J'ai fait arroser dans la chambre.
Va, dors! L'espoir luit comme un caillou dans un creux.
Ah, quand refleuriront les roses de septembre!

'Je suis venu, calme orphelin'

Gaspard Hauser chante

Je suis venu, calme orphelin,
Riche de mes seuls yeux tranquilles,
Vers les hommes des grandes villes:
Ils ne m'ont pas trouvé malin.

A vingt ans un trouble nouveau,
Sous le nom d'amoureuses flammes,
M'a fait trouver belles les femmes:
Elles ne m'ont pas trouvé beau.

Bien que sans patrie et sans roi
Et très brave ne l'étant guère,
J'ai voulu mourir à la guerre:
La mort n'a pas voulu de moi.

Suis-je né trop tôt ou trop tard?
Qu'est-ce que je fais en ce monde?
Ô vous tous, ma peine est profonde:
Priez pour le pauvre Gaspard!

'Un grand sommeil noir'

Un grand sommeil noir
Tombe sur ma vie:
Dormez, tout espoir,
Dormez, toute envie!

Je ne vois plus rien,
Je perds la mémoire
Du mal et du bien...
Ô la triste histoire!

Midday strikes. I've had water sprinkled round the room.
Go on, sleep. Hope shines like a stone in a hollow.
Ah, when will September roses flower again?

'Peaceful eyes my only wealth'

Gaspard Hauser* sings:

Peaceful eyes my only wealth
Calm orphan I arrived
Innocent
In the cities of men.

At twenty new stirrings—
Love's fever so-called—
Made women lovely
Me unlovely to them.

Stateless un-kinged
Brave coward
I went to war to die.
Death turned me down.

Was I born too early
Or too late? Or why at all?
People, I'm a pit of pain.
Say prayers for poor Gaspard.

'A great dark sleep'

A great dark sleep
Falls on my life.
Sleep hope,
Sleep desires.

I see nothing now
I forget what good
And evil are...
A sorry story.

Je suis un berceau
Qu'une main balance
Au creux d'un caveau:
Silence, silence!

'Le ciel est, par-dessus le toit'

Le ciel est, par-dessus le toit,
    Si bleu, si calme!
Un arbre, par-dessus le toit,
    Berce sa palme.

La cloche, dans le ciel qu'on voit,
    Doucement tinte.
Un oiseau sur l'arbre qu'on voit
    Chante sa plainte.

Mon Dieu, mon Dieu, la vie est là,
    Simple et tranquille.
Cette paisible rumeur-là
    Vient de la ville.

—Qu'as-tu fait, ô toi que voilà
    Pleurant sans cesse,
Dis, qu'as-tu fait, toi que voilà,
    De ta jeunesse?

'Je ne sais pourquoi'

Je ne sais pourquoi
    Mon esprit amer
D'une aile inquiète et folle vole sur la mer.
    Tout ce qui m'est cher,
    D'une aile d'effroi
Mon amour le couve au ras des flots. Pourquoi, pourquoi?

I'm a cradle
Rocked by a hand
Deep in a vault.
Quiet the quiet.

'The sky above the roof . . .'

The sky above the roof's
　　So blue so calm.
A branch above the roof's
　　Fanning the air.

The bell up there in the sky
　　Makes little sounds.
A bird up there in the tree
　　Sings its lament.

Dear God dear God life's there
　　Simple and quiet.
Those soft and distant sounds
　　Come from the town.

What have you done, you standing there
　　In floods of tears?
Tell me what have you done
　　With your young life?

'I don't know why'

I don't know why
　　My bitter soul
Crosses seas on crazed wings.
　　All I hold dear
　　Nestles below
Love's wing fearful on the waves. Why?

Mouette à l'essor mélancolique,
Elle suit la vague, ma pensée,
A tous les vents du ciel balancée,
Et biaisant quand la marée oblique,
Mouette à l'essor mélancolique.

Ivre de soleil
Et de liberté,
Un instinct la guide à travers cette immensité.
La brise d'été
Sur le flot vermeil
Doucement la porte en un tiède demi-sommeil.

Parfois si tristement elle crie
Qu'elle alarme au lointain le pilote,
Puis au gré du vent se livre et flotte
Et plonge, et l'aile toute meurtrie
Revole, et puis si tristement crie!

Je ne sais pourquoi
Mon esprit amer
D'une aile inquiète et folle vole sur la mer.
Tout ce qui m'est cher,
D'une aile d'effroi
Mon amour le couve au ras des flots. Pourquoi, pourquoi?

'Le son du cor . . .'

Le son du cor s'afflige vers les bois
D'une douleur on veut croire orpheline
Qui vient mourir au bas de la colline
Parmi la bise errant en courts abois.

L'âme du loup pleure dans cette voix
Qui monte avec le soleil qui décline
D'une agonie on veut croire câline
Et qui ravit et qui navre à la fois.

Soaring melancholy gull
Tracking my thought tracking waves
Riding every turbulence
Following the turn of the tide,
Soaring melancholy gull.

Drunk with sun
And freedom
Instinct guides it through the deep.
Summer's breeze
On crimson waves
Gently bears it warm and half-asleep.

Sometimes it gives sad cries
Alarming far-off pilots
Then lifts on a whim of air and floats
And plummets then wing-wounded
Soars again and again makes sad sounds.

I don't know why
My bitter soul
Crosses seas on crazed wings.
All I hold dear
Nestles below
Love's wing fearful on the waves. Why?

'A hunting-horn . . .'

A hunting-horn curls its distress
Over by the woods, orphaned pain
Fading at the foot of the hill
In the barking scavenging wind.

The wolf's soul cries inside this voice
Which lifts as the sun declines
In death-throe coquetry
Delight and dismay all at once.

Pour faire mieux cette plainte assoupie,
La neige tombe à longs traits de charpie
A travers le couchant sanguinolent,

Et l'air a l'air d'être un soupir d'automne,
Tant il fait doux par ce soir monotone
Où se dorlote un paysage lent.

'La tristesse, la langueur . . .'

La tristesse, la langueur du corps humain
M'attendrissent, me fléchissent, m'apitoient.
Ah! surtout quand des sommeils noirs le foudroient,
Quand les draps zèbrent la peau, foulent la main!

Et que mièvre dans la fièvre du demain,
Tiède encor du bain de sueur qui décroît,
Comme un oiseau qui grelotte sur un toit!
Et les pieds, toujours douloureux du chemin!

Et le sein, marqué d'un double coup de poing!
Et la bouche, une blessure rouge encor,
Et la chair frémissante, frêle décor!

Et les yeux, les pauvres yeux si beaux où point
La douleur de voir encore du fini!...
Triste corps! Combien faible et combien puni!

'La bise se rue . . .'

La bise se rue à travers
Les buissons tout noirs et tout verts,
Glaçant la neige éparpillée
Dans la campagne ensoleillée.
L'odeur est aigre près des bois,
L'horizon chante avec des voix,
Les coqs des clochers des villages

The better to hush this lament
Snow falls in long strips of gauze
Down the sunset smeared with blood.

The air has airs of autumn sighing
So mild is this monotone evening
Wrapped round a slow land.

'The sadness, the languor . . .'

The sadness, the languor of the human body
Move me to pity, melt and weaken me—
Most of all when dark sleep strikes it down,
When sheets stripe skin, press down on hands.

How frail it is in the fever of tomorrow,
Still warm from evaporating sweat,
Like a bird shivering on a roof!
And then the feet, painful still from walking,

And the breast, double-marked by fists,
The mouth, a still-red wound,
And trembling flesh, a fragile arrangement.

And the eyes, poor eyes, so beautiful, pricked
With the pain of seeing nothing but this world...
Sad body, so sad, and punished so much!

'A cold wind . . .'

A cold wind hurls itself at
Dark green and black bushes
Turning bits of snow to ice
In the sunlit countryside.
Over by the woods the air's sharp.
Voices wake horizons up.
And village weathervanes

Luisent crûment sur les nuages.
C'est délicieux de marcher
A travers ce brouillard léger
Qu'un vent taquin parfois retrousse.
Ah! fi de mon vieux feu qui tousse!
J'ai des fourmis plein les talons.
Debout, mon âme, vite, allons!
C'est le printemps sévère encore,
Mais qui par instant s'édulcore
D'un souffle tiède juste assez
Pour mieux sentir les froids passés
Et penser au Dieu de clémence...
Va, mon âme, à l'espoir immense!

'L'échelonnement des haies'

L'échelonnement des haies
Moutonne à l'infini, mer
Claire dans le brouillard clair
Qui sent bon les jeunes baies.

Des arbres et des moulins
Sont légers sur le vert tendre
Où vient s'ébattre et s'étendre
L'agilité des poulains.

Dans ce vague d'un Dimanche
Voici se jouer aussi
De grandes brebis aussi
Douces que leur laine blanche.

Tout à l'heure déferlait
L'onde, roulée en volutes,
De cloches comme des flûtes
Dans le ciel comme du lait.

Stickney, 75

Cast raw bright light onto the clouds.
It's wonderful to walk
Through this thin mist lifted
Sometimes by a teasing wind.
Enough of my old fire coughing in its grate.
I'm itching to make a move now.
Up up, my soul, no more delays.
Severe Spring's still with us,
But growing gentler by the hour
In breaths of air just warm enough
To make past cold keener
And recall God's mercy...
Soul, give yourself up to the greatness of hope.

'Uneven rows . . .'

Uneven rows of hedges
Unfold forever like clear
Waves billowing under clear
Haze scented with young berries.

There are trees, there are mills,
Standing light on tender green
Where frolicking, gambolling
Colts play and stretch out.

In this Sunday haze,
See as well big ewes at play,
Ewes as soft as
Their coats of white wool.

A short while ago,
Leaping fluting sound
Spiralled from the belfry
Up into a milky sky.

Stickney, 1875

Jadis et Naguère

Pierrot

A Léon Valade

Ce n'est plus le rêveur lunaire du vieil air
Qui riait aux aïeux dans les dessus de porte;
Sa gaîté, comme sa chandelle, hélas! est morte,
Et son spectre aujourd'hui nous hante, mince et clair.

Et voici que parmi l'effroi d'un long éclair
Sa pâle blouse a l'air, au vent froid qui l'emporte,
D'un linceul, et sa bouche est béante, de sorte
Qu'il semble hurler sous les morsures du ver.

Avec le bruit d'un vol d'oiseaux de nuit qui passe,
Ses manches blanches font vaguement par l'espace
Des signes fous auxquels personne ne répond.

Ses yeux sont deux grands trous où rampe du phosphore
Et la farine rend plus effroyable encore
Sa face exsangue au nez pointu de moribond.

Kaléidoscope

A Germain Nouveau

Dans une rue, au cœur d'une ville de rêve,
Ce sera comme quand on a déjà vécu:
Un instant à la fois très vague et très aigu...
Ô ce soleil parmi la brume qui se lève!

Ô ce cri sur la mer, cette voix dans les bois!
Ce sera comme quand on ignore des causes:
Un lent réveil après bien des métempsychoses:
Les choses seront plus les mêmes qu'autrefois

Pierrot*

To Léon Valade*

No more is he the moonstruck dreamer of old songs
Laughing at his forebears from door-top bas-reliefs.
His sense of fun like his candle is dead alas
And lean and bright today his ghost is haunting us.

He stands there like a long and frightful flash.
His pale tunic in the cold air moving it
Is like a winding-sheet and his mouth gapes so it's
Like a silent yell as worms begin their work.

Sounding like a flock of birds by night
His vague white sleeves fill the air with mad signs,
Crazy signs no one will answer.

His eyes are hollow pits where phosphorus ignites
And his pasty face with its death's-door pointed nose
Is made more chilling still by thickly plastered flour.

Kaleidoscope*

To Germain Nouveau*

On a street in the heart of a city of dreams
It will be like life already lived:
A moment at once precise and vague...
Oh, that sun inside the rising mist

And that cry on the sea, that voice in the woods!
It will be like moments of mystery:
Slow waking from metempsychosis.
More than before things will be the same

Dans cette rue, au cœur de la ville magique
Où des orgues moudront des gigues dans les soirs,
Où les cafés auront des chats sur les dressoirs,
Et que traverseront des bandes de musique.

Ce sera si fatal qu'on en croira mourir:
Des larmes ruisselant douces le long des joues,
Des rires sanglotés dans le fracas des roues,
Des invocations à la mort de venir,

Des mots anciens comme un bouquet de fleurs fanées!
Les bruits aigres des bals publics arriveront,
Et des veuves avec du cuivre après leur front,
Paysannes, fendront la foule des traînées

Qui flânent là, causant avec d'affreux moutards
Et des vieux sans sourcils que la dartre enfarine,
Cependant qu'à deux pas, dans des senteurs d'urine,
Quelque fête publique enverra des pétards.

Ce sera comme quand on rêve et qu'on s'éveille!
Et que l'on se rendort et que l'on rêve encor
De la même féerie et du même décor,
L'été, dans l'herbe, au bruit moiré d'un vol d'abeille.

Dizain mil huit cent trente

Je suis né romantique et j'eusse été fatal
En un frac très étroit aux boutons de métal
Avec ma barbe en pointe et mes cheveux en brosse.
Hablant español, très loyal et très féroce,
L'œil idoine à l'œillade et chargé de défis.
Beautés mises à mal et bourgeois déconfits
Eussent bondé ma vie et soûlé mon cœur d'homme
Pâle et jaune, d'ailleurs, et taciturne comme
Un infant scrofuleux dans un Escurial...
Et puis j'eusse été si féroce et si loyal!

On this street in the heart of the magic town.
Barrel-organs will grind out evening jigs;
Cats will sprawl on cupboard-tops
In cafés favoured by buskers.

It will seem the fatal hour has come;
Soft gulleys of tears down cheeks,
Sobbing laughter in the clatter of wheels,
Voices pleading for death,

Old words like bouquets of faded flowers.
There'll be metallic dance-hall noise,
Widowed peasant-women with sufficient brass
To have a go at unsavoury girls

Chatting idly with unsavoury young men
And un-haired pensioners with skin complaints
While a stone's-throw away in a smell of piss
Firecrackers will bang—the sound of fun.

It will be like emerging from a dream,
Like falling into sleep again and into new dreams
Of the self-same fairy-land, the same decor—
Summer, grass, the silk sound of bees on the wing.

Ten lines on 1830

I'm a born Romantic and would've been dynamite
In tight dress-coat with metal buttons
Pointed beard and close-cropped hair
Habla-ing Español, utterly loyal and fierce
With dare-you-to eyes made for meaningful looks.
Gorgeous girls led astray, ill-at-ease bourgeois
Would've filled the life and drugged the masculine
Heart of this pale and jaundiced man,
Taciturn as a scrofulous kid in some Escorial...*
And then how fierce and loyal I'd have been!

Sonnet boiteux

A Ernest Delahaye

Ah! vraiment c'est triste, ah! vraiment ça finit trop mal.
Il n'est pas permis d'être à ce point infortuné.
Ah! vraiment c'est trop la mort du naïf animal
Qui voit tout son sang couler sous son regard fané.

Londres fume et crie. Ô quelle ville de la Bible!
Le gaz flambe et nage et les enseignes sont vermeilles.
Et les maisons dans leur ratatinement terrible
Épouvantent comme un sénat de petites vieilles.

Tout l'affreux passé saute, piaule, miaule et glapit
Dans le brouillard rose et jaune et sale des Sohos
Avec des *indeeds* et des *all rights* et des *haôs*.

Non vraiment c'est trop un martyre sans espérance,
Non vraiment cela finit trop mal, vraiment c'est triste:
Ô le feu du ciel sur cette ville de la Bible!

Art poétique

A Charles Morice

De la musique avant toute chose,
Et pour cela préfère l'Impair
Plus vague et plus soluble dans l'air,
Sans rien en lui qui pèse ou qui pose.

Il faut aussi que tu n'ailles point
Choisir tes mots sans quelque méprise:
Rien de plus cher que la chanson grise
Où l'Indécis au Précis se joint.

Limping sonnet

To Ernest Delahaye*

It's really very sad that things aren't working out well.
It shouldn't be allowed, to suffer as I am now.
It's really much too much this death of naïve creatures
Who see all their blood flow out beneath their fading eyes.

The smoke and cries of London, that biblical city!
The gas flares up and swims, the signs are painted crimson,
And houses standing there, all shrunken back terribly,
Cause fear as though they were a club of aged women.

The awful past jumps up, it whimpers miaows and bow-wows
Among the dirty pink and yellow fogs of Soho
With its 'indeeds' with its 'all rights' with its 'good evenings'.

No really, it's too much a martyr's hopeless torture,
No really, it's too sad, no really things are too bad—
Fire-coal sky hanging over that biblical city!

The art of poetry

To Charles Morice*

Let's hear the music first and foremost,
And that means no more one-two-one-twos...
Something more vague instead, something lighter
Dissolving in air, weightless as air.

When you choose your words, no need to search
In strict dictionaries for pinpoint
Definitions. Better the subtle
And heady Songs of Imprecision.

C'est des beaux yeux derrière des voiles,
C'est le grand jour tremblant de midi,
C'est, par un ciel d'automne attiédi,
Le bleu fouillis des claires étoiles!

Car nous voulons la Nuance encor,
Pas la Couleur, rien que la nuance!
Oh! la nuance seule fiance
Le rêve au rêve et la flûte au cor!

Fuis du plus loin la Pointe assassine,
L'Esprit cruel et le Rire impur,
Qui font pleurer les yeux de l'Azur,
Et tout cet ail de basse cuisine!

Prends l'éloquence et tords-lui son cou!
Tu feras bien, en train d'énergie,
De rendre un peu la Rime assagie.
Si l'on n'y veille, elle ira jusqu'où?

Ô qui dira les torts de la Rime?
Quel enfant sourd ou quel nègre fou
Nous a forgé ce bijou d'un sou
Qui sonne creux et faux sous la lime?

De la musique encore et toujours!
Que ton vers soit la chose envolée
Qu'on sent qui fuit d'une âme en allée
Vers d'autres cieux à d'autres amours.

Que ton vers soit la bonne aventure
Éparse au vent crispé du matin
Qui va fleurant la menthe et le thym...
Et tout le reste est littérature.

Imagine fine eyes behind a veil,
Imagine the shimmer of high noon,
Imagine, in skies cooled for autumn,
Blue entanglements of lucent stars.

No, what we must have is more Nuance.
Colour's forbidden, only Nuance!
Nuance alone writes the harmonies
Of dream and dream, of woodwind and brass.

Clever-clever phrases are deadly,
So too are rapier Wit and cheap Laughs,
Ubiquitous garlic of bad cooks,
Only fit to fill blue air with tears.

Grip eloquence by the throat and squeeze
It to death. And while you're about it
You might corral that runaway, Rhyme,
Or you'll get Rhyme Without End, Amen.

Who will denounce that criminal, Rhyme?
Tone-deaf children or crazed foreigners
No doubt fashioned its paste jewellery,
Tinplate on top, hollow underneath.

Music, more music, always music!
Create verse which lifts and flies away,
Verse of a soul that has taken off
Into other stratospheres of love.

You must let your poems ride their luck
On the back of the sharp morning air
Touched with the fragrance of mint and thyme...
And everything else is LIT-RIT-CHER.

Allégorie

A Jules Valadon

Despotique, pesant, incolore, l'Été,
Comme un roi fainéant présidant un supplice,
S'étire par l'ardeur blanche du ciel complice
Et bâille. L'homme dort loin du travail quitté.

L'alouette au matin, lasse, n'a pas chanté,
Pas un nuage, pas un souffle, rien qui plisse
Ou ride cet azur implacablement lisse
Où le silence bout dans l'immobilité.

L'âpre engourdissement a gagné les cigales
Et sur leur lit étroit de pierres inégales
Les ruisseaux à moitié taris ne sautent plus.

Une rotation incessante de moires
Lumineuses étend ses flux et ses reflux...
Des guêpes, çà et là, volent, jaunes et noires.

Vers pour être calomnié

A Charles Vignier

Ce soir je m'étais penché sur ton sommeil.
Tout ton corps dormait chaste sur l'humble lit,
Et j'ai vu, comme un qui s'applique et qui lit,
Ah! j'ai vu que tout est vain sous le soleil!

Qu'on vive, ô quelle délicate merveille,
Tant notre appareil est une fleur qui plie!
Ô pensée aboutissant à la folie!
Va, pauvre, dors! moi, l'effroi pour toi m'éveille.

Allegory

To Jules Valadon*

Heavy, blank, despotic Summer, like a world-weary
Monarch authorizing a spot of torture,
Stretches out on the sky's scorched white,
Its accomplice, then yawns. A man sleeps, far from his work.

The morning skylark's been too tired to sing.
Not a cloud, not a breath of air, nothing
To crease this seamless expanse of blue
Where silence boils in stillness.

Harsh slumber has stilled the cicadas.
Half-empty streams can scarcely creep
Over thin and bumpy beds of stone.

A constant swim of light
Ripples rainbow sheets...
Zigzag wasps, yellow and black.

Libellous lines

To Charles Vignier*

That night I'd bent over you in your sleep.
Your whole body slept chastely on the humble bed,
And like a dedicated scholar I understood
That all on this earth is vanity.

That we're alive's a miracle;
We're as frail as wilting flowers.
Thinking leads to madness.
Sleep on, poor child. My fears for you keep me awake.

Ah! misère de t'aimer, mon frêle amour
Qui vas respirant comme on expire un jour!
Ô regard fermé que la mort fera tel!

Ô bouche qui ris en songe sur ma bouche,
En attendant l'autre rire plus farouche!
Vite, éveille-toi. Dis, l'âme est immortelle?

Luxures

A Léo Trézenik

Chair! ô seul fruit mordu des vergers d'ici-bas,
Fruit amer et sucré qui jutes aux dents seules
Des affamés du seul amour, bouches ou gueules,
Et bon dessert des forts, et leurs joyeux repas,

Amour! le seul émoi de ceux que n'émeut pas
L'horreur de vivre, Amour qui presses sous tes meules
Les scrupules des libertins et des bégueules
Pour le pain des damnés qu'élisent les sabbats,

Amour, tu m'apparais aussi comme un beau pâtre
Dont rêve la fileuse assise auprès de l'âtre
Les soirs d'hiver dans la chaleur d'un sarment clair,

Et la fileuse c'est la Chair, et l'heure tinte
Où le rêve étreindra la rêveuse,—heure sainte
Ou non! qu'importe à votre extase, Amour et Chair?

Vendanges

A Georges Rall

Les choses qui chantent dans la tête
Alors que la mémoire est absente,
Écoutez, c'est notre sang qui chante...
Ô musique lointaine et discrète!

Loving you is misery, fragile love
Drawing breath now just as one day we expire.
Ah, your closed look which death will make its own!

Your mouth laughs its dreams onto my mouth
As it waits for other wilder laughter.
Quick, wake up. Tell me, how immortal is the soul?

Lusts

To Léo Trézenik*

Flesh! The one fruit we bite in this world's orchards,
Tart and sugared fruit spurting juice onto teeth
Hungry only for love. Mouths, throats,
Strong men's rich desserts, their meal of joy,

Love! The one wave of emotion for those unmoved
By the horror of life. Love, your millstone grinds
Prudes' and libertines' scruples
To make the black bread of damnation.

Love, to me you also seem a handsome shepherd,
The kind a weaver dreams about beside her fire
On winter evenings warmed by bright wine,

And the weaver is the Flesh, and the hour comes
When the dream will grip the dreamer—holy hour
Or not, does it change your ecstasy, Love and Flesh?

Harvests

To Georges Rall*

The things that sing in the head
When memory's absent.
Listen, it's the singing of our blood...
Such distant music, so discreet.

Écoutez! c'est notre sang qui pleure
Alors que notre âme s'est enfuie,
D'une voix jusqu'alors inouïe
Et qui va se taire tout à l'heure.

Frère du sang de la vigne rose,
Frère du vin de la veine noire,
Ô vin, ô sang, c'est l'apothéose!

Chantez, pleurez! Chassez la mémoire
Et chassez l'âme, et jusqu'aux ténèbres
Magnétisez nos pauvres vertèbres.

Langueur

A Georges Courteline

Je suis l'Empire à la fin de la décadence,
Qui regarde passer les grands Barbares blancs
En composant des acrostiches indolents
D'un style d'or où la langueur du soleil danse.

L'âme seulette a mal au cœur d'un ennui dense.
Là-bas on dit qu'il est de longs combats sanglants.
Ô n'y pouvoir, étant si faible aux vœux si lents,
Ô n'y vouloir fleurir un peu cette existence!

Ô n'y vouloir, ô n'y pouvoir mourir un peu!
Ah! tout est bu! Bathylle, as-tu fini de rire?
Ah! tout est bu, tout est mangé! Plus rien à dire!

Seul, un poème un peu niais qu'on jette au feu,
Seul, un esclave un peu coureur qui vous néglige,
Seul, un ennui d'on ne sait quoi qui vous afflige!

Listen, it's the crying of our blood
When our soul's taken flight,
A voice unheard before,
Soon to go quiet.

Blood-brother of rosy vines,
Brother of the black vein's wine,
Apotheosis of blood and wine!

Sing, cry. Send memory packing,
See off the soul. Let's hypnotize
Our poor bones into nothingness.

Languor

To Georges Courteline*

I'm the Empire* at the end of decadence,*
Watching great and white barbarians pass by
As I doodle my lazy acrostics
Scribed in gold beneath a play of languid light.

Lonely soul weighted down by ennui.
There, they say, it's long and bloody war.
Ah, what if slow and weak desire stopped
Trying to make life sing with colour?

What if the need to die there went?
Everything's been drunk. Stop laughing, Bathyllus.*
Everything's been consumed. Nothing left to say,

Just a silly poem for the fire,
Just a wanton slave neglecting you,
Just afflictions of ennui sprung from God knows where.

Paysage

Vers Saint-Denis c'est bête et sale la campagne.
C'est pourtant là qu'un jour j'emmenai ma compagne.
Nous étions de mauvaise humeur et querellions.
Un plat soleil d'été tartinait ses rayons
Sur la plaine séchée ainsi qu'une rôtie.
C'était pas trop après le Siège: une partie
Des 'maisons de campagne' était à terre encor.
D'autres se relevaient comme on hisse un décor,
Et des obus tout neufs encastrés aux pilastres
Portaient écrit autour: Souvenir des désastres.

Le Poète et la Muse

La Chambre, as-tu gardé leurs spectres ridicules,
Ô pleine de jour sale et de bruits d'araignées?
La Chambre, as-tu gardé leurs formes désignées
Par ces crasses au mur et par quelles virgules?

Ah fi! Pourtant, chambre en garni qui te recules
En ce sec jeu d'optique aux mines renfrognées
Du souvenir de trop de choses destinées,
Comme ils ont donc regret aux nuits, aux nuits
      d'Hercules!

Qu'on l'entende comme on voudra, ce n'est pas ça:
Vous ne comprenez rien aux choses, bonnes gens.
Je vous dis que ce n'est pas ce que l'on pensa.

Seule, ô chambre qui fuis en cônes affligeants,
Seule, tu sais! mais sans doute combien de nuits
De noce auront déviginé leurs nuits, depuis!

Landscape

Saint-Denis's* a dirty stupid stretch of land.
Still, that's where one day I took my lady friend.
We were out of sorts, and bickering.
A flat sun plastered butter-rays
On a plain as dry as toast.
It wasn't long after the Siege.*
Some flattened 'country houses'
Hadn't been rebuilt. Others looked like stage sets.
Scrawled on unexploded shells embedded in pilasters
Ran these words: 'Souvenir of the Disasters'.

The Poet and the Muse*

Bedroom, do you guard their ridiculous ghosts,
Room of dirty light and spiders' sounds?
Room, have you kept their shape which sundry stains
And smudges outline on the wall?

No matter. Yet, furnished room receding
In sharp optics, frowning at the memory
Of so many destinies,
What regrets must they have on Herculean
    nights!

Make of it what you will, it isn't that:
Good people, you don't understand a thing.
I tell you it isn't what you thought.

Room, receding painfully in shadow-cones,
You alone surely know what wedding nights
Have laid to rest virginities since then!

Crimen amoris

A Villiers de l'Isle-Adam

Dans un palais, soie et or, dans Ecbatane,
De beaux démons, des Satans adolescents,
Au son d'une musique mahométane,
Font litière aux Sept Péchés de leurs cinq sens.

C'est la fête aux Sept Péchés: ô qu'elle est belle!
Tous les Désirs rayonnaient en feux brutaux;
Les Appétits, pages prompts que l'on harcèle,
Promenaient des vins roses dans des cristaux.

Des danses sur des rhythmes d'épithalames
Bien doucement se pâmaient en longs sanglots
Et de beaux chœurs de voix d'hommes et de femmes
Se déroulaient, palpitaient comme des flots,

Et la bonté qui s'en allait de ces choses
Était puissante et charmante tellement
Que la campagne autour se fleurit de roses
Et que la nuit paraissait en diamant.

Or le plus beau d'entre tous ces mauvais anges
Avait seize ans sous sa couronne de fleurs.
Les bras croisés sur les colliers et les franges,
Il rêve, l'œil plein de flammes et de pleurs.

En vain la fête autour se faisait plus folle,
En vain les Satans, ses frères et ses sœurs,
Pour l'arracher au souci qui le désole,
L'encourageaient d'appels de bras caresseurs:

Il résistait à toutes câlineries,
Et le chagrin mettait un papillon noir
A son cher front tout brûlant d'orfèvreries.
Ô l'immortel et terrible désespoir!

Crime of love

To Villiers de l'Isle-Adam*

In an Ecbatana palace, all gold and silks,
Demonic beauties, adolescent Satans,
Indulge in every Deadly Sin
To the music of the East.

Beautiful Feast of the Sins!
Desires shine with brutal fiery light.
Like harassed servants appetites
Go round decanting bright red wines.

Dances floating on wedding-song cadences
Sway in a long swoon of sobs.
Men and women sing in great chorales,
Sing music trembling like the sea.

So full of deep enchantment
Is the sweetness of these things
That the countryside blooms with roses
And night is a diamond.

The loveliest of these bad angels
Is aged sixteen and crowned with flowers.
Arms folded over ruffs and fringes
He dreams, his eyes ablaze with tears.

He pays no heed to the cavorting.
His sibling Satans try in vain
To lure him out of desolation
With a welcome of wide-open arms.

He doesn't fall for blandishments.
Distress places its black butterfly
On that face forever set
To burn with anguish and despair.

Il leur disait: 'Ô vous, laissez-moi tranquille!'
Puis, les ayant baisés tous bien tendrement,
Il s'évada d'avec eux d'un geste agile,
Leur laissant aux mains des pans de vêtement.

Le voyez-vous sur la tour la plus céleste
Du haut palais avec une torche au poing?
Il la brandit comme un héros fait d'un ceste:
D'en bas on croit que c'est une aube qui point.

Qu'est-ce qu'il dit de sa voix profonde et tendre
Qui se marie au claquement clair du feu
Et que la lune est extatique d'entendre?
'Oh! je serai celui-là qui créera Dieu!

Nous avons tous trop souffert, anges et hommes,
De ce conflit entre le Pire et le Mieux.
Humilions, misérables que nous sommes,
Tous nos élans dans le plus simple des vœux.

Ô vous tous, ô nous tous, ô les pécheurs tristes,
Ô les gais Saints, pourquoi ce schisme têtu?
Que n'avons-nous fait, en habiles artistes,
De nos travaux la seule et même vertu!

Assez et trop de ces luttes trop égales!
Il va falloir qu'enfin se rejoignent les
Sept Péchés aux Trois Vertus Théologales!
Assez et trop de ces combats durs et laids!

Et pour réponse à Jésus qui crut bien faire
En maintenant l'équilibre de ce duel,
Par moi l'enfer dont c'est ici le repaire
Se sacrifie à l'Amour universel!'

La torche tombe de sa main éployée,
Et l'incendie alors hurla s'élevant,
Querelle énorme d'aigles rouges noyée
Au remous noir de la fumée et du vent.

He tells them: 'Let me be',
Kisses each one tenderly, then
Tears himself away, leaving them
There, holding just scraps of his clothing.

Do you see him on the highest tower
Of that high palace, torch in hand?
It's raised like a winning fighter's fist.
From below it's like dawn breaking.

What's he saying in that soft dark voice,
Deep with sounds of snapping fires
That send moons orbiting with joy?
'Oh yes, I'll be the one who creates God!

Men, angels, we've suffered too long
In this battle of Good and Evil.
Miserable worms that we are, our impulses
Must be trimmed to one simple wish.

You, us, sad sinners all,
Happy saints, why this stubborn rift?
We're skilled artists. Why haven't we
Made common cause of all our works?

Enough of battles unresolved.
Now at least the Deadly Sins
And the Theological Virtues must unite.
Enough of brutal ugly war.

I'll tell Jesus, who thought it best
To keep the duel balanced,
That I'll sacrifice Hell to Universal Love,
Hell which thought that it was safe with me.'

The torch falls from his open hand.
The rising fire begins its screams.
Quarrels of red eagles are lost
In black tides of smoke and wind.

L'or fond et coule à flots et le marbre éclate;
C'est un brasier tout splendeur et tout ardeur;
La soie en courts frissons comme de l'ouate
Vole à flocons tout ardeur et tout splendeur.

Et les Satans mourants chantaient dans les flammes,
Ayant compris, comme ils s'étaient résignés!
Et de beaux chœurs de voix d'hommes et de femmes
Montaient parmi l'ouragan des bruits ignés.

Et lui, les bras croisés d'une sorte fière,
Les yeux au ciel où le feu monte en léchant,
Il dit tout bas une espèce de prière,
Qui va mourir dans l'allégresse du chant.

Il dit tout bas une espèce de prière,
Les yeux au ciel où le feu monte en léchant...
Quand retentit un affreux coup de tonnerre,
Et c'est la fin de l'allégresse et du chant.

On n'avait pas agréé le sacrifice:
Quelqu'un de fort et de juste assurément
Sans peine avait su démêler la malice
Et l'artifice en un orgueil qui se ment.

Et du palais aux cent tours aucun vestige,
Rien ne resta dans ce désastre inouï,
Afin que par le plus effrayant prodige
Ceci ne fût qu'un vain rêve évanoui...

Et c'est la nuit, la nuit bleue aux mille étoiles;
Une campagne évangélique s'étend,
Sévère et douce, et, vagues comme des voiles,
Les branches d'arbre ont l'air d'ailes s'agitant.

De froids ruisseaux courent sur un lit de pierre;
Les doux hiboux nagent vaguement dans l'air
Tout embaumé de mystère et de prière;
Parfois un flot qui saute lance un éclair.

Molten gold flows in floods, marble bursts.
It's a splendour of incandescence.
Shimmers of silk flutter like wisps
Of incandescence and splendour.

Dying Satans sing in the flames.
They've understood, they're resigned.
Splendid choirs of women and men
Rise in the storm and the lava-spew.

He, arms crossed and full of pride,
Eyes lifted to the flames in the sky,
Utters a soft prayer,
Lost in the joy of song.

He utters a soft prayer,
Eyes lifted to the flames in the sky...
Then a wild thunderclap's heard,
Ending song and joy.

The sacrifice has been refused.
A strong true force
Has seen straight through the plan,
The ploy, the self-deluding arrogance.

After the great fall, no trace remains
Of the palace and its hundred towers.
This fearsome act of God will clear
The lingering smoke of burnt-up dreams...

Now, it's blue star-strewn night;
A landscape of angels soft and severe
Stretches out. Vague as veils
Branches seem like moving wings.

Cold waters course over stone beds;
Gentle owls row through dim air
Scented with mystery and prayer;
Sometimes light glances off water.

La forme molle au loin monte des collines
Comme un amour encore mal défini,
Et le brouillard qui s'essore des ravines
Semble un effort vers quelque but réuni.

Et tout cela comme un cœur et comme une âme,
Et comme un verbe, et d'un amour virginal,
Adore, s'ouvre en une extase et réclame
Le Dieu clément qui nous gardera du mal.

A soft shape rises in the distant hills
Like amorphous love;
Mist rising from ravines
Searching out the true goal.

And all this like a heart, a soul,
Like the word innocent with love,
Opens out in adoration and asks
The God of Mercy to keep us all from evil.

Amour

Écrit en 1875
A Edmond Lepelletier

J'ai naguère habité le meilleur des châteaux
Dans le plus fin pays d'eau vive et de coteaux:
Quatre tours s'élevaient sur le front d'autant d'ailes,
Et j'ai longtemps, longtemps habité l'une d'elles.
Le mur, étant de brique extérieurement,
Luisait rouge au soleil de ce site dormant,
Mais un lait de chaux, clair comme une aube qui pleure,
Tendait légèrement la voûte intérieure.
Ô diane des yeux qui vont parler au cœur,
Ô réveil pour les sens éperdus de langueur,
Gloire des fronts d'aïeuls, orgueil jeune des branches,
Innocence et fierté des choses, couleurs blanches!
Parmi des escaliers en vrille, tout aciers
Et cuivres, luxes brefs encore émaciés,
Cette blancheur bleuâtre et si douce, à m'en croire,
Que relevait un peu la longue plinthe noire,
S'emplissait tout le jour de silence et d'air pur
Pour que la nuit y vînt rêver de pâle azur.
Une chambre bien close, une table, une chaise,
Un lit strict où l'on pût dormir juste à son aise,
Du jour suffisamment et de l'espace assez,
Tel fut mon lot durant les longs mois là passés,
Et je n'ai jamais plaint ni les mois ni l'espace,
Ni le reste, et du point de vue où je me place
Maintenant que voici le monde de retour,
Ah! vraiment, j'ai regret aux deux ans dans la tour!
Car c'était bien la paix réelle et respectable,
Ce lit dur, cette chaise unique et cette table,
La paix où l'on aspire alors qu'on est bien soi,
Cette chambre aux murs blancs, ce rayon sobre et coi,
Qui glissait lentement en teintes apaisées,

Written in 1875

To Edmond Lepelletier*

Once I lived in the best chateau
Set in a softness of water and hills.
Four towers rose from its four-winged front;
One was my residence for long long days.
The outer walls of brick
Shone red in the sun of this sleepy site.
But inside, gleaming like moist dawn
Whitewash lightly brushed the chamber-walls.
Such reveilles of eyes wanting to speak to the heart,
Such refreshment of senses half-dead with fatigue,
Glory-browed ancestors, the branches' young pride,
Proud innocence of things, and the white!
Among corkscrew staircases of steel
And copper—brief wizened luxury—
The soft blue-tinted whiteness
In contrast to the long black plinth
Was filled all day with silence and pure air
Setting the stage for night to dream in blue.
A tight-shut room, a table, a chair,
A narrow bed, barely adequate,
Sufficient light, room to move—
Such was my fate for long months there.
I've never complained at this unwilling
Suspension of time, space, everything,
And from where I am now, back in the world,
I'll own I miss my two years in the tower.
That was real respectable peace.
The harsh bed, the one chair, the table,
The peace you need to be yourself,
White-walled room with sober muted light
Filtering quiet tints, not a huge

Au lieu de ce grand jour diffus de vos croisées.
Car, à quoi bon le vain appareil et l'ennui
Du plaisir, à la fin, quand le malheur a lui
(Et le malheur est bien un trésor qu'on déterre),
Et pourquoi cet effroi de rester solitaire
Qui pique le troupeau des hommes d'à présent,
Comme si leur commerce était bien suffisant?
Questions! Donc, j'étais heureux avec ma vie,
Reconnaissant de biens que nul, certes, n'envie.
(Ô fraîcheur de sentir qu'on n'a pas de jaloux!
Ô bonté d'être cru plus malheureux que tous!)
Je partageais les jours de cette solitude
Entre ces deux bienfaits, la prière et l'étude,
Que délassait un peu de travail manuel.
Ainsi les Saints! J'avais aussi ma part de ciel,
Surtout quand, revenant au jour, si proche encore,
Où j'étais ce mauvais sans plus qui s'édulcore
En la luxure lâche aux farces sans pardon,
Je pouvais supputer tout le prix de ce don:
N'être plus là, parmi les choses de la foule,
S'y dépensant, plutôt dupe, pierre qui roule,
Mais de fait un complice à tous ces noirs péchés,
N'être plus là, compter au rang des cœurs cachés,
Des cœurs discrets que Dieu fait siens dans le silence,
Sentir qu'on grandit bon et sage, et qu'on s'élance
Du plus bas au plus haut en essors bien réglés,
Humble, prudent, béni, la croissance des blés!—
D'ailleurs, nuls soins gênants, nulle démarche à faire.
Deux fois le jour ou trois, un serviteur sévère
Apportait mes repas et repartait muet.
Nul bruit. Rien dans la tour jamais ne remuait
Qu'une horloge au cœur clair qui battait à coups larges.
C'était la liberté (la seule!) sans ses charges,
C'était la dignité dans la sécurité!
Ô lieu presque aussitôt regretté que quitté,
Château, château magique où mon âme s'est faite,
Frais séjour où se vint apaiser la tempête
De ma raison allant à vau-l'eau dans mon sang,
Château, château qui luis tout rouge et dors tout blanc,

Diffuse light entering through casements.
Fine things become dross, pleasure boring
When misfortune shines like unearthed treasure.
Why does the fear of solitude
So terrorize modern man?
As if human company were enough!
Questions! I was happy then and grateful
For good things envied by no other.
(How sweet to know one has no rivals!
How good to be thought worse off than anyone!)
I shared my days of solitude
Between twin blessings of study and prayer,
Relieved from time to time by manual work.
The life of the Saints, my own corner of Heaven,
As became plain to me, once back in the real world
(Which thought me middling bad, no worse,
And given to weak-willed selfish pleasure),
Where I saw the true worth of this gift:
Namely, to be outside the throng, not duped, not
Wasting myself, mossless as a rolling stone,
Keeping my distance, safe among the hidden
Discreet souls God silently claims for Himself;
To feel myself grow in wisdom and goodness, vaulting
High with measured leaps;
Humble, prudent, blessed—good corn thriving!
No silly distractions, no moves to make...
Two or three times a day, my no-nonsense warder
Brought in my meals and left without a word.
Not a sound in the tower, nothing except
The generous striking of a stout-hearted clock.
This was freedom (the only kind!), no dues to pay;
Dignity within security!
No sooner had I left than I missed the place,
Magical chateau where my soul was composed,
Cool tranquillity where the storm pounding
The badlands of my chaos blew itself out;
White and glow-red sleepless chateau,
You're the lingering taste of good fruit
Which quenches fever's residue of thirst.

Comme un bon fruit de qui le goût est sur mes lèvres
Et désaltère encor l'arrière-soif des fièvres,
Ô sois béni, château d'où me voilà sorti
Prêt à la vie, armé de douceur et nanti
De la Foi, pain et sel et manteau pour la route
Si déserte, si rude et si longue, sans doute,
Par laquelle il faut tendre aux innocents sommets.
Et soit aimé l'AUTEUR de la Grâce, à jamais!

Stickney, Angleterre

Bournemouth

A Francis Poictevin

Le long bois de sapins se tord jusqu'au rivage,
L'étroit bois de sapins, de lauriers et de pins,
Avec la ville autour déguisée en village:
Chalets éparpillés rouges dans le feuillage
Et les blanches villas des stations de bains.

Le bois sombre descend d'un plateau de bruyère,
Va, vient, creuse un vallon, puis monte vert et noir
Et redescend en fins bosquets où la lumière
Filtre et dore l'obscur sommeil du cimetière
Qui s'étage bercé d'un vague nonchaloir.

A gauche la tour lourde (elle attend une flèche)
Se dresse d'une église invisible d'ici;
L'estacade très loin; haute, la tour, et sèche:
C'est bien l'anglicanisme impérieux et rêche
A qui l'essor du cœur vers le ciel manque aussi.

Il fait un de ces temps ainsi que je les aime,
Ni brume ni soleil! le soleil deviné,
Pressenti, du brouillard mourant dansant à même
Le ciel très haut qui tourne et fuit, rose de crème;
L'atmosphère est de perle et la mer d'or fané.

Chateau, may you be blessed for sending me out
Ready for life, strengthened by sweetness, armed
With Faith, bread, salt, and clothes for that road—
Empty, rough, endless—those foothills which surely
Lead to the high peaks of innocence.
And may the GIVER of Grace be loved forever!

Stickney, England

Bournemouth

To Francis Poictevin*

The long wood winds down banks,
Narrow wood of firs, laurels, and pines.
The town sits like a village,
Red chalets scattered among greenery,
Bathing-stations, white villas.

The dark wood descends from a gorse-covered plain,
Is lost, seen again; it scoops hollows then rises
Green and black, falls away in thin copses.
The graveyard: filtered light bronzes
Sombre vague easy rows of sleep.

To the left a solid tower (with as yet
No spire) rises from an unseen church.
In the distance a pier, and a tall dry tower—
The Anglican faith, imperious and severe.
Nothing about it to lift the heart.

The weather's the sort I like,
Neither mist nor sun. The sun's guessed-at,
Sensed. Fog fades, partnering the tall
Turning sky in a movement of pink and cream.
Air like pearl, sea like faded gold.

De la tour protestante il part un chant de cloche,
Puis deux et trois et quatre, et puis huit à la fois,
Instinctive harmonie allant de proche en proche,
Enthousiasme, joie, appel, douleur, reproche,
Avec de l'or, du bronze et du feu dans la voix;

Bruit immense et bien doux que le long bois écoute!
La Musique n'est pas plus belle. Cela vient
Lentement sur la mer qui chante et frémit toute,
Comme sous une armée au pas sonne une route
Dans l'écho qu'un combat d'avant-garde retient.

La sonnerie est morte. Une rouge traînée
De grands sanglots palpite et s'éteint sur la mer,
L'éclair froid d'un couchant de la nouvelle année
Ensanglante là-bas la ville couronnée
De nuit tombante, et vibre à l'ouest encore clair.

Le soir se fonce. Il fait glacial. L'estacade
Frissonne et le ressac a gémi dans son bois
Chanteur, puis est tombé lourdement en cascade
Sur un rhythme brutal comme l'ennui maussade
Qui martelait mes jours coupables d'autrefois:

Solitude du cœur dans le vide de l'âme,
Le combat de la mer et des vents de l'hiver,
L'Orgueil vaincu, navré, qui râle et qui déclame,
Et cette nuit où rampe un guet-apens infâme,
Catastrophe flairée, avant-goût de l'Enfer!...

Voici trois tintements comme trois coups de flûtes,
Trois encor! trois encor! l'*Angélus* oublié
Se souvient, le voici qui dit: Paix à ces luttes!
Le Verbe s'est fait chair pour relever tes chutes,
Une vierge a conçu, le monde est délié!

From the Protestant tower come bells, first
One then two three four then eight together,
Instinctive harmonies tightening.
Joy pain enthusiasm reproach appeal,
Gold and bronze and fire in their voice.

A wide, soft noise which the long wood hears.
No sweeter music. It comes to the sea
Slowly singing and trembling,
The way echoes made by marching feet
Are heard by fellow soldiers out ahead.

The bells have stopped. A red ribbon of sobs
Flutters, dies on the sea.
The cold brio of a New Year setting sun
Bloodies the town crested with early night.
A shimmer in the West, still bright.

Evening gathers, cold as ice. The pier
Shines. A belly of water in its singing
Wood has come flopping down
To a rough rhythm—like peevish ennui
Beating at me in the old days of guilt.

The heart's solitude in the soul's void.
The sea's struggle with winter winds.
Crushed Pride, loud with anger.
Night laying its awful ambush.
The whiff of catastrophe, foretaste of Hell...

Now three fluting chimes, then
Three more then another three—forgotten nagging
Angelus, proclaiming peace, an end to war.
The Word has been made flesh to raise you up again,
A virgin has conceived and the world is absolved.

Ainsi Dieu parle par la voie de *sa* chapelle
Sise à mi-côte à droite et sur le bord du bois...
Ô Rome, ô Mère! Cri, geste qui nous rappelle
Sans cesse au bonheur seul et donne au cœur rebelle
Et triste le conseil pratique de la Croix.

—La nuit est de velours. L'estacade laissée
Tait par degrés son bruit sous l'eau qui refluait.
Une route assez droite, heureusement tracée,
Guide jusque chez moi ma retraite pressée
Dans ce noir absolu sous le long bois muet.

Janvier 1877

Un veuf parle

Je vois un groupe sur la mer.
Quelle mer? Celle de mes larmes.
Mes yeux mouillés du vent amer
Dans cette nuit d'ombre et d'alarmes
Sont deux étoiles sur la mer.

C'est une toute jeune femme
Et son enfant déjà tout grand
Dans une barque où nul ne rame,
Sans mât ni voile, en plein courant...
Un jeune garçon, une femme!

En plein courant dans l'ouragan!
L'enfant se cramponne à sa mère
Qui ne sait plus où, non plus qu'en...
Ni plus rien, et qui, folle, espère
En le courant, en l'ouragan.

Espérez en Dieu, pauvre folle,
Crois en notre Père, petit.
La tempête qui vous désole,
Mon cœur de là-haut vous prédit
Qu'elle va cesser, petit, folle!

So God's voice is heard in God's chapel
Halfway up a hill to the right by the wood's edge...
Mother Rome! The cry, the endless beckoning
Of our only happiness gives rebellious
Sad hearts the counsel of the Cross.

Velvet night. Back there the pier buries
Its sounds in waves beneath an ebbing tide.
The path is less than straight. Happily its track
Guides me as I hurry home in pitch black
Below the long and silent wood.

January 1877

A widower speaks

I'm watching a group on the sea.
What sea? The sea of my tears.
My eyes smarting in sharp air
On this night of shade and alarm
Are two stars on the sea.

A young woman
And her child already tall
Are in a boat without oars
Mast or sail out in the current...
A young boy and a woman.

Out in the current in the storm.
The child clings tight to his mother
Who no longer knows what nor where...
Nor anything. Half-crazed her hopes lie
In the current in the storm.

Put your faith in God, frantic woman,
Have faith in our Father, little boy.
The tempest causing your despair
I sense from up here where I stand
Is ending, frantic woman, little boy.

Et paix au groupe sur la mer,
Sur cette mer de bonnes larmes!
Mes yeux joyeux dans le ciel clair,
Par cette nuit sans plus d'alarmes,
Sont deux bons anges sur la mer.

1878

Adieu

Hélas! je n'étais pas fait pour cette haine
Et pour ce mépris plus forts que moi que j'ai.
Mais pourquoi m'avoir fait cet agneau sans laine
Et pourquoi m'avoir fait ce cœur outragé?

J'étais né pour plaire à toute âme un peu fière,
Sorte d'homme en rêve et capable du mieux,
Parfois tout sourire et parfois tout prière,
Et toujours des cieux attendris dans les yeux;

Toujours la bonté des caresses sincères,
En dépit de tout et quoi qu'il y parût,
Toujours la pudeur des hontes nécessaires
Dans l'argent brutal et les stupeurs du rut;

Toujours le pardon, toujours le sacrifice!
J'eus plus d'un des torts, mais j'avais tous les soins.
Votre mère était tendrement ma complice,
Qui voyait mes torts et mes soins, elle, au moins.

Elle n'aimait pas que par vous je souffrisse.
Elle est morte et j'ai pleuré sur son tombeau;
Mais je doute fort qu'elle approuve et bénisse
La chose actuelle et trouve cela beau.

Et j'ai peur aussi, nous en terre, de croire
Que le pauvre enfant, votre fils et le mien,
Ne vénérera pas trop votre mémoire,
Ô vous sans égard pour le mien et le tien.

Peace to the group on the sea,
This good sea of tears.
Filled with joy in open skies
On this night which now is safe
My eyes are two good angels on the sea.

1878

Adieu

No, I wasn't born to feel this hate
Or this scorn beyond control.
Why was I born a naked fleeceless
Lamb? Why give me this tortured heart?

I was born to please souls touched with pride,
A dreamer capable of worthy acts
Sometimes lost in prayer sometimes bathed in smiles,
Soft horizons always in the eyes.

I offer a sincere embrace in spite of all,
In spite of how it looks. I was always fair
About the shameful brute necessities
Of money and narcosis of the bed.

Forgiveness always, always sacrifice.
I was bad when trying to be good,
Your indulgent mother my accomplice.
At least she saw my endless vacillations.

She didn't want me to suffer because of you.
When she died I wept on her grave
But if she were here I doubt she'd approve
Or admire or bless what our life has become.

Once we're dead and buried, I fear that the boy
The poor boy our son, yours and mine,
Will lose respect for your memory,
You, without respect for mine or his.

Je n'étais pas fait pour dire de ces choses,
Moi dont la parole exhalait autrefois
Un épithalame en des apothéoses,
Ce chant du matin où mentait votre voix.

J'étais, je suis né pour plaire aux nobles âmes,
Pour les consoler un peu d'un monde impur,
Cimier d'or chanteur et tunique de flammes,
Moi le Chevalier qui saigne sur azur,

Moi qui dois mourir d'une mort douce et chaste
Dont le cygne et l'aigle encor seront jaloux,
Dans l'honneur vainqueur malgré ce vous néfaste,
Dans la gloire aussi des Illustres Époux!

Novembre 1886

Parsifal

A Jules Tellier

Parsifal a vaincu les Filles, leur gentil
Babil et la luxure amusante—et sa pente
Vers la Chair de garçon vierge que cela tente
D'aimer les seins légers et ce gentil babil;

Il a vaincu la Femme belle, au cœur subtil,
Étalant ses bras frais et sa gorge excitante;
Il a vaincu l'Enfer et rentre sous sa tente
Avec un lourd trophée à son bras puéril,

Avec la lance qui perça le Flanc suprême!
Il a guéri le roi, le voici roi lui-même,
Et prêtre du très saint Trésor essentiel.

En robe d'or il adore, gloire et symbole,
Le vase pur où resplendit le Sang réel.
—Et, ô ces voix d'enfants chantant dans la coupole!

I wasn't born to say such things.
Once, my words carried on their breath
The perfection of a wedding-song
That morning song resonant with your lies.

I was born to please noble souls
And give them comfort in this impure world,
A plume of singing gold, a tunic of flames,
I the Cavalier, blood-red against azure,

I who must die a chaste and gentle death
To make swans and eagles jealous,
Death with honour despite the misfortune you brought,
Death in the glory of a couple deemed Illustrious!

November 1886

Parsifal*

To Jules Tellier*

Parsifal has conquered the Maidens, their sweet
Talk, their seductions. He's sidestepped
Flesh, soft murmur and high breasts,
Traps for virgin boys.

He's turned away from subtle beautiful Woman,
Open-armed and thrilling-breasted.
He's seen off the Devil. The young man returns
To his tent, in his arms a heavy prize—

The lance which pierced the supreme body's side.
He's cured the King, now he himself is king,
Priest of the holiest of Holy Treasures.

He venerates in golden robes that symbol,
That glory, that pure vessel where real Blood gleams.
—And then, those children's voices singing in the dome!*

Sonnet héroïque

La Gueule parle: 'L'or, et puis encore l'or,
Toujours l'or, et la viande, et les vins, et la viande,
Et l'or pour les vins fins et la viande, on demande
Un trou sans fond pour l'or toujours et l'or encor!'

La Panse dit: 'A moi la chute du trésor!
La viande, et les vins fins, et l'or, toute provende,
A moi! Dégringolez dans l'outre toute grande
Ouverte du seigneur Nabuchodonosor!'

L'œil est de pur cristal dans les suifs de la face:
Il brille, net et franc, près du vrai, rouge et faux,
Seule perfection parmi tous les défauts.

L'âme attend vainement un remords efficace,
Et dans l'impénitence agonise de faim
Et de soif, et sanglote en pensant à LA FIN.

1881

Lucien Létinois VIII

Ô l'odieuse obscurité
Du jour le plus gai de l'année
Dans la monstrueuse cité
Où se fit notre destinée!

Au lieu du bonheur attendu,
Quel deuil profond, quelles ténèbres!
J'en étais comme un mort, et tu
Flottais en des pensers funèbres.

La nuit croissait avec le jour
Sur notre vitre et sur notre âme,
Tel un pur, un sublime amour
Qu'eût étreint la luxure infâme;

Heroic sonnet

Throat: 'Gold and more gold
Always gold and meat and wine and meat
And gold for fine wines and viands
Gold and more gold from bottomless pits.'

Gut: 'This rush of treasure's mine.
Viands gold fine wine
Grist to my mill. Tumble into
Nebuchadnezzar's wide-mouth sack.'

Crystal gaze in a face of soot;
Frank clear almost truthful eye, red and false,
The one perfection in so many faults.

Impenitence. The soul seeks
Efficacious remorse—no luck. It's dying
Of thirst and hunger, tearful with thoughts of THE END.

1881

Lucien Létinois VIII

Hateful darkness
Of the year's brightest day
In our destiny's
Monstrous city.

Instead of the happiness
Expected, what gloom!
I was an automaton, you,
A drift of dismal dreams.

Night invaded the window's
Framed light, invaded our souls,
As though filth and lust
Had chased out pure love.

Et l'affreux brouillard refluait
Jusqu'en la chambre où la bougie
Semblait un reproche muet
Pour quelque lendemain d'orgie.

Un remords de péché mortel
Serrait notre cœur solitaire...
Puis notre désespoir fut tel
Que nous oubliâmes la terre,

Et que, pensant au seul Jésus
Né rien que pour nous ce jour même,
Notre foi prenant le dessus
Nous éclaira du jour suprême.

—Bonne tristesse qu'aima Dieu!
Brume dont se voilait la Grâce,
Crainte que l'éclat de son feu
Ne fatiguât notre âme lasse.

Délicates attentions
D'une Providence attendrie!...
Ô parfois encore soyons
Ainsi tristes, âme chérie!

Lucien Létinois IX

Tout en suivant ton blanc convoi, je me disais
Pourtant: C'est vrai, Dieu t'a repris quand tu faisais
Sa joie et dans l'éclair de ta blanche innocence,
Plus tard la Femme eût mis sans doute en sa puissance
Ton cœur ardent vers elle affrontée un moment
Seulement et t'ayant laissé le tremblement
D'elle, et du trouble en l'âme à cause d'une étreinte;
Mais tu t'en détournas bientôt par noble crainte
Et revins à la simple, à la noble Vertu,
Tout entier à fleurir, lys un instant battu
Des passions, et plus viril après l'orage,

And the stinking fog rolled
Into the room where candle-flame
Was silent reproach
After an orgy.

Remorse for a deadly sin*
Burned our solitude...
Despair dug so deep
We forgot this world

And remembered Jesus,
Born for us this very day.
Our faith revived
And shed its light on us.

Good sadness so loved by God!
Haze-shroud of Grace,
Fear its fire
Might exhaust our weakling souls.

Delicate attentiveness
Of warm Providence!
Pray we can be sad
Again, dear soul, like this!

Lucien Létinois IX

As I walked behind your white cortège, I had to tell myself
It's true, God called you in when you became
His joy, at the height of your innocence.
No doubt later Woman would have had you trapped
And straining after her. Offered for only
A second, she'd have left you to your trembling want,
Your soul in chaos because of a kiss.
But you turned away, lofty and reserved,
And came back to simple Virtue,
Noble and whole again, to flower like a lily
Briefly battered by passion. You rode the storm,

Plus magnifique pour le céleste suffrage
Et la gloire éternelle... Ainsi parlait ma foi.

Mais quelle horreur de suivre, ô toi! ton blanc convoi!

Lucien Létinois X

Il patinait merveilleusement,
S'élançant, qu'impétueusement!
R'arrivant si joliment vraiment!

Fin comme une grande jeune fille,
Brillant, vif et fort, telle une aiguille,
La souplesse, l'élan d'une anguille.

Des jeux d'optique prestigieux,
Un tourment délicieux des yeux,
Un éclair qui serait gracieux.

Parfois il restait comme invisible,
Vitesse en route vers une cible
Si lointaine, elle-même invisible...

Invisible de même aujourd'hui.
Que sera-t-il advenu de lui?
Que sera-t-il advenu de lui?

Lucien Létinois XII

Je te vois encore à cheval
Tandis que chantaient les trompettes,
Et ton petit air martial
Chantait aussi quand les trompettes;

Je te vois toujours en treillis
Comme un long Pierrot de corvée
Très élégant sous le treillis,
D'une allure toute trouvée;

Became a man splendidly ready for God
And everlasting glory... That's what my faith told me.

But what horror to walk behind your white cortège!

Lucien Létinois X

The way he skated, marvellously,
Up and away, impetuously,
Then back again, deliciously.

Like a tall young woman, elegant,
Like a sharp bright needle, brilliant,
Like a light-flashing eel, undulant.

Illusions, optical and magical,
Swirling movement, pyrotechnical,
The grace of glancing light, electrical.

Sometimes he seemed to stay out of sight,
Pure velocity in full flight
Towards a target out of sight...

Invisible then and to this day.
Where is he now? Where, today?
Where is he now? Where is he today?

Lucien Létinois XII

I see you still, on horseback,
While buglers played.
That little martial air of yours
Sat well with the trumpets.

I see you still, in dungarees
Like a long sentinel Pierrot,
Elegant in those fatigues,
In your own make-do style.

Je te vois autour des canons,
Frêles doigts dompteurs de colosses,
Grêle voix pleine de crés noms,
Bras chétifs vainqueurs de colosses;

Et je te rêvais une mort
Militaire, sûre et splendide,
Mais Dieu vint qui te fit la mort
Confuse de la typhoïde...

Seigneur, j'adore vos desseins,
Mais comme ils sont impénétrables!
Je les adore, vos desseins,
Mais comme ils sont impénétrables!

Lucien Létinois XVII

Ce portrait qui n'est pas ressemblant,
Qui fait roux tes cheveux noirs plutôt,
Qui fait rose ton teint brun plutôt,
Ce pastel, comme il est ressemblant!

Car il peint la beauté de ton âme,
La beauté de ton âme un peu sombre,
Mais si claire au fond que, sur mon âme,
Il a raison de n'avoir pas d'ombre.

Tu n'étais pas beau dans le sens vil
Qu'il paraît qu'il faut pour plaire aux dames,
Et, pourtant, de face et de profil,
Tu plaisais aux hommes comme aux femmes.

Ton nez certes n'était pas si droit,
Mais plus court qu'il n'est dans le pastel,
Mais plus vivant que dans le pastel,
Mais aussi long et droit que de droit.

I see you among the guns,
Giant's fingers blasting everything,
Harsh voice blaring out loved names,
Stunted and triumphant arms of giants.

I dreamed a military death for you,
A sure and splendid death,
But God decreed
The typhoid victim's ragged death...

Dear Lord, I venerate your ways,
But how inscrutable they are.
I venerate your ways,
But how inscrutable they are.

Lucien Létinois XVII

This portrait,* a poor likeness—
Contriving to make your dark hair
Too ginger, your swarthy skin too pink—
Is an excellent likeness in fact.

Because it paints the beauty
Of your soul, dark yet limpid
Making my own soul live
In the fullness of your light.

You weren't handsome in that vulgar way
Women like, so it is said.
And yet in profile or full-face,
Your looks were pleasing to both sexes.

Your nose certainly wasn't so straight,
And shorter than the picture shows,
More living than in the picture,
But none the less long and straight enough.

Ta lèvre et son ombre de moustache
Fut rouge moins qu'en cette peinture
Où tu n'as pas du tout de moustache,
Mais c'est ta souriance si pure.

Ton port de cou n'était pas si dur,
Mais flexible, et d'un aigle et d'un cygne;
Car ta fierté parfois primait sur
Ta douceur dive et ta grâce insigne.

Mais tes yeux, ah! tes yeux, c'est bien eux,
Leur regard triste et gai, c'est bien lui,
Leur éclat apaisé, c'est bien lui.
Ces sourcils orageux, que c'est eux!

Ah! portrait qu'en tous les lieux j'emporte
Où m'emporte une fausse espérance,
Ah! pastel spectre, te voir m'emporte
Où? parmi tout, jouissance et transe!

Ô l'élu de Dieu, priez pour moi,
Toi qui sur terre étais mon bon ange;
Car votre image, plein d'alme émoi,
Je la vénère d'un culte étrange.

Lucien Létinois XVIII

Âme, te souvient-il, au fond du paradis,
De la gare d'Auteuil et des trains de jadis
T'amenant chaque jour, venus de La Chapelle?
Jadis déjà! Combien pourtant je me rappelle
Mes stations au bas du rapide escalier
Dans l'attente de toi, sans pouvoir oublier
Ta grâce en descendant les marches, mince et leste
Comme un ange le long de l'échelle céleste,
Ton sourire amical ensemble et filial,
Ton serrement de main cordial et loyal,
Ni tes yeux d'innocent, doux mais vifs, clairs et sombres,

Your upper lip smudged with hair
Was not so red as in this picture
Where no trace of moustache shows—
But your inner smile is there.

You didn't hold your head so stiffly,
But naturally, half-eagle, half-swan.
Your proud bearing sometimes hid
Radiant sweetness, remarkable grace.

But your eyes, yes, that's them exactly,
Their sparkling sadness perfectly caught,
Their restful brilliance caught perfectly.
Those thunderstorm brows, that's exactly them.

Ah, that portrait I carry
Everywhere false hopes take me,
Crayoned ghost, just to see you takes me where?
Anywhere, everywhere, pleasure, dream.

Now that God's taken you, pray for me,
You who were my guardian angel here on earth.
Your image, which sustains and moves me,
I worship with the rites of some strange cult.

Lucien Létinois XVIII

Dear soul, there in Paradise, do you recall
The station at Auteuil,* those bygone trains
Which came from La Chapelle, bringing you each day?
Time past so soon! How I remember
My vigils at the foot of rapid stairs,
Waiting for you, my mind full of you
Full of grace as you descended,
Airy as an angel on Heaven's ladder,
A friend, a smiling son.
Then your warm, loyal handshake,
Innocent eyes, soft but bright, clear, dark,

Qui m'allaient droit au cœur et pénétraient mes ombres.
Après les premiers mots de bonjour et d'accueil,
Mon vieux bras dans le tien, nous quittions cet Auteuil
Et, sous les arbres pleins d'une gente musique,
Notre entretien était souvent métaphysique.
Ô tes forts arguments, ta foi du charbonnier!
Non sans quelque tendance, ô si franche! à nier,
Mais si vite quittée au premier pas du doute!
Et puis nous rentrions, plus que lents, par la route
Un peu des écoliers, chez moi, chez nous plutôt,
Y déjeuner de rien, fumailler vite et tôt,
Et dépêcher longtemps une vague besogne.

Mon pauvre enfant, ta voix dans le Bois de Boulogne!

Lucien Létinois XXIV

Ta voix grave et basse
Pourtant était douce
Comme du velours,
Telle, en ton discours,
Sur de sombre mousse
De belle eau qui passe.

Ton rire éclatait
Sans gêne et sans art,
Franc, sonore et libre,
Tel, au bois qui vibre,
Un oiseau qui part
Trillant son motet.

Cette voix, ce rire
Font dans ma mémoire
Qui te voit souvent
Et mort et vivant,
Comme un bruit de gloire
Dans quelque martyre.

Piercing my heart's shadows.
A few words of greeting, then
My ancient arm linked in yours, we left Auteuil
And under trees filled with gentle music,
Our talk often waxed metaphysical.
The passion of your arguments, that simple faith,
That naïve need sometimes to deny it,
The quick refusal to walk the path of doubt...
We set off dawdling down roundabout routes
Which led us back to my room,
Or rather ours. We improvised lunch, had quick smokes,
Then spun out for an age some vague and pointless task.

My poor dear boy, your voice in the Bois de Boulogne!

Lucien Létinois XXIV

Your voice was low and grave,
Soft too,
Like velvet, sounding
When you spoke
Like lovely water
Over dark moss.

Your sudden laughter
Was open, artless,
Frank, musical, free,
Like the song of a bird
Ready for flight
In a rustle of trees.

That voice, that laughter
Are like sounds of glory
Rising like martyrs
Filling my head
Which rings with the memory
Of you alive, you dead.

Ma tristesse en toi
S'égaie à ces sons
Qui disent: 'Courage!'
Au cœur que l'orage
Emplit des frissons
De quel triste émoi!

Orage, ta rage,
Tais-la, que je cause
Avec mon ami
Qui semble endormi,
Mais qui se repose
En un conseil sage...

Batignolles

Un grand bloc de grès; quatre noms: mon père
Et ma mère et moi, puis mon fils bien tard
Dans l'étroite paix du plat cimetière
Blanc et noir et vert, au long du rempart.

Cinq tables de grès; le tombeau nu, fruste,
En un carré long, haut d'un mètre et plus,
Qu'une chaîne entoure et décore juste,
Au bas du faubourg qui ne bruit plus.

C'est de là que la trompette de l'ange
Fera se dresser nos corps ranimés
Pour la vie enfin qui jamais ne change,
Ô vous, père et mère et fils bien-aimés.

My sadness
Brightens with these sounds
Giving courage
To the heart which the storm
Fills with the shudder
Of sad emotion.

Storm, still your rage,
And let me speak
With my friend
Who seems asleep
But who rests
In wise counsel...

Batignolles

A large block of stone. Four names. My father,
My mother, myself, and much later
My son in the narrow peace of the flat
White and black and green cemetery by the wall.

Five stone slabs; the rough, bare tomb.
Big and square, a metre high or more,
Fenced off by a chain, the one ornament,
At the edge of the city, now silent.

It's here the angel's trumpet-call
Will bring our corpses back to life. They'll rise,
Fit at last for life without end,
Dear father, dear mother, dear son.

Parallèlement

Allégorie

Un très vieux temple antique s'écroulant
Sur le sommet indécis d'un mont jaune,
Ainsi qu'un roi déchu pleurant son trône,
Se mire, pâle, au tain d'un fleuve lent.

Grâce endormie et regard somnolent,
Une naïade âgée, auprès d'un aulne,
Avec un brin de saule agace un faune,
Qui lui sourit, bucolique et galant.

Sujet naïf et fade qui m'attristes,
Dis, quel poète entre tous les artistes,
Quel ouvrier morose t'opéra,

Tapisserie usée et surannée,
Banale comme un décor d'opéra,
Factice, hélas! comme ma destinée?

Pensionnaires

L'une avait quinze ans, l'autre en avait seize;
Toutes deux dormaient dans la même chambre.
C'était par un soir très lourd de septembre:
Frêles, des yeux bleus, des rougeurs de fraise.

Chacune a quitté, pour se mettre à l'aise,
La fine chemise au frais parfum d'ambre.
La plus jeune étend les bras, et se cambre,
Et sa sœur, les mains sur ses seins, la baise,

Puis tombe à genoux, puis devient farouche
Et tumultueuse et folle, et sa bouche
Plonge sous l'or blond, dans les ombres grises;

Allegory

An ancient temple in decay
On the blurred summit of some yellow hill,
Like a fallen king crying for his throne,
Looks at itself reflected in slow water.

In floating graceful somnolence
By an alder-tree an ancient nymph
Teases a Faun with a willow-wisp;
The Faun smiles back, bucolic, gallant.

You sadden me, tired and naïve subject.
Tell me, among all artists, what poet
What moody artisan made you,

Faded time-worn tapestry
As banal as a theatre-set,
As false as my destiny?

Boarders

One girl was fifteen, the other a year older.
They'd been given beds together in one room.
Picture, on a sultry evening in September,
Slenderness, blue eyes, strawberry blush.

Wanting more freedom, each one's removed
Her thin blouse scented with amber.
The younger one opens her arms, and stretches.
Her sister's hands go to her breasts and she kisses

Her, falls to her knees, turns wild and then wilder,
Tumultuously plunging her mouth
Under that light gold, blind intoxication...

Et l'enfant, pendant ce temps-là, recense
Sur ses doigts mignons des valses promises,
Et, rose, sourit avec innocence.

Printemps

Tendre, la jeune femme rousse,
Que tant d'innocence émoustille,
Dit à la blonde jeune fille
Ces mots, tout bas, d'une voix douce:

'Sève qui monte et fleur qui pousse,
Ton enfance est une charmille:
Laisse errer mes doigts dans la mousse
Où le bouton de rose brille,

Laisse-moi, parmi l'herbe claire,
Boire les gouttes de rosée
Dont la fleur tendre est arrosée, —

Afin que le plaisir, ma chère,
Illumine ton front candide
Comme l'aube l'azur timide.'

Été

Et l'enfant répondit, pâmée
Sous la fourmillante caresse
De sa pantelante maîtresse;
'Je me meurs, ô ma bien-aimée!

Je me meurs; ta gorge enflammée
Et lourde me soûle et m'oppresse;
Ta forte chair d'où sort l'ivresse
Est étrangement parfumée;

During which time the other one counts
Waltzes-to-come on her sweet little fingertips,
And, flushing, and innocent, smiles.

Spring

The young redhead, tender, aroused
By so much innocence
Says these low, soft words
To the light-haired girl:

'So young and such magic in your growing
Garden of saps and flowers...
Let my fingers move through moss
Where the rosebud glistens.

Let me find in new grass
Dewdrops to drink,
The fragile flower's refreshment,

So that pleasure, pure and simple, my sweet,
May flood with light your open face
Like dawn in a bashful sky.'

Summer

Swept on a tingling tide
Of breathless caresses,
The drugged child replied:
'I want to die,

I'm going to die
In the splendour of your breasts,
I'm giddy, I'm drunk
On the smell of you.

Elle a, ta chair, le charme sombre
Des maturités estivales,—
Elle en a l'ambre, elle en a l'ombre;

Ta voix tonne dans les rafales,
Et ta chevelure sanglante
Fuit brusquement dans la nuit lente.'

A la Princesse Roukhine

'Capellos de Angelos.'
(Friandise espagnole)

C'est une laide de Boucher
Sans poudre dans sa chevelure,
Follement blonde et d'une allure
Vénuste à tous nous débaucher.

Mais je la crois mienne entre tous,
Cette crinière tant baisée,
Cette cascatelle embrasée
Qui m'allume par tous le bouts.

Elle est à moi bien plus encor
Comme une flamboyante enceinte
Aux entours de la porte sainte,
L'alme, la dive toison d'or!

Et qui pourrait dire ce corps
Sinon moi, son chantre et son prêtre,
Et son esclave humble et son maître
Qui s'en damnerait sans remords,

Son cher corps rare, harmonieux,
Suave, blanc comme une rose
Blanche, blanc de lait pur, et rose
Comme un lys sous de pourpres cieux?

Your skin casts spells
Dark as ripe summer:
It's all shadow and amber.

Your voice comes through storms,
And your hair, bright as blood,
Flies in the slow night.'

To Princess Roukhine*

'Cabellos de ángel'

(Fruit conserve;*
Spanish delicacy)

She's one of Boucher's* ugly women.
Hair unpowdered, she's
Extravagantly blond, a charming
Invitation to debauchery.

But I think that mane of hair so often kissed
Is mine more than anyone's—
Those tumbling waves of fire
Igniting the whole of me.

Beyond that it's mine,
A flamboyant frame
Surrounding hallowed doors—
Superb Golden Fleece, breathing life.

And who can speak of this body
If not me, its cantor, its high priest,
Its humble servant, its master?
I'd gladly suffer hell for that body.

Those rare harmonies, sweet
And white as white roses,
White as new milk and pink
As lilies against purple skies.

Cuisses belles, seins redressants,
Le dos, les reins, le ventre, fête
Pour les yeux et les mains en quête
Et pour la bouche et tous les sens?

Mignonne, allons voir si ton lit
A toujours sous le rideau rouge
L'oreiller sorcier qui tant bouge
Et les draps fous. Ô vers ton lit!

Séguidille

Brune encore non eue,
Je te veux presque nue
Sur un canapé noir
Dans un jaune boudoir,
Comme en mil huit cent trente.

Presque nue et non nue
A travers une nue
De dentelles montrant
Ta chair où va courant
Ma bouche délirante.

Je te veux trop rieuse
Et très impérieuse,
Méchante et mauvaise et
Pire s'il te plaisait,
Mais si luxurieuse!

Ah, ton corps noir et rose
Et clair de lune! Ah, pose
Ton coude sur mon cœur,
Et tout ton corps vainqueur,
Tout ton corps que j'adore!

Fine thighs, proud breasts,
Back, hips, belly, a feast
For eyes and searching hands,
For mouth, for all the senses.

Delicious woman, let's see if your bed*
Still has below its red hangings
That nightshade pillow* full of its own life,
And wild sheets... Oh please, let's find your bed!

Seguidilla*

Dusky woman still not had
I want you naked almost
Lying on a black settee
In an ochre-painted private room
Circa 1830.

Almost naked and not naked
Through a cloud
Of lace revealing
Your skin which I run
My mad mouth over.

I want you lost in laughter
I want you to take charge
Wicked to the end
Worse if you wish
Serpentine with lust.

Ah, that pink and ebony
Moon-bright body... Place
Your elbow on my heart
And that triumphant body
That adorable body.

Ah, ton corps, qu'il repose
Sur mon âme morose
Et l'étouffe s'il peut,
Si ton caprice veut,
Encore, encore, encore!

Splendides, glorieuses,
Bellement furieuses
Dans leurs jeunes ébats,
Fous mon orgueil en bas
Sous tes fesses joyeuses!

A Mademoiselle ***

Rustique beauté
Qu'on a dans les coins,
Tu sens bon les foins,
La chair et l'été.

Tes trente-deux dents
De jeune animal
Ne vont point trop mal
A tes yeux ardents.

Ton corps dépravant
Sous tes habits courts,
—Retroussés et lourds,
Tes seins en avant,

Tes mollets farauds,
Ton buste tentant,
—Gai, comme impudent,
Ton cul ferme et gros,

Nous boutent au sang
Un feu bête et doux
Qui nous rend tout fous,
Croupe, rein et flanc.

Let your body lie full-length
On my gloomy soul
Try to smother it
If the mood takes you—
Again and again and again.

Under those glorious and splendid
And beautifully frenzied
Alive-with-such-youth
Buttocks of joy
Find a place for my pride.

To Mademoiselle ***

Rustic beauty
Had in corners,
Sweet smell of hay
Summer and skin.

Your thirty-two young
Animal teeth
Go well enough
With your hot eyes.

Body to deprave
In that short dress—
Heavy corseted
Breasts proclaiming,

Clever glimpse of leg,
Mouth-watering bust—
Impudent happy
Large and firm arse.

All this lights a magic
Crazy fire in our veins
Driving us mad—
Hips midriff waist.

Le petit vacher
Tout fier de son cas,
Le maître et ses gas,
Les gas du berger,

Je meurs si je mens,
Je les trouve heureux.
Tous ces culs-terreux,
D'être tes amants.

Impression fausse

Dame souris trotte,
Noire dans le gris du soir,
Dame souris trotte
Grise dans le noir.

On sonne la cloche,
Dormez, les bons prisonniers!
On sonne la cloche:
Faut que vous dormiez.

Pas de mauvais rêve,
Ne pensez qu'à vos amours.
Pas de mauvais rêve:
Les belles toujours!

Le grand clair de lune!
On ronfle ferme à côté.
Le grand clair de lune
En réalité!

Un nuage passe,
Il fait noir comme en un four.
Un nuage passe.
Tiens, le petit jour!

The little cattle-lad*
Pleased as Punch
The shepherd-boys
The gaffer and his bunch—

Strike me dead if I lie—
Don't know they're born,
Farmyard have-nots
Having you.

False impression

Dame Mouse scampers
Black against the evening's grey.
 Dame Mouse scampers
 Grey on black.

Sound of a bell.
Time to sleep my jail-birds!
 Sound of a bell.
 You must sleep.

Dream no bad dreams.
Think of nothing else but love.
 Dream no bad dreams.
 Always women!

Wonderful moon!
Loud snoring next to me.
 Wonderful moon
 Shining for real.

A cloud floats past.
It's as dark in here as an oven.
 A cloud floats past.
 Nearly dawn.

Dame souris trotte,
Rose dans les rayons bleus.
Dame souris trotte:
Debout, paresseux!

Autre

La cour se fleurit de souci
    Comme le front
    De tous ceux-ci
    Qui vont en rond
En flageolant sur leur fémur
    Débilité
    Le long du mur
    Fou de clarté.

Tournez, Samsons sans Dalila,
    Sans Philistin,
    Tournez bien la
    Meule au destin.
Vaincu risible de la loi,
    Mouds tour à tour
    Ton cœur, ta foi
    Et ton amour!

Ils vont! et leurs pauvres souliers
    Font un bruit sec,
    Humiliés,
    La pipe au bec.
Pas un mot ou bien le cachot
    Pas un soupir,
    Il fait si chaud
    Qu'on croit mourir.

Dame Mouse scampers
Pink in the rising blue.
Dame Mouse scampers.
Rise and shine!

Another

In the exercise-yard care
   Flowers*
   Like the faces
   Of these men walking
Round and round on jelly legs;
   Fragility
   Along the walls
   Crazed with brightness.

Round and round, you un-Dalilahed Samsons,*
   Un-Philistined,
   Turn the millstone
   Of destiny.
Derisory victims of the law,
   Grind one by one
   Your heart your faith
   Your love.

They shuffle on, wretched shoes
   Scraping round,
   Humiliated,
   Pipe in mouth.
Not a word or else it's solitary
   Confinement.
   No air. Heat
   You think you'll die.

J'en suis de ce cirque effaré,
   Soumis d'ailleurs
   Et préparé
   À tous malheurs.
Et pourquoi si j'ai contristé
   Ton vœu têtu,
   Société,
   Me choierais-tu?

Allons, frères, bons vieux voleurs,
   Doux vagabonds,
   Filous en fleurs,
   Mes chers, mes bons,
Fumons philosophiquement,
   Promenons-nous
   Paisiblement:
   Rien faire est doux.

Réversibilités

Totus in maligno positus

Entends les pompes qui font
   Le cri des chats.
Des sifflets viennent et vont
   Comme en pourchas.
Ah, dans ces tristes décors
Les Déjà sont les Encors!

Ô les vagues Angélus!
   (Qui viennent d'où?)
Vois s'allumer les Saluts
   Du fond d'un trou.
Ah, dans ces mornes séjours
Les Jamais sont les Toujours!

I'm in this circus of scarecrows
   Obedient
   And prepared for
   Any trouble.
Just because you're aggrieved I've flouted
   Your wilful laws,
   Society,
   Why cast me out?

Come, comrades, brothers, good my rogues,
   Gentle vagrants,
   My radiant
   Partners in crime,
Let's smoke a philosophical pipe
   And walk about
   In peace and quiet.
   Indolence is bliss.

Reversibilities

Everything lies in wickedness*

   Pumps going like
     Yelling cats,
   Whistle-shriek chasing
     Whistle-shriek.
   In these sad decors,
   Already is Again!

   And the vague Angelus
     (Coming from where?).
   Salvation glowing
     Deep in a hole.
   In these drab places
   Never is Always!

Quels rêves épouvantés,
    Vous, grands murs blancs!
Que de sanglots répétés,
    Fous ou dolents!
Ah, dans ces piteux retraits
Les Toujours sont les Jamais!

Tu meurs doucereusement,
    Obscurément,
Sans qu'on veille, ô cœur aimant,
    Sans testament!
Ah, dans ces deuils sans rachats
Les Encors sont les Déjàs!

Tantalized

L'aile où je suis donnant juste sur une gare,
J'entends de nuit (mes nuits sont blanches) la bagarre
Des machines qu'on chauffe et des trains ajustés,
Et vraiment c'est des bruits de nids répercutés
A des dieux de fonte et de verre et gras de houille.
Vous n'imaginez pas comme cela gazouille
Et comme l'on dirait des efforts d'oiselets
Vers des vols tout prochains à des cieux violets
Encore et que le point du jour éclaire à peine.
Ô ces wagons qui vont dévaler dans la plaine!

Invraisemblable mais vrai

Las! je suis à l'Index et dans les dédicaces
Me voici Paul V... pur et simple. Les audaces
De mes amis, tant les débiteurs sont des saints,
Doivent éliminer mon nom de leurs desseins.
Extraordinaire et saponaire tonnerre
D'une excommunication que je vénère
Au point d'en faire des fautes de quantité!

What dreams of terror,
   Great white walls,
What tides of tears,
   Plaintive or wild!
In these abject recesses
Always is Never!

Insipidly you die,
   Loving heart,
Unknown and unattended,
   No legacy.
In this grief of no redemption
Again is Already!

Tantalized

From my cell-block overlooking the station,
Night after sleepless night I hear the engines
Quarrelling as they're stoked up; I hear shunting,
And it's like birds'-nest noises bounced
Into skies of molten metal and glass and coal.
You can't imagine the cheeping and chirping;
It sounds like little birds contemplating
Little test-flights in violet skies
Which dawn has not yet roused from sleep.
—Ah, those trains about to race across the plain!

Incredible but true

Oh hell, I'm on the Index;* and in dedications
I'm referred to just as Paul V.* My brave
Friends (sanctimonious Judases)
No doubt reckon I'm beyond the pale.
Amazing and deep-cleansing thunder
Of an excommunication I embrace
More I'm sure than I should.

Vrai, si je n'étais pas (forcément) désisté
Des choses, j'aimerais, surtout m'étant contraire,
Cette pudeur du moins si rare de libraire.

Le Dernier dizain

O Belgique qui m'as valu ce dur loisir,
Merci! J'ai pu du moins réfléchir et saisir
Dans le silence doux et blanc de tes cellules
Les raisons qui fuyaient comme des libellules
A travers les roseaux bavards d'un monde vain,
Les raisons de mon être éternel et divin,
Et les étiqueter comme en un beau musée
Dans les cases en fin cristal de ma pensée.
Mais, ô Belgique, assez de ce huis-clos têtu!
Ouvre enfin, car c'est bon pour une fois, sais-tu!

Bruxelles, août 1873–Mons, janvier 1875

A la manière de Paul Verlaine

C'est à cause du clair de la lune
Que j'assume ce masque nocturne
Et de Saturne penchant son urne
Et de ces lunes l'une après l'une.

Des romances sans paroles ont,
D'un accord discord ensemble et frais,
Agacé ce cœur fadasse exprès,
Ô le son, le frisson qu'elles ont!

Il n'est pas que vous n'ayez fait grâce
A quelqu'un qui vous jetait l'offense:
Or, moi, je pardonne à mon enfance
Revenant fardée et non sans grâce.

True, if I weren't forced into retirement,
I'd adopt (especially since it's just not me)
The bookish person's rare and bashful modesty.

Ten last lines

Thanks, Belgium, for the enforced rest.
At least I've had time to reflect
In the sweet white silence of your cells,
And arrange those tatters of my real self
Flitting like dragonflies among the breezy reeds
Of a frivolous world—the religious me,
Labelled now like some museum piece
Displayed in my mind's crystal cabinets.
But, Belgium, enough now of this solitary
Confinement. Just this once, now, open sesame!

Brussels, August 1873–Mons, January 1875

In the manner of Paul Verlaine

Because the moon is shining bright
I assume this mask of night
And of Saturn tilting up its urn
And of these moons, soon one, one more soon.

Songs without words have, in fresh and
Altogether jarring harmonies,
Annoyed this purposely sick heart.
Oh, the trembling, the sounds that abound!

It's not that you haven't forgiven
Someone who's given you offence.
Me, I pardon my remembered childhood
All brushed and combed and not without its share of grace.

Je pardonne à ce mensonge-là
En faveur en somme du plaisir
Très banal drôlement qu'un loisir
Douloureux un peu m'inocula.

Limbes

L'imagination, reine,
Tient ses ailes étendues,
Mais la robe qu'elle traîne
A des lourdeurs éperdues.

Cependant que la Pensée,
Papillon, s'envole et vole,
Rose et noir clair, élancée
Hors de la tête frivole.

L'Imagination, sise
En son trône, ce fier siège!
Assiste, comme indécise,
A tout ce preste manège,

Et le papillon fait rage,
Monte et descend, plane et vire:
On dirait dans un naufrage
Des culbutes du navire.

La reine pleure de joie
Et de peine encore, à cause
De son cœur qu'un chaud pleur noie,
Et n'entend goutte à la chose.

Psyché Deux pourtant se lasse.
Son vol est la main plus lente
Que cent tours de passe-passe
Ont faite toute tremblante.

I'm ready to forgive that untruth
In favour of a very strangely
Ordinary pleasure
Painful freedom has injected me with.

Limbo

Queen Imagination
Stretches out her wings
But drags robes
Heavy with madness.

Meanwhile butterfly
Thought wings out
Of the empty head,
A pink and black volley.

Imagination, enthroned
On her proud seat,
Caught in two minds,
Watches this ballet.

The butterfly loops loops,
Weaves glides drops,
A stricken ship
Pitching in the storm.

The Queen cries with joy
And pain too because
Her tear-choked heart
Understands not a thing.

But Psyche II's* tiring.
Her flight's a slow
Hand trembling after
Too much legerdemain.

Hélas, voici l'agonie!
Qui s'en fût formé l'idée?
Et tandis que, bon génie
Plein d'une douceur lactée,

La bestiole céleste
S'en vient palpiter à terre,
La Folle-du-Logis reste
Dans sa gloire solitaire!

Lombes

Deux femmes des mieux m'ont apparu cette nuit.
Mon rêve était au bal, je vous demande un peu!
L'une d'entre elles maigre assez, blonde, un œil bleu,
Un noir et ce regard mécréant qui poursuit.

L'autre, brune au regard sournois qui flatte et nuit,
Seins joyeux d'être vus, dignes d'un demi-dieu!
Et toutes deux avaient, pour rappeler le jeu
De la main chaude, sous la traîne qui bruit,

Des bas de dos très beaux et d'une gaîté folle
Auxquels il ne manquait vraiment que la parole,
Royale arrière-garde aux combats du plaisir.

Et ces Dames—scrutez l'armorial de France—
S'efforçaient d'entamer l'orgueil de mon désir,
Et n'en revenaient pas de mon indifférence.

Vouziers (Ardennes), 13 avril–23 mai 1885

La Dernière Fête galante

Pour une bonne fois séparons-nous,
Très chers messieurs et si belles mesdames.
Assez comme cela d'épithalames,
Et puis là, nos plaisirs furent trop doux.

Here's death, sad to say.
Who'd have thought?
As the heaven-bent insect,
Like a valiant genie

Filled with milky sweetness,
Flutters to the ground,
Wild imagination stays high
In solitary splendour!

Loins

Last night in my dreams two fabulous women
Came to me during a ball (I ask you, a ball!).
One was rather thin and blond, with one blue eye,
The other black. She had a haunting pagan look.

The second was dark and sly and promised harm.
Breasts thrilled to be seen, breasts for a god.
Curving backs—described by hot hands—
Under their dresses' swish and sweep

Plunged with such beauty and such wild joy,
Song without words, so to speak,
Royal rearguard on the battlefield of love.

And these Belles Dames—study France's coat of arms—
Did what they could to prick me into life,
Astonished that I didn't give a damn.

Vouziers* (Ardennes), 13 April–23 May 1885

The last 'Fête galante'

Let's have done, let's go our separate ways,
Lovely ladies, esteemed gentlemen.
Enough of these come-to-bed songs.
Yes, agreed, it's been too much fun for words.

Nul remords, nul regret vrai, nul désastre!
C'est effrayant ce que nous nous sentons
D'affinités avecque les moutons
Enrubannés du pire poétastre.

Nous fûmes trop ridicules un peu
Avec nos airs de n'y toucher qu'à peine.
Le Dieu d'amour veut qu'on ait de l'haleine,
Il a raison! Et c'est un jeune Dieu.

Séparons-nous, je vous le dis encore.
Ô que nos cœurs qui furent trop bêlants,
Dès ce jourd'hui réclament, trop hurlants,
L'embarquement pour Sodome et Gomorrhe!

Guitare

Le pauvre du chemin creux chante et parle.
Il dit: 'Mon nom est Pierre et non pas Charle,
Et je m'appelle aussi Duchatelet.
Une fois je vis, moi, qu'on croit très laid,
Passer vraiment une femme très belle.
(Si je la voyais telle, elle était telle.)
Nous nous mariâmes au vieux curé.
On eut tout ce qu'on avait espéré,
Jusqu'à l'enfant qu'on m'a dit vivre encore.
Mais elle devint la pire pécore
Indigne même de cette chanson,
Et certain beau soir quitta la maison
En emportant tout l'argent du ménage
Dont les trois quarts étaient mon apanage.
C'était une voleuse, une sans-cœur,
Et puis, par des fois, je lui faisais peur.
Elle n'avait pas l'ombre d'une excuse,
Pas un amant ou par rage ou par ruse.
Il paraît qu'elle couche depuis peu
Avec un individu qui tient lieu
D'époux à cette femme de querelle.
Faut-il la tuer ou prier pour elle?'

No remorse, no regrets, nothing's been lost.
Frightening, the extent to which we feel
Affinity with the worst hack shepherding
His verses like prize sheep.

We were a touch too ridiculous
With our don't-come-too-close affectations,
The god of love says take deep breaths and take
The plunge, and he's so right, this god of youth.

So once more then, let's go our separate ways.
Let our bleating hearts cease
Their endless bah-bahs. Now's the time to book berths
On the next boat to Sodom and Gomorrah.*

Guitar

The poor man of the hollow road sings and speaks.
He says: 'I'm called Pierre, not Charle.
And my other name's Duchatelet.*
Me, hideous me, I once saw
Such a lovely woman pass by.
(That's how I saw her, that's what she was).
A kindly old priest married us.
All our hopes were fulfilled,
Even a child, who they say still lives.
But she became too silly for words,
Not worthy even of these lines.
One fine night she upped and left the house
Taking with her all the petty cash,
Most of which was strictly mine.
Heartless thief who claimed
She sometimes found me frightening.
She hadn't got the least excuse,
No lover taken out of rage or on the sly.
The word is she now sleeps
With some Tom, Dick, or Harry who's
Stand-in husband to this yack-yack wife.
Should I kill her? Pray for her? Which?'

Et le pauvre sait très bien qu'il priera,
Mais le diable parierait qu'il tuera.

'Ces passions . . .'

Ces passions qu'eux seuls nomment encore amours
Sont des amours aussi, tendres et furieuses,
Avec des particularités curieuses
Que n'ont pas les amours certes de tous les jours.

Même plus qu'elles et mieux qu'elles héroïques,
Elles se parent de splendeurs d'âme et de sang
Telles qu'au prix d'elles les amours dans le rang
Ne sont que Ris et Jeux ou besoins érotiques,

Que vains proverbes, que riens d'enfants trop gâtés,
—'Ah! les pauvres amours banales, animales,
Normales! Gros goûts lourds ou frugales fringales,
Sans compter la sottise et des fécondités!'

—Peuvent dire ceux-là que sacre le haut Rite,
Ayant conquis la plénitude du plaisir,
Et l'insatiabilité de leur désir
Bénissant la fidélité de leur mérite.

La plénitude! Ils l'ont superlativement:
Baisers repus, gorgés, mains privilégiées
Dans la richesse des caresses repayées,
Et ce divin final anéantissement!

Comme ce sont les forts et les forts, l'habitude
De la force les rend invaincus au déduit.
Plantureux, savoureux, débordant, le déduit!
Je le crois bien qu'ils l'ont la pleine plénitude!

The poor man firmly thinks he'll pray,
But the clever money's on murder.

'These passions . . .'

These passions they alone call love
Are love indeed, tender, full of fire,
With curiosities beyond
The realm of what is known as normal love.

Better than that kind and more heroic,
They set their souls and blood with jewels.
Alongside these passions, rank-and-file love's
A party game, or mere erotic needs,

Or pious maxims, or spoiled brats' whims.
'Pathetic ordinary normal animal
Love! Gorging or starving itself,
The mindless treadmill of reproduction.'

Those who take their own High Church's sacraments
Can say this, having conquered pleasure's heights.
Eternal desire's the blessing enjoyed
By those who stay true to what they are.

The heights! They've conquered Everests:
Kiss-drunk, hands licensed
To touch treasures received and exchanged;
Then final glorious oblivion!

They belong to the tribe of the strong;
Strength is their habit, they're unbowed by love's demands,
Never full, yet full to overflowing,
In the aromatic plant-house of desire.

Et pour combler leurs vœux, chacun d'eux tour à tour
Fait l'action suprême, a la parfaite extase,
—Tantôt la coupe ou la bouche et tantôt le vase—
Pâmé comme la nuit, fervent comme le jour.

Leurs beaux ébats sont grands et gais. Pas de ces crises:
Vapeurs, nerfs. Non, des jeux courageux, puis d'heureux
Bras las autour du cou, pour de moins langoureux
Qu'étroits sommeils à deux, tout coupés de reprises.

Dormez, les amoureux! Tandis qu'autour de vous
Le monde inattentif aux choses délicates,
Bruit ou gît en somnolences scélérates,
Sans même, il est si bête! être de vous jaloux.

Et ces réveils francs, clairs, riants, vers l'aventure
De fiers damnés d'un plus magnifique sabbat?
Et salut, témoins purs de l'âme en ce combat
Pour l'affranchissement de la lourde nature!

Laeti et errabundi

Les courses furent intrépides
(Comme aujourd'hui le repos pèse!)
Par les steamers et les rapides.
(Que me veut cet at home obèse?)

Nous allions,—vous en souvient-il,
Voyageur où ça disparu?—
Filant légers dans l'air subtil,
Deux spectres joyeux, on eût cru!

Car les passions satisfaites
Insolemment outre mesure
Mettaient dans nos têtes des fêtes
Et dans nos sens, que tout rassure,

And in a final act of wish-fulfilment, each
In turn knows sublime ecstasy—
Be it the cup or the mouth or the vase—*
Abandoned as night, ardent as day.

The naked beauty of joyful love
Free and willed. Courageous games,
Arms around necks in narrow sleep for two,
Less prone to peace than repetition.

So sleep on, lovers. Meanwhile, all around,
A world careless of things delicate
Bangs and thumps or drowses in wickedness
Without the brains to be jealous of you.

And what of those laughing reveilles,
The adventures awaiting the proud lost souls
Of prouder sabbaths? Bless the soul's pure witnesses
Struggling to throw off nature's great constraint!

Footloose and fancy free*

A flurry of escapades
(The sheer boredom today!),
Mad flits by boat and train.
(No loosened waistbands by warm firesides!)

We went about—remember,
Traveller vanished God knows where?—
Like acrobats on threads of air
For all the world a pair of happy ghosts.

Because passion
Slaked beyond anything ever dreamt
Filled our heads with carnivals.
Youth friendship everything

Tout, la jeunesse, l'amitié,
Et nos cœurs, ah! que dégagés
Des femmes prises en pitié
Et du dernier des préjugés,

Laissant la crainte de l'orgie
Et le scrupule au bon ermite,
Puisque quand la borne est franchie
Ponsard ne veut plus de limite.

Entre autres blâmables excès
Je crois que nous bûmes de tout,
Depuis les plus grands vins français
Jusqu'à ce faro, jusqu'au stout,

En passant par les eaux-de-vie
Qu'on cite comme redoutables,
L'âme au septième ciel ravie,
Le corps, plus humble, sous les tables.

Des paysages, des cités
Posaient pour nos yeux jamais las;
Nos belles curiosités
Eussent mangé tous les atlas.

Fleuves et monts, bronzes et marbres,
Les couchants d'or, l'aube magique,
L'Angleterre, mère des arbres,
Fille des beffrois, la Belgique,

La mer, terrible et douce au point,—
Brochaient sur le roman très cher
Que ne discontinuait point
Notre âme—et *quid* de notre chair?...—

Le roman de vivre à deux hommes
Mieux que non pas d'époux modèles,
Chacun au tas versant des sommes
De sentiments forts et fidèles.

Flattered our senses.
And then how free our hearts were
Of pitiable women!
Free of the final prejudice

We left the righteous hermit to tremble
About sex performed with gay abandon—
For once they've crossed the Rubicon,
Even sticklers for rules throw the rule-book away.

Among our shameful excesses
We drank everything going,
France's finest vintages
Belgian beers and stouts

Fire-water brandies
Reputed for their clout.
Our spirits were in seventh heaven.
Less lofty our bodies lay beneath the table.

Landscapes and cities stretched out
Beneath our eager eyes.
Our splendid curiosity
Demanded every map and atlas.

Rivers and mountains bronze and marble statues
Golden sunsets magic dawns
England motherland of trees
Belgium issued from belfries

The sea pitching from terror to sweetness—
These things bound our endless book
The great saga of our souls...
And then what of the flesh?

Unfolding story of two men's lives
Together, not like man and wife,
But better, each bringing
New strengths and loyalties.

L'envie aux yeux de basilic
Censurait ce mode d'écot:
Nous dînions du blâme public
Et soupions du même fricot.

La misère aussi faisait rage
Par des fois dans le phalanstère:
On ripostait par le courage,
La joie et les pommes de terre.

Scandaleux sans savoir pourquoi
(Peut-être que c'était trop beau)
Mais notre couple restait coi
Comme deux bons porte-drapeau,

Coi dans l'orgueil d'être plus libres
Que les plus libres de ce monde,
Sourd aux gros mots de tous calibres,
Inaccessible au rire immonde.

Nous avions laissé sans émoi
Tous impédiments dans Paris,
Lui quelques sots bernés, et moi
Certaine princesse Souris,

Une sotte qui tourna pire...
Puis soudain tomba notre gloire,
Tels, nous, des maréchaux d'empire
Déchus en brigands de la Loire,

Mais déchus volontairement!
C'était une permission,
Pour parler militairement,
Que notre séparation,

Permission sous nos semelles,
Et depuis combien de campagnes!
Pardonnâtes-vous aux femelles?
Moi, j'ai peu revu ces compagnes,

Envy with its metal stab
Attacked our way of doing things.
We ate from the pot of universal blame,
Then returned for more.

When poverty spread
Through our pioneer community,
We answered with fortitude
Joy and good helpings of potatoes.

We spelt scandal—why, we didn't know
(Too beautiful for most, perhaps),
But stayed cool under fire
Like exemplary standard-bearers

Calm in the pride of being freer
Than those who think they're freest,
Deaf to their high–decibel slanders
Impervious to their smutty jokes.

We slipped the leash of Paris
Without a backward glance
(In his case) at a bunch of bigots,
(In mine) a certain Sugar-Mouse

Princess, who started stupid and got worse...
Suddenly our glory days were over.
We were like famous Admirals
Turned pirate on the Loire.

But we took that course by choice.
Militarily speaking,
We had leave
To disappear.

The wind was in our heels.
What campaigns we fought!
Did you forgive the female
Of the species? Me, I've hardly seen

Assez toutefois pour souffrir.
Ah, quel cœur faible que mon cœur!
Mais mieux vaut souffrir que mourir
Et surtout mourir de langueur.

On vous dit mort, vous. Que le Diable
Emporte avec qui la colporte
La nouvelle irrémédiable
Qui vient ainsi battre ma porte!

Je n'y veux rien croire. Mort, vous,
Toi, dieu parmi les demi-dieux!
Ceux qui le disent sont des fous.
Mort, mon grand péché radieux,

Tout ce passé brûlant encore
Dans mes veines et ma cervelle
Et qui rayonne et qui fulgore
Sur ma ferveur toujours nouvelle!

Mort tout ce triomphe inouï
Retentissant sans frein ni fin
Sur l'air jamais évanoui
Que bat mon cœur qui fut divin!

Quoi, le miraculeux poème
Et la toute-philosophie,
Et ma patrie et ma bohème
Morts? Allons donc! tu vis ma vie!

Ballade de la mauvaise réputation

Il eut des temps quelques argents
Et régala ses camarades
D'un sexe ou deux, intelligents
Ou charmants, ou bien les deux grades,
Si que dans les esprits malades
Sa bonne réputation
Subit que de dégringolades!
Lucullus? Non. Trimalcion.

Any, yet enough to cause me pain.
My heart! Call that feeble thing a heart?
Suffering's better than any kind of death,
Especially death by yearning.

They say you're dead. To hell
With both the message and the messenger.
My ears won't hear doom thump
Its fists against my door.

I don't want to believe it. Dead, you,
You, a god among mere demi-gods?
Those who say you're dead are mad.
Dead, you, my great and radiant sin,*

While all our past life burns
In my head and my blood,
White heat forging
New and blinding passion?

Dead, our great unprecedented
Gravity-defying triumph
Winging through restless air which moves
To the beating of my god-like heart?

The miraculous poem,
The ultimate philosophy,
My country, my Bohemia,
All gone? No, you live my life.

Bad name ballad

For a while he had money
Spent on good times with friends
Of one sex or two,
Friends who were charming or clever
Or both so that certain sick people
Grabbed hold of his good name
And trampled it underfoot.
Lucullus?* No. Trimalchio.*

Sous ses lambris, c'étaient des chants
Et des paroles point trop fades.
Éros et Bacchos indulgents
Présidaient à ces sérénades
Qu'accompagnaient des embrassades.
Puis chœurs et conversation
Cessaient pour des fins peu maussades.
Lucullus? Non. Trimalcion.

L'aube pointait et ces méchants
La saluaient par cent aubades
Qui réveillaient au loin les gens
De bien, et par mille rasades.
Cependant de vagues brigades
—Zèle ou dénonciation?—
Verbalisaient chez des alcades.
Lucullus? Non. Trimalcion.

ENVOI

Prince, ô très haut marquis de Sade,
Un souris pour votre scion
Fier derrière sa palissade.
Lucullus? Non. Trimalcion.

Caprice

O poète, faux pauvre et faux riche, homme vrai,
Jusqu'en l'extérieur riche et pauvre pas vrai,
(Dès lors, comment veux-tu qu'on soit sûr de ton cœur?)
Tour à tour souple drôle et monsieur somptueux,
Du vert clair plein d'"espère' au noir componctueux,
Ton habit a toujours quelque détail blagueur.

Lively talk and music
Filled his lavish rooms.
Indulgent Eros* and Bacchus*
Orchestrated
Serenades of love.
Then song and chatter
Made way for other cheerful things.
Lucullus? No. Trimalchio.

Dawn blinked, and this rowdy crowd,
Glasses raised, brought in the day
On a chorus fit to wake
Good folk for miles around.
But faceless vigilantes
(Pure motives? A settling of scores?)
Were naming names to magistrates.
Lucullus? No. Trimalchio.

ENVOI

Prince, Highness, great Marquis de Sade,*
Smile on your latest offshoot
Standing proud behind his palisade.
Lucullus? No. Trimalchio.

Caprice

Poet, pseudo-rich man, pseudo-poor, man of truth,
False appearance of wealth and poverty
(Can we be sure henceforth of your heart?),
At times compliant, at others strange then
Splendid again... From 'hopeful' green to guilty black
Your clothes always contain some hidden joke.

Un bouton manque. Un fil dépasse. D'où venue
Cette tache—ah ça, malvenue ou bienvenue?—
Qui rit et pleure sur le cheviot et la toile?
Nœud noué bien et mal, soulier luisant et terne.
Bref, un type à se pendre à la Vieille-Lanterne
Comme à marcher, gai proverbe, à la belle étoile,

Gueux, mais pas comme ça, l'homme vrai, le seul vrai.
Poète, va, si ton langage n'est pas vrai,
Toi l'es, et ton langage, alors! Tant pis pour ceux
Qui n'auront pas aimé, fous comme autant de tois,
La lune pour chauffer les sans femmes ni toits,
La mort, ah, pour bercer les cœurs malechanceux,

Pauvres cœurs mal tombés, trop bons et très fiers, certes!
Car l'ironie éclate aux lèvres belles, certes,
De vos blessures, cœurs plus blessés qu'une cible,
Petits sacrés-cœurs de Jésus plus lamentables!
Va, poète, le seul des hommes véritables,
Meurs sauvé, meurs de faim pourtant le moins possible.

Ballade Sappho

Ma douce main de maîtresse et d'amant
Passe et rit sur ta chère chair en fête,
Rit et jouit de ton jouissement.
Pour la servir tu sais bien qu'elle est faite,
Et ton beau corps faut que je le dévête
Pour l'enivrer sans fin d'un art nouveau
Toujours dans la caresse toujours prête.
Je suis pareil à la grande Sappho.

Laisse ma tête errant et s'abîmant
A l'aventure, un peu farouche, en quête
D'ombre et d'odeur et d'un travail charmant
Vers les saveurs de ta gloire secrète.
Laisse rôder l'âme de ton poète
Partout par là, champ ou bois, mont ou vau,
Comme tu veux et si je le souhaite.
Je suis pareil à la grande Sappho.

A missing button. A hanging thread. What caused
That stain? Suspect, is it? Maybe not?
Worsted and tweed to make you laugh and cry.
Dull or shiny shoes. Cravat well or badly tied.
The sort that hangs itself from lamp-posts,
Or, as the saying goes, takes to the road,

A beggar, but not in that sense—the one true man.
Poet, if your language isn't exactly true,
You are—your language too, therefore! Bad luck for those
As crazed as you, who've never loved
The moon, bringer of warmth to the destitute,
Or death, the luckless hearts' swaddling clothes,

Poor good proud hearts fallen on bad times!
Irony no doubt flowers on your wounds'
Fine lips, you hearts more pierced than target-rings,
Sad little sacred hearts in Jesus.
Poet, the one authentic man,
Die saved but not starved if you can.

Sappho* ballad

My gentle hand, a lover's hand, a mistress's,
Glides and smiles its way across the festival
Of your skin. Such pleasure in your pleasure.
You know my hand was meant to serve you.
You know I must unclothe your splendour
To send it with a new art's skilful strokes
Into rapture, then more rapture.
I am like great Sappho.

Let my wild head wander and burrow
Where it will, in search of shadow
And smell and the charmed work to be done
Among the flavours of your secret glory.
Let the soul of your poet roam
Where it will, fields woods hills
As you wish and as I so much want.
I am like great Sappho.

Je presse alors tout ton corps goulûment,
Toute ta chair contre mon corps d'athlète
Qui se bande et s'amollit par moment,
Heureux du triomphe et de la défaite
En ce conflict du cœur et de la tête.
Pour la stérile étreinte où le cerveau
Vient faire enfin la nature complète
Je suis pareil à la grande Sappho.

ENVOI

Prince ou princesse, honnête ou malhonnête,
Qui qu'en grogne et quel que soit son niveau,
Trop su poète ou divin proxénète,
Je suis pareil à la grande Sappho.

Projet en l'air

A Ernest Delahaye

Il fait bon supinément,
　　Mi-dormant,
Dans l'aprication douce
D'un déjeuner modéré,
　　Digéré
Sur un lit d'herbe et de mousse,

Bon songer et bon rêver
　　Et trouver
Toute fin et tout principe
Dans les flocons onduleux,
　　Roses, bleus
Et blancs d'une lente pipe.

Then hungrily I press my athlete's body
Against the length of yours.
Hard and soft again, happily
It knows victory and defeat
In the battle fought by heart and head.
In the sterile embrace where human will
Completes Nature,
I am like great Sappho.

ENVOI

Prince or Princess, dishonest or straight,
Whatever kind of person may complain,
Famous poet or wonderful white-slaver,
I am like great Sappho.

Up in the air
To Ernest Delahaye*

It's so good when you're lying*
    Half-asleep
In the sweet post-prandial glow*
Of a lunch that was just right.
    Digestion
On a bed of grass and moss.

It's good to drift and dream
    And find first
Principles and last ends
In the pink and blue and white
    Tobacco
Drawing nice and slowly in your pipe.

L'éternel problème ainsi
    Éclairci,
Philosopher est de mise
Sur maint objet réclamant
    Moindrement
La synthèse et l'analyse...

Je me souviens que j'aimais
    A jamais
(Pensais-je à seize ans) la Gloire,
A Thèbes pindariser,
    Puis oser
Ronsardiser sur la Loire,

Ou bien être un paladin
    Gai, hautain,
Dur aux félons, qui s'avance
Toujours la lance en arrêt!
    J'ai regret
A ces bêtises d'enfance...

La femme? En faut-il encor?
    Ce décor
Trouble un peu le paysage
Simple, petit et surtout
    De bon goût
Qu'à la fin prise le sage.

A vingt ans, même à trente ans,
    J'eus le temps
De me plaire aux mines gentes,
Et d'écouter les propos
    Faux mais beaux,
Sexe alme, que tu nous chantes...

The eternal problem thus
   Clarified,
Philosophy's the very thing
To tackle things which need
   A pinch of
Synthesis, analysis...

I recall I was in love
   Forever
(So I thought aged sixteen) with Fame...
To write like Pindar* in Thebes,
   Then dare to
Flow like Ronsard* down the Loire,

Or become a light-hearted
   Haughty Knight,
Tough on crime, always going
Forward, lance at the ready!
   I regret
This childhood foolishness.

Women? Necessary still?
   That prospect
Disturbs somewhat the simple
Small and more than anything tasteful
   Perspective,
Which wisdom values in the end.

Aged twenty or even thirty,
   I had time
To take pleasure in sweet looks
And listen to the false but
   Lovely words
Earth-mothers sang to us...

La Politique, ah, j'en fis!
　　Mon avis?
Zut et bran! L'amitié seule
Est restée, avec l'espoir
　　De me voir
Un jour sauvé de la gueule

De cet ennui sans motif
　　Par trop vif,
Qui des fois bâille, l'affreuse!
Et de m'endormir, que las!
　　Dans tes bras,
Éternité bienheureuse.

Tire-lire et chante-clair!
　　Voix de l'air
Et des fermes, cette aurore
Que la mort nous révéla,
　　Dites-la
Si douce d'un los sonore!

Politics? I got involved.
   My verdict?
Utter tripe. Friendship only
Has endured, hope as well
   That one day
I'll find myself rescued from

The jaws of pointless, over-
   Sharp ennui
Given to mammoth yawning bouts.
I hope I'll lay my weary head
   In your lap,
Eternity of happiness.

Songs of cockerels, songs of larks!
   Sounds in air
And in farmyards, this dawn
Which death has revealed to us,
   Recount its
Sweetness in a song of praise!

Dédicaces

Souvenir de Manchester

A Theodore C. London

Je n'ai vu Manchester que d'un coin de Salford,
Donc très mal et très peu, quel que fût mon effort
A travers le brouillard et les courses pénibles
Au possible, en dépit d'hansoms inaccessibles
Presque, grâce à ma jambe male et mes pieds bots.
N'importe, j'ai gardé des souvenirs plus beaux
De cette ville que l'on dit industrielle,—
Encore que de telle ô qu'intellectuelle
Place où ma vanité devait se pavaner
Soi-disant mieux—et dussiez-vous vous étonner
Des semblantes naïvetés de cette épître,
Ô vous! quand je parlais du haut de mon pupitre
Dans cette salle où l'élite' de Manchester
Applaudissait en Verlaine l'auteur d'*Esther*,
Et que je proclamais, insoucieux du pire
Ou du meilleur, mon culte énorme pour Shakspeare.

30 janvier 1894

A Arthur Rimbaud

Mortel, ange ET démon, autant dire Rimbaud,
Tu mérites la prime place en ce mien livre,
Bien que tel sot grimaud t'ait traité de ribaud
Imberbe et de monstre en herbe et de potache ivre.

Les spirales d'encens et les accords de luth
Signalent ton entrée au temple de mémoire
Et ton nom radieux chantera dans la gloire,
Parce que tu m'aimas ainsi qu'il le fallut.

Manchester remembered

To Theodore C. London*

I've only seen Manchester from somewhere in Salford.*
Little therefore, and not well despite my best
Endeavours in the fog, on trying journeys,
Notwithstanding cabs which my club-footed
Gammy leg nearly made me miss.
No matter. I've better memories
Of this so-called filthy town
Than of a lofty seat of learning*
Where it seems I was meant
To parade my vanity. And should you
Raise eyebrows at what seems this screed's naïvety,
Please remember it was you folk who, when
Ex-cathedra I addressed Manchester's elite,
Saluted in Verlaine the author of *Esther**
While I ploughed on, cloth-eared,
Declaring my huge regard for Will Shakespeare.*

30 January 1894

To Arthur Rimbaud

Mortal angel AND devil—Rimbaud in short.
You deserve pride of place in my book
Even though some stupid hacks thought you a fresh-faced
Monster, drunken schoolboy, a disgrace.

Spirals of incense-smoke and lute notes herald
Your entry into the halls of memory,
And your radiant name will sing in glory
Because you loved me the way love must be.

Les femmes te verront grand jeune homme très fort,
Très beau d'une beauté paysanne et rusée,
Très désirable, d'une indolence qu'osée!

L'histoire t'a sculpté triomphant de la mort
Et jusqu'aux purs excès jouissant de la vie,
Tes pieds blancs posés sur la tête de l'Envie!

A Arthur Rimbaud

Sur un croquis de lui par sa sœur

Toi mort, mort, mort! Mais mort du moins tel que tu veux,
En nègre blanc, en sauvage splendidement
Civilisé, civilisant négligemment...
Ah, mort! Vivant plutôt en moi de mille feux

D'admiration sainte et de souvenirs feux
Mieux que tous les aspects vivants même comment
Grandioses! De mille feux brûlant vraiment
De bonne foi dans l'amour chaste aux fiers aveux.

Poète qui mourus comme tu le voulais,
En dehors de ces Paris-Londres moins que laids,
Je t'admire en ces traits naïfs de ce croquis,

Don précieux à l'ultime postérité
Par une main dont l'art naïf nous est acquis,
Rimbaud! *pax tecum sit, Dominus sit cum te!*

A A. Duvigneaux

Trop fougueux adversaire de l'orthographe phonétique

É coi vréman, bon Duvignô,
Vou zôci dou ke lé zagnô
É meïeur ke le pin con manj,
Vou metr' an ce courou zétranj

Women will see in you a tall and strong young man
With all the countryman's cunning beauty,
Outrageously indolent and so much desired.

History has cast you as the conqueror of death,
Lover of life to pure excess,
Your white feet placed on Envy's head.

To Arthur Rimbaud

(On a sketch made of him by his sister)

You, dead! Dead! But dead at least the way
You wanted: white Negro, splendidly civilized
Savage, civilizing as you went...
Dead? I'd say burning brightly on in me

With holy fires of awe-struck recollection,
Fiercer than the greatest living lights.
A thousand flames burning with the true faith
Of chaste love, ardently declared.

You, the poet who died the way you wished
Far from those awful Paris–London trips.
I'm full of wonder at this portrait's naïve touch,

A precious gift to ultimate posterity,
Done by a hand whose naïve art belongs to us.
The Lord be with you, Rimbaud. Go in peace.

To A. Duvigneaux*

(Fiery opponent of phonetic script and scribes)

A whirr, door to good Duvignô,
Ewe as dough—sigh, Lazar Lamb,
Farce wheater than our deli-bread,
Oo aye, get (yawn!) nick (curse!) inert whist?

Contr (e) ce tâ de brav (e) jan
O fon plus bête ke méchan
Drapan leur linguistic étic
Dan l'ortograf (e) fonétic?

Kel ir (e) donc vou zambala?
Vizavi de cé zoizola
Sufi d'une parol (e) verde.

Et pour leur prouvé sans déba
Kil é dé mo ke n'atin pa
Leur sistem (e), dizon-leur:...

Oo aye, have it in for those ad-men,
Morse stew-pit than Mall-ish—us?
Hoo, air there! Linger, whiz-stick arts!
On there! Fo! Net-ticks, leaves.

Vi, let the bar-studs get two yew?

Oo, any ordealing with ease, jerks,
These slang (ooh!) age-doctors, nothing (ooh!) irks.

This slot, main ever, gets truck off—
But closure rears, and they'll...!!

Bonheur

'La vie est bien sévère'

La vie est bien sévère
A cet homme trop gai:
Plus le vin dans le verre
Pour le sang fatigué,

Plus l'huile dans la lampe
Pour les yeux et la main,
Plus l'envieux qui rampe
Pour l'orgueil surhumain,

Plus l'épouse choisie
Pour vivre et pour mourir,
En qui l'on s'extasie
Pour s'aider à souffrir,

Hélas! et plus les femmes
Pour le cœur et la chair,
Plus la Foi, sel des âmes,
Pour la peur de l'Enfer,

Et ni plus l'Espérance
Pour le ciel mérité
Par toute la souffrance!
Rien! Si! La Charité:

Le pardon des offenses
Comme un déchirement,
L'abandon des vengeances
Comme un délaissement;

Changer au mieux le pire,
A la méchanceté
Déployant son empire
Opposer la bonté;

'Life's harsh'

Life's harsh
For the easy-going man.
No more wine
To fire the jaundiced blood.

Little life left
In flickering eyes, limp hands,
No more rampant envy,
Superhuman pride,

No more spouse chosen
'Til death us do part,
To hide reality
And make life bearable,

Damn it, no more women
For the needs of heart and flesh,
No more Faith, astringency
Of souls confronting Hell.

And no more hope either
Of Heaven
Merited through suffering.
Nothing? Not so: there's Charity.

Trespasses forgiven
Like a tear,
Revenge abandoned
Like a loss.

Change worst to best,
Challenge evil's
Vast empire
With goodness.

Peser, se rendre compte,
Faire la part de tous,
Boire la bonne honte,
Être toujours plus doux...

Quelque chaleur va luire
Pour ce cœur fatigué,
La vie un peu sourire
A cet homme si gai,

Et puisque je pardonne,
Mon Dieu, pardonnez-moi,
Ornant l'âme enfin bonne
D'espérance et de foi.

'Maintenant, au gouffre . . .'

Maintenant, au gouffre du Bonheur!

Mais avant le glorieux naufrage
Il faut faire à cette mer en rage
Quelque sacrifice et quelque honneur.

Jettes-y, dans cette mer terrible,
Ouragan de calme, flot de paix,
Tes songes creux, tes rêves épais,
Et tous les défauts, comme d'un crible,

(Car de gros vices tu n'en as plus.
Quant aux défauts, foule vénielle
Contaminante, ivraie et nielle,
Tu les as tous on ne peut pas plus.)

Jettes-y tes petites colères,
—Garde les grandes pour les cas vrais,—
Les scrupules excessifs après,
—Les extrêmes, que tu les tolères!—

Weigh things up, be aware,
Make allowances for all,
Know the virtues of shame,
Be kinder then kinder...

A glow of warmth
Will wrap this tired heart,
Life will bestow thin smiles
On this easy-going man,

And since I forgive,
Lord, forgive me,
Deck my soul, at last made good,
In hope and faith.

'Now, into the chasm . . .'

Now, into the chasm of Happiness!

But, before the ship goes gloriously
Down, this broiling sea
Needs honour and sacrifice.

Into the terrible sea,
Hurricane of calm, great swell of peace,
Throw your hollow thoughts, your crowded dreams,
Sift through your failings,

(Since you no longer have bad vices.
As for peccadilloes, venial
Poisoners, contamination, blight,
You're riddled with them all up to the hilt.)

Give up your petty fits of pique.
Keep the big ones for emergencies.
Try not to be too delicate.
Put up with extremes.

Jette la moindre velléité
De concupiscence, quelle qu'elle
Soit, femmes ou vin ou gloire, ah, quelle
Qu'elle soit, qu'importe en vérité!

Jette-moi tout ce luxe inutile
Sans soupir, au contraire en chantant,
Jette sans peur, au contraire! étant
Lors délesté d'un luxe inutile.

Jette à l'eau! que légers nous dansions
En route pour l'entonnoir tragique
Que nul atlas ne cite ou n'indique,
Sur la mer des Résignations.

'Rompons! Ce que j'ai dit . . .'

Rompons! Ce que j'ai dit je ne le reprends pas.
Puisque je le pensai c'est donc que c'était vrai.
Je le garderai, jusqu'au jour où je mourrai,
Total, intégral, pur, en dépit des combats

De la rancœur très haute et de l'orgueil très bas.
Mais comme un fier métal qui sort du minerai
De vos nuages à la fin je surgirai,
Je surgis, amitiés d'ennuis et de débats...

Ô pour l'affection toute simple et si douce
Où l'âme se blottit comme en un nid de mousse!
Et fi donc de la sale 'âme parisienne'!

Vive l'esprit français, d'Artois jusqu'en Gascogne,
De la Champagne et de l'Argonne à la Bourgogne
Et vive un cœur, morbleu! dont un cœur se souvienne!

Extinguish every tiny flicker
Of lust for whatever,
Women, drink, fame, etc.,
What does any of it matter?

Abandon pointless luxury
Without regrets—sing indeed
As you do so fearlessly. Jettison
Excess baggage of abundance.

Into the drink! As we near
The tragic brink
Not shown on any map, let's dance
Across the Sea of Resignation.

'Let's end it . . .'

Let's end it. What I said I won't take back.
Since it's what I thought it must be true.
That's how things will stay until I die,
Total pure complete, despite the war

Between high rancour and abject pride.
But like a noble metal which the ore yields
One day I'll detach myself—indeed now—
From murky friendships and arguments...

What I'd give for simple kind affection,
A nest of moss for the soul to hide in.
No more of that awful 'soul of Paris' stuff!

Long live the spirit of France, from Artois to Gascony,
Champagne and Argonne to Burgundy,*
And long live a heart another should remember!

'J'ai dit à l'esprit vain . . .'

J'ai dit à l'esprit vain, à l'ostentation,
L'Ilion de l'orgueil futile, la Sion
De la frivolité sans cœur et sans entrailles,
La citadelle enfin du Faux: 'Croulez, murailles
Ridicules et pis, remparts bêtes et pis,
Contrescarpes, sautez comme autant de tapis
Qu'un valet matinal aux fenêtres secoue,
Fossés que l'eau remplit, concrétez-vous en boue,
Qu'il ne reste plus rien qu'un souvenir banal
De tout votre appareil, et que cet arsenal,
Chics fougueux et froids, mots secs, phrase redondante,
Et cætera, se rende à l'émeute grondante
Des sentiments enfin naturels et réels.'
Ah, j'en suis revenu, des 'dandysmes' 'cruels'
Vrais ou faux, dans la vie (accident ou coutume)
Ou dans l'art ou tout bêtement dans le costume.
Le vêtement de son état avec le moins
De taches et de trous possible, apte aux besoins,
Aux tics, aux chics qu'il faut, le linge, mal terrible
D'empois et d'amidon, le plus fréquent possible,
Et souple et frais autour du corps dispos aussi,
Voilà pour le costume, et quant à l'art, voici:

L'art tout d'abord doit être et paraître sincère
Et clair, absolument: c'est la loi nécessaire
Et dure, n'est-ce pas, les jeunes, mais la loi;
Car le public, non le premier venu, mais moi,
Mais mes pairs et moi, par exemple, vieux complices,
Nous, promoteurs de vos, de nos pauvres malices,
Nous autres qu'au besoin vous sauriez bien chercher,
Le vrai, le seul Public qu'il faille raccrocher,
Le Public, pour user de ce mot ridicule,
Dorénavant il bat en retraite et recule
Devant vos trucs un peu trop niais d'aujourd'hui,
Tordu par le fou rire ou navré par l'ennui.
L'art, mes enfants, c'est d'être absolument soi-même.

'I said to that vain spirit . . .'

I said to that vain spirit, ostentation,
The Ilion* of futile pride, the Zion*
Of feeble and heartless frivolity,
The citadel, in a word, of Falsity:
'Fall, you worse-than-ridiculous
Walls, you preposterous ramparts;
Counterscarps, jump like carpets
Shaken at windows by early-morning
Domestics; ditches, muddy your rising waters,
Let nothing remain beyond flat memories
Of your sparkle, and let that impassioned
Yet icy bag of technical tricks—sarcastic word,
Bombastic phrase, etc.—be split by growling
Rebellions of feeling, true and real at last.'
I'm through with 'cruel' and 'dandy', affected
Or not, a question of habit or chance in life
And in art and (ridiculously) in clothes.
Wear whatever has a minimum of holes
Or stains, suited simply to what you're about,
In your own style. Your shirt, that tyranny of starch,
Should be fresh and soft to the touch.
So much for matters sartorial. Now, Art:

Art first of all must be seen to be sincere
And absolutely clear. It's a harsh
And necessary law, eh, you youngsters,
But it's the law. Because I and my peers,
Not any Tom Dick or Harry,
We're the ones who champion your miserable squibs,
And ours, we're the ones you'd have to turn to,
The one true Public (pardon the word) to win over.
The Public: creased up with laughter or rigid
With boredom, it's abandoning you, thanks to
Those silly games you're over-fond of now. No,
The art, my dears, is to be absolutely yourself.
Whoever loves me should follow me, who follows

Et qui m'aime me suive, et qui me suit qu'il m'aime,
Et si personne n'aime ou ne suit, allons seul
Mais traditionnel et soyons notre aïeul!
Obéissons au sang qui coule dans nos veines
Et qui ne peut broncher en conjectures vaines,
Flux de verve gauloise et flot d'aplomb romain
Avec, puisqu'un peu Franc, de bon limon germain.
Moyennant cette allure et par cette assurance
Il pourra bien germer des artistes en France.
Mais, plus de vos fioritures, bons petits,
Ni de ce pessimisme et ni du cliquetis
De ce ricanement comme d'armes faussées,
Et ni de ce scepticisme en sottes fusées;
Autrement c'est la mort et je vous le prédis
De ma voix de bonhomme, encore un peu, Jadis.
Foin d'un art qui blasphème et fi d'un art qui pose,
Et vive un vers *bien* simple, autrement, c'est la prose.
La Simplicité, —c'est d'ailleurs l'*avis rara*, —
Ô la Simplicité, tout-puissant qui l'aura
Véritable, au service, en outre, de la Vie.
Elle vous rend bon, franc, vous demi-déifie,
Que dis-je? elle vous déifie en Jésus-Christ
Par l'opération du même Saint-Esprit
Et l'humblesse sans nom de son Eucharistie,
Sur les siècles épand l'ordre et la sympathie,
Règne avec la candeur et lutte par la foi,
Mais la foi tout de go, sans peur et sans émoi
Ni de ces grands raffinements des exégètes.

Elle trempe les cœurs, rassérène les têtes,
Enfante la vertu, met en fuite le mal
Et fixerait le monde en son état normal,
N'était la Liberté que Dieu dispense aux âmes
Et dont, le premier homme et nous, nous abusâmes
Jusqu'aux tristes excès où nous nous épuisons
Dans des complexités comme autant de prisons.

Et puis, c'est l'unité désirable et suprême.
On vit simple, comme on naît simple, comme on aime

Should love me, and if no one fits the bill,
I'll go alone, as antiquated as my forebears.
We must obey the call of our blood
Which won't be re-routed down dead-end byways.
Its flow of Gallic verve and Roman steadfastness
Is mixed (Frankish legacy) with good German clay.
Provided this flair, this assurance prevail,
True artists will emerge in France.
But good people, please, no more fancy frills,
No more pessimism, no more metallic sneers,
Bashing like buckled swords,
No more scepticism with its silly jeers.
Otherwise it's death, let me warn you
In my best Old Fogey voice.
No more art which blasphemes or strikes poses.
Long live good and simple art, or else it's prose.
If you truly have simplicity, that rare bird,
You'll be all-powerful,
On the side of life.
It makes you honest, good, a sort of demi-god—
What am I saying? it'll make you live in Christ,
Through the intervention of the Holy Ghost,
The humility of the Eucharist.
It spreads order and fellow-feeling,
Its reign is open, its fight won by faith,
Without fuss, calm and fearless,
Free of obfuscating exegesis.

It fills hearts, calms brains,
Creates virtue, routs evil,
And would keep the world this way
Were it not for the freedom God's given us,
Abused by Adam and ourselves,
Tangling us in labyrinths
Of sad excess.

And it's the unity most to be desired, the best.
You live simply, the way you're born simply

Quand on aime vraiment et fort, et comme on hait
Et comme l'on pardonne, au bout, lorsque l'on est
Purement, nettement simple et l'on meurt de même,
Comme on naît, comme on vit, comme on hait, comme
    on aime!

Car aimer c'est l'Alpha, fils, et c'est l'Oméga
Des simples que le Dieu simple et bon délégua
Pour témoigner de lui sur cette sombre terre
En attendant leur vol calme dans sa lumière.

Oui, d'être absolument soi-même, absolument!
D'être un brave homme épris de vivre, et réclamant
Sa place à toi, juste soleil de tout le monde,
Sans plus se soucier, naïveté profonde!
De ce tiers, l'apparat, que du fracas, ce quart,
Pour le costume, dans la vie et quant à l'art;
Dédaigneux au superlatif de la réclame,
Un digne homme amoureux et frère de la Femme,
Élevant ses enfants pour ici-bas et pour
Leur lot gagné dûment en le meilleur Séjour,
Fervent de la patrie et doux aux misérables,
Fier pourtant, partant, aux refus inexorables
Devant les préjugés et la banalité
Assumant à l'envi ce masque dégoûté
Qui rompt la patience et provoque la claque
Et, pour un peu, ferait défoncer la baraque!
Rude à l'orgueil tout en pitoyant l'orgueilleux,
Mais dur au fat et l'écrasant d'un mot joyeux
S'il juge toutefois qu'il en vaille la peine
Et que sa nullité soit digne de l'aubaine.

Oui, d'être et de mourir loin d'un siècle gourmé
Dans la franchise, ô vivre et mourir enfermé,
Et s'il nous faut, par surcroît, de posthumes socles,
Gloire au poète pur en ces jours de monocles!

And love when you love properly, the way you hate
And finally forgive when you're purely
Soundly simple and die that way too,
The way you're born live hate love!

Love, Alpha and Omega of simplicity,
Delegates of a good simple God,
Down here on this dark Earth as his witness
Pending calm elevation to his light.

Yes, be absolutely yourself, absolutely,
A decent human being in love with life,
Asking you, fair sun of all the world, for leave
To live carefree in profound naïvety!
Some people are neurotic about their lives,
Others about their art.
Archly contemptuous of advertisers' wiles,
Here's a decent man, lover and friend of women,
Raising his children in this world
And preparing them for the next,
Ardently patriotic and kind to fellow-sufferers,
But proud in the face of constant reversals.
A man who, faced with prejudice and mediocrity,
Assumes that perfect mask of disgust
Which tries patience and leads to fisticuffs,
Or even to civil disobedience over nothing at all!
He's tough on pride while pitying the proud,
But he crushes pompous fools
With a choice phrase, if he can be bothered
Or if he thinks his target worth the compliment.

Yes, exist and die well shot of this self-righteous
Puffed-up age, live and die locked up,
And if on top of that we need posthumous pedestals,
Glory to the pure poet in these days of monocles!

'La neige à travers la brume'

La neige à travers la brume
Tombe et tapisse sans bruit
Le chemin creux qui conduit
A l'église où l'on allume
Pour la messe de minuit.

Londres sombre flambe et fume:
Ô la chère qui s'y cuit
Et la boisson qui s'ensuit!
C'est Christmas et sa coutume
De minuit jusqu'à minuit.

Sur la plume et le bitume,
Paris bruit et jouit.
Ripaille et Plaisant Déduit
Sur le bitume et la plume
S'exaspèrent dès minuit.

Le malade en l'amertume
De l'hospice où le poursuit
Un espoir toujours détruit
S'épouvante et se consume
Dans le noir d'un long minuit...

La cloche au son clair d'enclume
Dans la tour fine qui luit,
Loin du péché qui nous nuit,
Nous appelle en grand costume
A la messe de minuit.

'L'amitié! . . .'

L'amitié! Mais entre homme et femme elle est divine
Elle n'empêche rien, aussi bien, des rapports
Nécessaires, et sous les mieux séants dehors
Abrite les secrets aimables qu'on devine.

'Snow in the mist'

Snow in the mist
Spreads silent carpets
Down the path which leads
To the church lit
For midnight mass.

Dark London of flames and smoke,
Good food on the stove,
Drink to follow.
It's Christmas, the custom
Of midnight to midnight.

In its beds and on its streets
Paris has its noisy fun.
Revelry and sweet embrace
In streets and beds rise to peaks
As midnight strikes.

Patients in bleak hospitals
Are racked and thwarted
By false hopes of remission,
Consumed with dread
In midnight's corridor darkness...

The bell's clear anvil strikes
In the lighted slender tower,
Far from sin and its wages,
Calling us in all our finery,
Summoning us to midnight mass.

'Friendship! . . .'

Friendship! Between men and women it's sublime,
And, what's more, impedes none of the requisite
Dealings. Behind the most correct exterior
It harbours lovely secrets we can guess at.

Nous mettrions chacun du nôtre, elle très fine,
Moi plus naïf, et bien réglés en chers efforts,
Lesdits rapports dès lors si joyeux sans remords
Dans la simplesse ovine et la raison bovine.

Si le bonheur était d'ici, ce le serait!
Puis nous nous en irions sans l'ombre d'un regret,
La conscience en paix et de l'espoir plein l'âme,

Comme les bons époux d'il n'y a pas longtemps,
Quand l'un et l'autre d'être heureux étaient contents
Qui vivaient, sans le trop chanter, l'épithalame.

'Vous m'avez demandé . . .'

A Monsieur Borély

Vous m'avez demandé quelques vers sur 'Amour',
Ce mien livre, d'émoi cruel et de détresse,
Déjà loin dans mon Œuvre étrange qui se presse
Et dévale, flot plus amer de jour en jour.

Qu'en dire, sinon: 'Poor Yorick!' ou mieux 'Poor
Lelian!' et pauvre âme à tout faire, faiblesse,
Mollesse par des fois, et caresse et paresse,
Ou tout à coup partie en guerre comme pour

Tout casser d'un passé si pur, si chastement
Ordonné par la beauté des calmes pensées,
Et pour damner tant d'heures en Dieu dépensées.

Puis il revient, mon Œuvre, las d'un tel ahan,
Pénitent, et tombant à genoux, mains dressées...
Priez avec et pour le pauvre Lelian!

It needs our best endeavours; she, more subtle,
I, more naïve; both of us pulling together.
Then, these said dealings would be free of guilt,
Full of joy, simple as sheep, sound as an ox.

If happiness were possible this would be it.
And off we'd go without remorse,
Conscience at peace, souls full of hope

Like married couples of not so long ago,
Happy to be happy,
Singing wedding-songs, pianissimo.

'You asked me for . . .'

To Monsieur Borély*

You asked me for some lines on *Love*,
My collection of verse on pain and distress,
Part of my strange Œuvre's distant past, spilling
Down in wide lagoons of bile.

What to say about it then, except 'Poor Yorick',*
'Poor Lelian',* rather, that general-purpose soul,
Weak sometimes, soft, stroked and doing not a stroke,
Or suddenly up and away, off to wage war

On everything in its pure past life,
Chaste and controlled by calm thought's beauty,
As though damning to Hell all that time spent with God.

Now, tired of this travail, here's the Œuvre again,
On its knees like a penitent, hands clasped...
Say prayers with, and say prayers for that poor Lelian.

'La cathédrale est majestueuse'

La cathédrale est majestueuse
Que j'imagine en pleine campagne
Sur quelque affluent de quelque Meuse
Non loin de l'Océan qu'il regagne,

L'Océan pas vu que je devine
Par l'air chargé de sels et d'arômes.
La croix est d'or dans la nuit divine
D'entre l'envol des tours et des dômes.

Des angélus font aux campaniles
Une couronne d'argent qui chante.
De blancs hiboux, aux longs cris graciles,
Tournent sans fin de sorte charmante.

Des processions jeunes et claires
Vont et viennent de porches sans nombre,
Soie et perles de vivants rosaires,
Rogations pour de chers fruits d'ombre.

Ce n'est pas un rêve ni la vie,
C'est ma belle et ma chaste pensée,
Si vous voulez, ma philosophie,
Ma mort bien mienne ainsi déguisée.

'I imagine'

I imagine
A great cathedral lost in fields
On some tributary of some Meuse*
Near the Ocean which it finds.

I sense
The unseen Ocean and salty air,
A holy night, a cross of gold
Among flights of towers and domes.

The Angelus garlands the bell-towers
With silver song.
White owls turning and wheeling
In charmed air shape their slender calls.

Bright youthful processions
Move in and out of endless porches,
Silk and pearl living rosaries,
Rogations for blessed fruit in need of light.

This is neither dream nor real life.
It's my chaste and naked thought,
My philosophy if you like,
My very own death disguised.

Chansons pour Elle

'Compagne savoureuse . . .'

Compagne savoureuse et bonne
A qui j'ai confié le soin
Définitif de ma personne,
Toi mon dernier, mon seul témoin,
Viens çà, chère, que je te baise,
Que je t'embrasse long et fort,
Mon cœur près de ton cœur bat d'aise
Et d'amour pour jusqu'à la mort:
    Aime-moi,
    Car, sans toi,
    Rien ne puis,
    Rien ne suis.

Je vais gueux comme un rat d'église
Et toi tu n'as que tes dix doigts;
La table n'est pas souvent mise
Dans nos sous-sols et sous nos toits;
Mais jamais notre lit ne chôme,
Toujours joyeux, toujours fêté
Et j'y suis le roi du royaume
De ta gaîté, de ta santé!
    Aime-moi,
    Car, sans toi,
    Rien ne puis,
    Rien ne suis.

Après nos nuits d'amour robuste
Je sors de tes bras mieux trempé,
Ta riche caresse est la juste,
Sans rien de ma chair de trompé,
Ton amour répand la vaillance
Dans tout mon être, comme un vin,

'Delectable companion'

Delectable companion,
Good woman fully in command
Of my person,
My last my only ally,
Come to me that I may kiss you
Long and hard.
My heart beats next to yours
With eternal love and pleasure.
    Love me—
    Without you
    I'm lost
    I don't exist.

Me, poor as a church mouse;
You, offering only the sweat of your brow.
In our basements, under our roofs,
We scarcely ever set a table,
Though our bed's never unemployed
Hung with its garlands of joy.
There, I'm Crown Prince
Of your laughter, your health.
    Love me—
    Without you
    I'm lost
    I don't exist.

After vigorous nights of love
I surface from your arms,
Refreshed. Such caresses!
Not an ounce of my flesh's
Been cheated. Your love makes me
Audacious, like a wine,

Et, seule, tu sais la science
De me gonfler un cœur divin.
   Aime-moi,
   Car, sans toi,
   Rien ne puis,
   Rien ne suis.

Qu'importe ton passé, ma belle,
Et qu'importe, parbleu! le mien:
Je t'aime d'un amour fidèle
Et tu ne m'as fait que du bien.
Unissons dans nos deux misères
Le pardon qu'on nous refusait
Et je t'étreins et tu me serres
Et zut au monde qui jasait!
   Aime-moi,
   Car, sans toi,
   Rien ne puis,
   Rien ne suis.

'Or, malgré ta cruauté'

Or, malgré ta cruauté
Affectée, et l'air très faux
De sale méchanceté
Dont, bête, tu te prévaux,

J'aime ta lasciveté!

Et quoiqu'en dépit de tout
Le trop factice dégoût
Que me dicte ton souris
Qui m'est, à mes dams et coût,

Rouge aux crocs blancs de souris!

Je t'aime comme l'on croit,
Et mon désir fou qui croît,

And only you know the secret
Formulae to fill my heart perfectly.
   Love me—
   Without you
   I'm lost
   I don't exist.

Who gives a fig for your past, my rose,
And who for God's sake thinks of mine?
I love you with courtly fidelity,
You who've done me nothing but good.
Let's add to our joint poverty
The forgiveness withheld from us.
I'll clasp you and you'll clasp me,
And to Hell with all the tittle-tattle.
   Love me—
   Without you
   I'm lost
   I don't exist.

'Now, despite . . .'

Now, despite your put-on cruelty
And that oh-so-very-phoney air
Of nasty wickedness
You stupidly indulge,

I love your lechery,

Despite my contrived
Disgust at your smile
(To die for, hell and damnation!),

Your red smile white with tiny fangs.

I love you blind as faith,
And my desire which grows

Tel un champignon des prés,
S'érige ainsi que le Doigt

D'un Terme là tout exprès.

Donc, malgré ma cruauté
Affectée, et l'air très faux
De pire méchanceté,
Dont, bête, je me prévaux,

Aime ma simplicité.

'Es-tu brune ou blonde?'

Es-tu brune ou blonde?
Sont-ils noirs ou bleus,
Tes yeux?
Je n'en sais rien mais j'aime leur clarté profonde,
Mais j'adore le désordre de tes cheveux.

Es-tu douce ou dure?
Est-il sensible ou moqueur,
Ton cœur?
Je n'en sais rien mais je rends grâce à la nature
D'avoir fait de ton cœur mon maître et mon vainqueur.

Fidèle, infidèle?
Qu'est-ce que ça fait,
Au fait
Puisque toujours dispose à couronner mon zèle
Ta beauté sert de gage à mon plus cher souhait.

'Je ne t'aime pas en toilette'

Je ne t'aime pas en toilette
Et je déteste la voilette,
Qui m'obscurcit tes yeux, mes cieux,

Wild as a mushroom
Is as straight as

An accusing finger.

So, despite my put-on cruelty,
That oh-so-very-phoney air
Of the worst spite
I stupidly indulge,

Love my simplicity.

'Blond or dark-haired . . .'

Blond or dark-haired, which are you?
    Your eyes,
  Are they dark or blue?
I don't know, but I adore their deep lucidity,
I love your hair's disorder.

  Soft or hard, which are you?
    Your heart,
  Is it warm or full of scorn?
I don't know, but I thank nature
For making it my conqueror.

  Are you faithful, yes or no?
    In fact
  Does it matter
Since your beauty, always ready to reward
My passion, is the token of my fondest wish?

'I can't bear you . . .'

I can't bear you all dressed up,
Nor can I stand that hat and veil
Which hide your eyes, my open skies.

Et j'abomine la 'tournure'
Parodie et caricature,
De tels tiens appas somptueux.

Je suis hostile à toute robe
Qui plus ou moins cache et dérobe
Ces charmes, au fond les meilleurs:
Ta gorge, mon plus cher délice,
Tes épaules et la malice
De tes mollets ensorceleurs.

Fi d'une femme trop bien mise!
Je te veux, ma belle, en chemise,
—Voile aimable, obstacle badin,
Nappe d'autel pour l'alme messe,
Drapeau mignard vaincu sans cesse
Matin et soir, soir et matin.

'J'ai rêvé de toi . . .'

J'ai rêvé de toi cette nuit:
Tu te pâmais en mille poses
Et roucoulais des tas de choses...

Et moi, comme on savoure un fruit
Je te baisais à bouche pleine
Un peu partout, mont, val ou plaine.

J'étais d'une élasticité,
D'un ressort vraiment admirable:
Tudieu, quelle haleine et quel râble!

Et toi, chère, de ton côté,
Quel râble, quelle haleine, quelle
Elasticité de gazelle...

And I loathe that 'bustle' thing,
A caricature
Of what your sumptuous glories really are.

I can't abide those frocks and skirts
Which pretty much disguise
Your fundamental charms:
Those unsurpassed delights, my rapture,
Your breasts,
And your shoulders, then the mischief,
The bewitchment of your legs.

To hell with female elegance!
You my joy, I want in a chemise,
Delicious open veil forbidding entry,
Altar-cloth of a reverential cult,
Charming ensign repeatedly rolled up,
First in the morning then again at night.

'I dreamed of you . . .'

I dreamed of you last night.
You were trying pose after pose
In a long sigh of contentment...

My roaming tongue tasted the full,
The succulent fruit you are,
Probing everything.

I was supple as an oiled
Spring, a coil
Unleashed rewound unleashed.

You my love were as live
And light as a gazelle,
Quick and strong...

Au réveil ce fut, dans tes bras,
Mais plus aiguë et plus parfaite,
Exactement la même fête!

'Je fus mystique . . .'

Je fus mystique et je ne le suis plus,
(La femme m'aura repris tout entier)
Non sans garder des respects absolus
Pour l'idéal qu'il fallut renier.

Mais la femme m'a repris tout entier!

J'allais priant le Dieu de mon enfance
(Aujourd'hui c'est toi qui m'as à genoux).
J'étais plein de foi, de blanche espérance,
De charité sainte aux purs feux si doux.

Mais aujourd'hui tu m'as à tes genoux!

La femme, par toi, redevient LE maître,
Un maître tout-puissant et tyrannique,
Mais qu'insidieux! feignant de tout permettre
Pour en arriver à tel but satanique...

Ô le temps béni quand j'étais ce mystique!

When I woke up in your arms,
There were more festivities,
More piquant now and closer to perfection.

'I was a mystic . . .'

I was a mystic for a while. Not now.
Woman's taken vacant possession.
But I've withheld the deeds
Of respect for ideals I've renounced.

But woman's taken vacant possession!

Once I prayed to the God of my youth.
Now it's you who've brought me to my knees.
I was full of faith and snow-white hope
And sweet-glow charity.

But now I'm down there clasping your knees!

Because of you woman's in command again
Issuing tyrannical decrees,
Not seeming to,
A way of doing Satan's work for him...

Ah, those sacred days of mysticism!

Liturgies intimes

A Charles Baudelaire

Je ne t'ai pas connu, je ne t'ai pas aimé,
Je ne te connais point et je t'aime encor moins:
Je me chargerais mal de ton nom diffamé,
Et si j'ai quelque droit d'être entre tes témoins,

C'est que, d'abord, et c'est qu'ailleurs, vers les Pieds joints
D'abord par les clous froids, puis par l'élan pâmé
Des femmes de péché—desquelles ô tant oints,
Tant baisés, chrême fol et baiser affamé!—

Tu tombas, tu prias, comme moi, comme toutes
Les âmes que la faim et la soif sur les routes
Poussaient belles d'espoir au Calvaire touché!

—Calvaire juste et vrai, Calvaire où, donc, ces doutes,
Ci, çà, grimaces, art, pleurent de leurs déroutes.
Hein? mourir simplement, nous, hommes de péché.

To Charles Baudelaire

I never knew you, never loved you.
I don't know you still and love you even less.
Your disreputable name would not sit well
On my shoulders. If I've some rights to be

Your witness, it's because you were prostrate in prayer
Before the Feet held first by cold nails
Then by the fainting rush of sinful women—
Those Feet so much anointed by holy oil,

So kissed by parched mouths—prostrate, like me, like all
Thirsting famished souls made beautiful by hope
As they grope their way towards the dreadful Cross,

The one true Calvary, the Calvary where
Darting doubt, art, grimaces lose their way
And weep. A simple death then, for simple men?

Odes en son honneur

'Et maintenant, aux Fesses!'

Et maintenant, aux Fesses!
Je veux que tu confesses,
Muse, ces miens trésors
Pour quels—et tu t'y fies—
Je donnerais cent vies
Et, riche, tous mes ors
Avec un tas d'encors.

Mais avant la cantate
Que mes âme et prostate
Et mon sang en arrêt
Vont dire à la louange
De son cher Cul que l'ange...
Ô déchu! saluerait,
Puis il l'adorerait,

Posons de lentes lèvres
Sur les délices mièvres
Du dessous des genoux,
Souple papier de Chine,
Fins tendons, ligne fine
Des veines sans nul pouls
Sensible, il est si doux!

Et maintenant, aux Fesses!
Déesses de déesses,
Chair de chair, beau de beau,
Seul beau qui nous pénètre
Avec les seins, peut-être,
D'émoi toujours nouveau
Pulpe dive, alme peau!

'And now, buttocks!'

And now, buttocks!
Muse, I'll have you own to
This treasure
Of treasures, which (oh yes)
I'd give my life a hundred times for,
And all I own
A hundred times again.

But before the cantatas
Which my soul, my prostate
And my stagnant blood
Are going to praise
Her dear Arse with (an arse
Which the fallen angel
Would lovingly salute),

Let slow lips linger
On those delights
The backs of the knee,
Fine-tendoned rice-paper
Vein-traceries
Whose tiny pulse
Eludes.

And now, buttocks!
Greatest goddess of all,
Flesh's nec plus ultra,
The best perhaps (with breasts),
The one beauty that never fails
To take our breath away,
The tissue of life.

Elles sont presque ovales,
Presque rondes. Opales,
Ambres, roses (très peu)
S'y fondent, s'y confondent
En blanc mat que répondent
Les noirs, roses par jeu,
De la raie au milieu.

Déesses de déesses!
Du repos en liesses,
De la calme gaîté,
De malines fossettes
Ainsi que des risettes,
Quelque perversité
Dans que de majesté!...

Et quand l'heure est sonnée
D'unir ma destinée
A son destin fêté,
Je puis aller sans crainte
Et bien tenter l'étreinte
Devers l'autre côté:
Leur concours m'est prêté.

Je me dresse, et je presse,
Et l'une et l'autre fesse
Dans mes heureuses mains.
Toute leur ardeur donne,
Leur vigueur est la bonne
Pour aider aux hymens
Des soirs aux lendemains...

Ce sont les reins ensuite,
Amples, nerveux, qu'invite
L'amour aux seuls élans
Qu'il faille dans ce monde,
C'est le dos gras et monde,
Satin tiède, éclairs blancs,
Ondulements troublants.

They're oval, almost,
Almost round. Opal,
Amber and pink tints
Melt and merge,
Matt white, answered by
The central parting's
Black and playful pink.

Greatest goddess,
Gala of repose,
Calm fun and games,
Artful dimples
Sly as smiles,
Perversity
In majesty...

And when the moment comes
For my luck to reach
Its laughing apogee,
I'll push my luck
Happily round the other side,
With full consent, of course.

Up I get and squeeze
With glad hands
One buttock then the other.
They respond with warmth
And strength, just right
To steer love through night
And into day.

Then, it's the sensitive back's
Broad slopes brought to life
By the one sort of love
This world needs.
The wholesome back,
Warm and satin-white,
Curves and disturbs.

Et c'est enfin la nuque
Qu'il faudrait être eunuque
Pour n'avoir de frissons,
La nuque damnatrice,
Folle dominatrice
Aux frissons polissons
Que nous reconnaissons.

Ô nuque proxénète,
Vaguement déshonnête
Et chaste vaguement,
Frisons, joli symbole
Des voiles de l'Idole
De ce temple charmant,
Frisons chers doublement!

Last, a nape
To make the hair on every neck
Stand up (except a eunuch's),
A nape to suffer Hell for,
Dictating madnesses
To the jellified will,
Thrills we know too well.

Nape with that vague
Dishonesty, that vague
False innocence of the pimp,
Let us tangle,
Lovely symbol of the temple
Idol's veil, worshipped
A hair's breadth away.

Le Livre posthume

Dernier espoir

Il est un arbre au cimetière
Poussant en pleine liberté,
Non planté par un deuil dicté,—
Qui flotte au long d'une humble pierre.

Sur cet arbre, été comme hiver,
Un oiseau vient qui chante clair
Sa chanson tristement fidèle.
Cet arbre et cet oiseau c'est nous:

Toi le souvenir, moi l'absence
Que le temps—qui passe—recense...
Ah, vivre encore à tes genoux!

Ah, vivre encor! Mais quoi, ma belle,
Le néant est mon froid vainqueur...
Du moins, dis, je vis dans ton cœur?

Last hope

In the graveyard a tree
Not there to honour any dead
Grows free
Swaying beside a bare stone wall.

On this tree summer and winter
Alike a bird sings its clear
Sad song of faithfulness.
This tree, this bird, they're us:

You're the memory I'm the absence
Which passing time clocks up... Ah
To be once more before you on my knees!

Live again! But there it is
My angel, I'm beaten by the chill of nothingness.
Tell me, do I live in your heart at least?

Dans les limbes

'Hélas! tu n'es pas vierge . . .'

Hélas! tu n'es pas vierge ni
Moi non plus. Surtout tu n'es pas
La Vierge Marie, et mes pas
Marchent très peu vers l'infini

De Dieu; mais l'infini d'amour,
Et l'amour c'est toi, cher souci,
Ils y courent, surtout d'ici,
Lieu blême où sanglote le jour.

Ils y courent comme des fous,
Saignant de n'être pas ailés,
Puis s'en reviennent désolés
De la porte fermée à tous

Espoirs certains, et résistant
A tels efforts pour t'enfin voir
En plein grand jour par un beau soir
Mué tôt en nuit douce tant!

Ah! Limbes où non baptisés
Du platonisme patient
Vont, pitoyablement criant
Et pleurant, mes désirs brisés.

Décembre 1892

'Alas, you're no virgin'

Alas, you're no virgin,
Me neither. Above all you're no
Virgin Mary and my own feet
Hardly tread the path

To God. But love's
Infinity is you
My dear concern. My steps move
Your way, eager to quit
This sad place of thin light.

My steps run frantically your way,
Bloodied by the rough terrain,
Then return disconsolate,
The door slammed on all

My hopes, fending off
My efforts to see you at last
In a wide evening's glorious light
Changed sweetly into night.

Ah, limbo where my wrecked desires
Roam unconsecrated by
Patient Platonism and cry
Fit to break your heart.

December 1892

'Aux tripes d'un chien pendu'

Aux tripes d'un chien pendu
Tu m'assimiles parfois,
M'engueulant de cette voix
Idoine à ce propos dû.

Tu me dis, robuste et grasse,
Assez souvent, qu'un beau jour
Ce sera si bien mon tour
Que le diable en crierait grâce!

Mon tour d'écoper, car tu
Ne te mouches pas du pied
Pour manier comme il sied
La gifle, et c'est ta vertu

De n'avoir pas peur d'un homme,
Fût-il fort comme un millier,
Et ton geste familier
Tu n'en es pas économe...

Ainsi nous nous disputons
(Tu me disputes du moins),
Prenant les dieux à témoins,
Sacrant, jurant, puis battons

En retraite l'un vers l'autre
Après tel combat fatal,
Distraction d'hôpital,
Bonne fille et bon apôtre.

En retraite, oui, nous battons
L'un vers l'autre et nous baisons
Sur la bouche, et ces façons,
Je les aime encore mieux que des coups de bâtons.

Décembre 1892

'Sometimes you liken me . . .'

Sometimes you liken me to
The gut of a hanged dog,
And berate me in that voice
So perfect for the job.

There you go, you strapping lass,
Telling me that one fine day
My turn will come
And when it does...!

My turn to get it in the neck—
A propos of which, you certainly know
How to dish it out.
Your great strength's

That you're not scared of any man,
Be he as strong as Hercules.
And you're quite the virtuoso
Of the vulgar sign, the filthy gesture...

And so we have our quarrels
(Or rather you have yours),
Effing and blinding
'By God, I swear I'll...', until we beat

Retreats into each other's arms
(Good girl, sweet boy, pure humbug),
Wiped out by almost mortal combat
In our sick-bay sideshow.

Yes, defeated we crash into
Each other's arms, with kissing
On the mouth. I much
Prefer all these things to kicks in the crotch.

December 1892

Épigrammes

'J'admire l'ambition . . .'

J'admire l'ambition du Vers Libre
—Et moi-même que fais-je en ce moment
Que d'essayer d'émouvoir l'équilibre
D'un nombre ayant deux rhythmes seulement?

Il est vrai que je reste dans ce nombre
Et dans la rime, un abus que je sais
Combien il pèse et combien il encombre,
Mais indispensable à notre art français

Autrement muet dans la poésie
Puisque le langage est sourd à l'accent.
Qu'y voulez-vous faire? Et la fantaisie
Ici perd ses droits: rimer est pressant.

Que l'ambition du Vers Libre hante
De jeunes cerveaux épris de hasards!
C'est l'ardeur d'une illusion touchante.
On ne peut que sourire à leurs écarts.

Gais poulains qui vont gambadant sur l'herbe
Avec une sincère gravité!
Leur cas est fou, mais leur âge est superbe.
Gentil vraiment, le Vers Libre tenté!

Au bas d'un croquis

(Siège de Paris)

Paul Verlaine (Félix Régamey *pingebat*)
Muet, inattentif aux choses de la rue,
Digère, cependant qu'au lointain on se bat,
Sa ration de lard et son quart de morue.

'I admire the ambitions . . .'

I admire the ambitions of free verse.
What's this now, if not a real attempt to
Tilt metre's spirit-level which (to mix
My metaphors) only has two forward gears?

All right, I stick too much to form and go
For rhyme as well, a mistake which I know
Weighs heavy and sounds like a hammer-blow,
But quite indispensable to French po—

Etry. Otherwise there'd be no accent
Since French is without iambs and spondees
And dactyls and anapaests. Fantasy's
No good. Therefore rhyme, inevitably.

Well, let the ambitions of free verse crowd
Younger poetic minds obsessed by chance.
They're wide of the mark but their hot-headed
Illusions are touching and make me smile.

These frisky colts go galloping along
Sincere and serious down to their hooves.
They've no leg to stand on except their proud
Youth. Charming really, free verse disallowed.

At the bottom of a sketch

(The Siege of Paris)*

Paul Verlaine (as seen in F. Régamey's painting),
Self-absorbed, oblivious to History's inexorable advance,
Gets, while people below are falling and fainting,
His gastric juices working on a plate of vol-au-vents.

Chair

Assonances galantes II

Là! je l'ai, ta photographie,
Quand t'étais cette galopine
Avec, jà, tes yeux de défi,

Tes petits yeux en trous de vrille,
Avec alors de fiers tétins
Promus en fiers seins aujourd'hui

Sous la longue robe si bien
Qu'on portait vers soixante-seize
Et sous la traîne et tous son train,

On devine bien ton manège
D'alors jà, cuisse alors mignonne,
Ce jourd'huy belle et toujours fraîche;

Hanches ardentes et luronnes,
Croupe et bas-ventre jamais las,
A présent le puissant appât,

Les appas, mûrs mais durs qu'appètent
Ma fressure quand tu es là
Et quand tu n'es pas là, ma tête!

Minuit

Et je t'attends en ce café,
Comme je le fis en tant d'autres,
Comme je le ferais, en outre,
Pour tout le bien que tu me fais.

Assonantal compliments II

There, I've got the photo of you
When you were that slightly loose
Thing with, even then, dare-you-to

Little drill-hole eyes
And what were then defiant
Bee-stings, promoted now to proud breasts

Beneath the long and fetching dress
Such as was worn in seventy-six.
Under its train and what it entails

Your stratagem's pretty plain
To see. It's all thighs. In those days they were
A treat, today they're fresh and splendid still.

Next, lewd inviting hips.
And then, down there, unfathomable
Attractions that still pull

Me down like ageing but still hard magnets
Which, when you're here, my guts
Crave, and when you're not, go to my head.

Midnight

And I wait for you in this café
As I've waited in so many more,
And shall doubtless do again,
For all the good you do me.

Tu sais, parbleu! que cela m'est
Égal aussi bien que possible:
Car, mon cœur, il n'est telles cibles...
Témoin les belles que j'aimais...

Et ce ne m'est plus un lapin
Que tu me poses, sale rosse,
C'est un civet que tu opposes
Vers midi à mes goûts sans frein.

Janvier 1895

Fog!

Pour Mme ***

Ce brouillard de Paris est fade,
On dirait même qu'il est clair
Au prix de cette promenade
Que l'on appelle Leicester Square.

Mais le brouillard de Londres est
Savoureux comme non pas autres;
Je vous le dis, et fermes et
Pires les opinions nôtres!

Pourtant dans ce brouillard hagard
Ce qu'il faut retenir quand même
C'est, en dépit de tout hasard,
Que je l'adore et qu'elle m'aime.

Just in case you're wondering,
I genuinely do not care.
My heart will simply aim elsewhere,
Viz., the pretty things I used to like...

It's one thing, you wretched cow,
To be late... It's damnwell midday now.
You've stood me up and I surmise
You're out to cut me down to size.

January 1895

Fog!

For Madame ***

This Paris fog is thin,
Almost as thin as air,
Compared to that promenade
Known as Leicester Square.*

But the London fog is
(Let me tell you quite
Freely and frankly)
Quite uniquely... tasty.

But in this blood-drained fog
One thing I should clearly see:
Whatever life may throw at us,
I adore her, she loves me.

Invectives

'Une folle entre . . .'

Une folle entre dans ma vie
Et je n'en suis pas étonné.
(À qui voulez-vous qu'on se fie?)
Une folle entre,—quelle envie!

Et pourtant j'avais ordonné
Patience et philosophie
A qui j'étais subordonné
Moyennant sa photographie.

Termes affreux! Rimes? Comment?
Mais n'est-il pas vraiment charmant
D'être à travers ce caractère,

Ce caractère qu'il faudrait
Renfoncer si l'on le voudrait...
Mais cette folle est mon affaire.

12 mai 1893

A la seule

Tu n'es guère qu'une coquine,
Qu'un abominable vaurien
Du sexe ennemi, mais combien
Je t'aime, tu le sais, gredine

Exquise qui me fis quel bien
Et me fais que de mal! J'opine
Pour ta mort... ou la mienne, ou bien
Pour les deux en même temps... Ni ne

'A madwoman . . .'

A madwoman enters my life and
I'm not surprised one little bit.
(All right, so who would *you* trust?)
She enters in a craze of lust,

Although I'd tried to counsel
Patience and wisdom
To this woman beneath whose boot
I lay, all because of a photograph.

Unacceptable terms! Rhymes? What, here, now?
But isn't it really charming
To exist through this character,

This type requiring, as it were,
Indents if desired...
But this madwoman's my affair.

12 May 1893

To the only one

Basically you're what's called loose,
A pretty worthless piece of trash,
A member of the sex we're warring with—
But as you know, whom I adore.

Sweet Jezebel who's done me good
And does me so much harm,
I pass on you the sentence of death...
On me, or why not both at once? Don't

Dis mot, ni surtout ne te tais!
Je bafouille en songes épais
(Ainsi que parlait Sainte-Beuve),

Quand tu n'es pas là je n'y suis
Pas non plus, et ce que je cuis
Dans mon jus! Reviens, ô ma Veuve!

Rêve

Je renonce à la poésie!
Je vais être riche demain.
A d'autres je passe la main:
Qui veut, qui veut m'être un Sosie?

Bel emploi, j'en prends à témoin
Les bonnes heures de balade
Où, rimaillant quelque ballade,
Je passais mes nuits tard et loin.

Sous la lune lucide et claire
Les ponts luisaient insidieux,
L'eau baignait de flots gracieux
Paris gai comme un cimetière.

Je renonce à tout ce bonheur
Et je lègue aux jeunes ma lyre!
Enfants, héritez mon délire,
Moi j'hérite un sac suborneur.

Réveil

Je reviens à la poésie!
La richesse décidément
Ne veut pas de mon dénuement,
Et c'est un triste dénouement.

Say a word, don't stay silent either.
My mind's gone. I'm floundering around
In clouds of dreams (the way Sainte-Beuve* used to).

When you're not here I'm quite at sea.
How I'm stewing in my juice!
Come back to me, my Widow-love!

Dream

I'm giving up poetry!
I'm going to get rich instead.
I'm handing the baton to someone else.
Who'd like to be my double? Roll up!

It's a good trade, honestly.
Witness all those happy hours spent
Drifting round at night,
Putting rhymes together.

'Neath yon moon's bright open eye
The stealthy bridges shone.
The water with its graceful waves
Bathed mournful Paris town.

I renounce this happiness
And leave my lyre to youth.
Children, take my lofty joy—
I've been seduced by loot.

Awakening

I'm coming back to poetry.
The world of riches doesn't want
My penury, so that's that—
Poignant dénouement.

A moi la provende choisie,
L'eau claire et pure et ce pain sec
Quotidien non sans, avec,
Un gent petit air de rebec!

A moi le lit problématique
Aux nuits blanches, aux rêves noirs,
A moi les éternels espoirs
Pavanés des matins aux soirs!

A moi l'éthique et l'esthétique!
Je suis le poète fameux
Rimant des vers pharamineux
A l'ombre d'un quinquet fumeux!

Je suis l'âme par Dieu choisie
Pour charmer mes contemporains
Par tels rares et fins refrains
Chantés à jeun, ô cieux sereins!

Je reviens à la poésie.

Back then to my chosen fare:
Pure, clean water with a daily
Ration of dry bread accompanied
By gentle tunes played on a lute.

I'll know sleepless nights again
In problem beds, and dark dark dreams.
I'll know again eternal hope's
Dawn-to-dusk seductions.

Ethics and aesthetics once more
I'll know. I'm the famous poet
Who magics up amazing rhymes
By the light of a smoky old lamp.

I'm the one chosen by God
To charm the people of my times
With rarefied and fine refrains;
My hunger hymns the peace of heaven.

I'm coming back to poetry.

Biblio-Sonnets

Les Quais

Quais de Paris! Beaux souvenirs! J'étais agile,
J'étais, sinon bien riche, à mon aise, en ces temps...
J'étais jeune et j'avais des goûts très militants,
Tel, un bon iconographobibliophile.

Loin de moi l'orgueil sot de me prétendre habile,
Même alors! Mais c'étaient de précieux instants,
Perdus ou non dans des déboires persistants
Pour les prix... et le reste! Et pas la moindre bile!

La Seine s'allongeait—elle s'allonge encor—
Comme un serpent jaspé de vert, de noir et d'or...
Le vent frémit toujours... L'aimable paysage!...

Mais bouquiner, n'y plus songer! De vils pisteurs
Pour les libraires ont exercé leur ravage,
Et les boîtes ont fait la nique aux amateurs.

By the Seine

Paris down by the Seine—memories! I was
Agile then, not rich, but enough for my needs...
Young and in excessively militant mode,
Like a good iconographobibliophile.

I made no pompous claims for my talent,
Not even then. But those were precious moments,
Lost or not in the dogged disappointments
Of literary prizes etc.—And no rancour!

The Seine stretched out and stretches still,
Like a mottled snake, green black gold,
And the wind still moans... Charming vista!

But, good books? Here? Chez the bookanistes?* Forget it.
The vile piranhas of the trade have done their worst.
The wooden boxes shut out amateurs.

Poèmes divers

A PH . . .

Depuis ces deux semaines
Où j'ai failli mourir,
Ces heures jà lointaines
Qui m'ont tant fait souffrir,

Depuis ce temps, chérie,
Comme d'ailleurs depuis
Si longtemps, je marie
Nos cœurs, mais dès ces nuits

Où tu vis l'agonie
Où j'allais m'enlisant,
Elle semble bénie
A nouveau, l'âme, issant

Du tombeau pour sourire
A ta dive bonté.
Laisse-moi te le dire,
Je t'aime, en vérité,

Comme il me semble, bonne,
Que je n'ai pas aimé...
Reçois la fleur d'automne
Que voici. Parfumé

De peu, le cadeau sombre
Veut être aussi joyeux,
Laisse-m'en suivre l'ombre
Au soleil de tes yeux.

To PH . . .

Those two weeks
When I nearly died,
Those hours long since gone
Which caused me agony,

Since that time, my love,
And as it happens for
Many moons I've married
Our hearts, but since those nights

When you watched me
Drowning in pain,
Suddenly the soul
Seems blessed, issuant

From the tomb to smile
On your great goodness.
Let me say
That, yes, I love you,

Loveable girl, the way
I've never loved before...
Take this
Autumn flower, a light

Fragrance, a dark prize
Scenting happiness too.
Let me trace its shadow
In the sun of your eyes.

[1893]

Épilogue

En manière d'adieux à la poésie 'personnelle'

Ainsi donc, adieu, cher moi-même,
Que d'honnêtes gens ont blâmé,
Les pauvres! d'avoir trop aimé,
Trop flatté (dame, quand on aime!),

Adieu, cher moi, chagrin et joie
Dont j'ai, paraît-il, tant parlé
Qu'on n'en veut plus, que c'est réglé!
Désormais faut que je me noie

Au sein—comment dit-on cela?—
De l'Art Impersonnel, et, digne,
Que j'assume un sang-froid insigne
Pour te chanter, ô Walhalla,

Pour, Bouddha, célébrer tes rites
Et vos coutumes, tous pays!
Et, le mien de pays, ô hiss!
Dire tes torts et tes mérites,

Et dans des drames palpitants,
Parmi des romans synthétiques
Ou bien, alors, analytiques,
M'étendre en tropes embêtants!

Adieu, cher moi-même en retraite,
C'est un peu déjà du tombeau
Qui nous guigne à travers ce beau
Projet vers l'art de seule tête,

Adieu, le Cœur! Il n'en faut plus:
C'est un peu déjà de la terre
Sur la Tête... et son art... austère,
Que ces 'adieux irrésolus'.

Mars 1895

Epilogue

In the 'farewell to first-person poetry' style

So, it's farewell to dear old me,
Vilified by decent and, I dare say, envious
Folk for having loved and flattered much
Too much (but then that's love for you).

Farewell, dear old me, goodbye pain and joy,
On about which, it appears,
I have gone so long no one hears
Any more. So that's that. Now I must drown

In the milk of—what's the phrase?—
Impersonal Art. I must affect
Dignified and lofty sang-froid
To celebrate you, Valhalla,*

Or you, Buddha, and your rites
Or every country's local colour!
My own country? Well, boo and hiss!
I'm supposed to talk of your good

And bad points in exciting plays
Or in the pages of contrived novels,
Wax analytical, turn
Phrase after tedious phrase.

Farewell, evaporating me.
This fine talk of art which has to come
Only from the head smacks a touch of death
Eager to pull the plug on me.

Farewell, redundant Heart!
These 'irresolute goodbyes' suddenly
Sound like spadefuls of earth rattling
On the Head... and its austere art.

March 1895

Aegri somnia

Depuis dix ans, ma jambe gauche,
Tu me jouas combien de tours!
C'en est lassant, cela me fauche,
Cela va-t-il durer toujours?

Si je marche, je me figure
Que je traîne un boulet, forçat
Innocent, mais tu n'en as cure!
—Qui donc voulut que tant pesât

Derrière moi ce membre raide
Et douloureux? le diable ou Dieu?
Est-ce à mes péchés le remède,
L'expiation? Lors, c'est peu.

Ou bien Satan, jamais en faute
Quand il faut ne pas faire bien,
Veut-il tenter, invisible hôte,
Ma patience de chrétien?...

Bah! ce n'est rien. Dieu voit mon zèle
À souffrir en cet aujourd'hui,
Et ma jambe muée en aile,
Moi mort, m'essorera vers Lui.

16 mars 1895

Sites urbains

Prisonnier dans Paris pour beaucoup trop de causes,
Par ces temps chauds, je me console avec les choses
Qui sont à ma portée et ne coûtent pas trop,
Par exemple la rue où j'habite... trop haut,
Et son spectacle primitif, en quelque sorte,
Grâce à la bonhomie évidente qu'apporte
La pauvreté des gens à celle des voisins
Dans les rapports quotidiens qui font cousins.

Feverish dreams

For ten years now, left leg of mine,
You've played your tricks on me.
It tires me out, it knocks me flat.
Must I endure much more of it?

When I walk it feels as if
I'm dragging a ball and chain like a poor
Innocent convict, but what do you care?...
Whose idea was it that this stiff

And painful appendage should drag
So heavy behind me? Satan's
Or God's? Is this the remedy,
The expiation of my sins?

If it's expiation, fine. If it's Satan
(Always one to accentuate
The negative), he's lodged inside me,
Trying my Christian patience hard.

Bah, it's nothing. God knows my thirst for pain.
Once dead, my leg'll turn into a wing,
And then I'll fly straight up to Heaven
On what it was that was my limb.

16 March 1895

Urban sites

Imprisoned in Paris on these dog days
And for many reasons, I take comfort
In things close to hand and none too costly—
The sights in the street where I live
(Too high up), strangely primitive,
Thanks to poor folk's good cheer
Which swells the good cheer of their neighbours
In the daily bonds of brotherhood.

A droite, à gauche, vont s'échevelant des squares
Au vent quand même septembral, et des bagarres
De feuilles en déroute imitent les vols fous
D'oiseaux qui seraient plats et verts aux reflets roux,
S'agitant au-dessus des disputes point graves
D'ouvriers un peu gris, que le vin bleu rend braves
A l'excès, s'il s'agit d'un mot pris de travers.

Moi, je fume ma pipe et compose des vers,
Bonhomme, en jouissant de ces sites bonhomme,
Et quand tombe la nuit, je m'endors vite; et comme
Je rêvasse toujours, je rêve à des vers mieux,
Bien mieux que ceux de tout à l'heure, vers, grands
   Dieux
Pathétiques, profonds, clairs telle l'eau de roche,
Sans rien en eux qui bronche ou seulement qui cloche;
Des vers à faire un jour mon renom sans pareil
—Et dont je ne sais plus un mot à mon réveil...

To left and right, squares straggle
In Septembral winds and squabbles
Of airborne leaves mimic what might be
Flat russet-green birds in crazy flight
Above the trivial disputes
Of death-before-dishonour workmen
Gigantic with cheap wine.

Well disposed, I scribble lines
And smoke my pipe, happy in this fellowship,
And when night comes I quickly fall asleep.
In vague dreams good lines come to me,
Better than the earlier ones. Now they're great gods,
Full of feeling, clear as rock-pools,
Lithe and smooth and undulant,
Lines to make Verlaine the greatest poet yet,
Lines which when I wake I instantly forget.

EXPLANATORY NOTES

Premiers vers

Aspiration

The themes of flight and purity recall Baudelaire, whose hugely influential *Les Fleurs du mal* had first appeared in 1857.

3 *Rückert*: Friedrich Rückert (1788–1866), German poet.

To Don Quixote

This celebration of Cervantes's famous Knight Errant sees him as a hero of poetic inspiration, and not (as is more usual) as an emblem of reason gone hilariously adrift.

The Apollo of Pont-Audemer

Pont-Audemer is a modest Normandy town south of Honfleur. This ironical, yet somewhat tender, sonnet calls to mind certain of Rimbaud's early poems: 'Novel', 'To Music', and especially 'The sleeper in the valley'.

Golden lines

A sonnet about the poet's need to be impassive (like marble, in the last line), a central tenet of Parnassianism, which attracted Verlaine and many poets of his generation during the early and mid-1860s. Parnassianism, whose guiding hand was Leconte de Lisle (1819–94), was a reaction against the excessive subjectivity of Romanticism. It favoured a more disciplined, scientific approach to poetry. Verlaine contributed to *Le Parnasse contemporain*, the three volumes of which appeared in 1866, 1871, and 1876.

Poèmes saturniens

Nevermore

Title taken from Edgar Allan Poe's 'The Raven'. Verlaine used the same title for another poem later in *Poèmes saturniens*. This poem, 'My recurring dream', and 'Anguish' are all taken from the 'Melancholia' section of *Poèmes saturniens*. The section is dedicated to Ernest Boutier, an amateur violinist and writer on art.

My recurring dream

Generally considered one of Verlaine's most successful poems. Verlaine breaks up the rhythm of the alexandrine (twelve-syllable line) to good effect. This technically controlled poem displays some of the nostalgic and, it has to be said, self-centred and self-pitying feelings about women which inform much of Verlaine's poetry.

Anguish

The contempt for Nature is perhaps reminiscent of Baudelaire, arguably the first great poet of the modern city.

Sketch of Paris

The first appearance in Verlaine of the imparisyllabic line (in this case, it is the five syllables of each stanza's second line). Note, too, how Verlaine gives this poem exclusively masculine rhymes, i.e. there is no mute *e* in the rhyming element. This poem and 'Nightmare', 'Marine', and 'Night effect' are all taken from the 'Eaux-fortes' section (Etchings) of *Poèmes saturniens*. The section is dedicated to François Coppée (1842–1908), dramatist and poet of humble life.

17   *Plato*: Greek philosopher (*c*.429–347 BC).

Phidias: Greek sculptor (*c*.496–*c*.431 BC).

Salamis: naval battle (480 BC) in which the Greek confederation defeated the Persians, led by Xerxes.

Marathon: battle (490 BC) in which the Athenians defeated the Persians.

Nightmare

> *That horseman Of German ballads*: the horseman might well be an allusion to the vivid and popular ballad 'Lenore', by the German poet G.-A. Bürger (1747–94). In it, a hussar, on horseback with his fiancée, is reduced to a skeleton as they ride along—the fiancée's punishment for having cursed God.

Night effect

The influence of *Gaspard de la Nuit* by Aloysius Bertrand (1807–41), poet of the medieval and the bizarre, perhaps is felt here. The title of the section of *Poèmes saturniens* from which this poem is taken, 'Eaux-fortes' (Etchings), indicates its links with fine art. Verlaine produces a white-on-black effect, as in etching.

Setting suns

Note the interesting technique of repetition-with-change, a kind of circularity which makes the poem develop while seeming to stay still. Verlaine noted this procedure in Baudelaire, which he defined as 'painting an obsession'. This poem and 'Sentimental walk', 'Classic Walpurgis Night', 'Autumn song', and 'Right time for lovers' are all taken from the 'Paysages tristes' (Sad landscapes) section of *Poèmes saturniens*. The whole section is dedicated to Catulle Mendès (1841–1909), poet, dramatist, and leading light of the Parnassians.

Classic Walpurgis Night

Allusion to *Faust*, the verse tragedy by Goethe. The *Walpurgisnacht* is depicted in both the first part of *Faust* (1808) and the second (1832). Verlaine is alluding to Faust's encounter with characters from ancient mythology.

23 *Lenôtre*: André Lenôtre [Le Nôtre] (1613–1700), architect and designer of some of France's great formal gardens, including Versailles and part of Fontainebleau.

Tannhäuser: music-drama by Richard Wagner. The first Paris production of *Tannhäuser* was in 1861.

25 *Watteau*: Jean-Antoine Watteau (1684–1721), celebrated painter. His depictions of slightly risqué pastoral scenes are the inspiration for many poems by Verlaine.

Raffet: Denis-Auguste-Marie Raffet (1804–60), black and white artist and lithographer.

Autumn song

One of Verlaine's most exquisite and famous poems, of astonishing lightness and delicacy. The shortness of the lines, three and four syllables, the brevity of the poem itself, built on the pathetic fallacy which sees autumnal depression and personal sadness as functions of each other, give an effect of intangibility. Parnassian impassivity has disappeared in favour of naked—if vague—emotion.

Woman and cat

This poem and 'Mr Pomp and Circumstance' are from the 'Caprices' section of *Poèmes saturniens*. The section is dedicated to the obscure poet and critic Henry Winter (dates unknown), a contemporary of Verlaine.

Mr Pomp and Circumstance

The fictitious Joseph Prudhomme was created by Henri Monnier (1805–77), writer and caricaturist. Prudhomme was fat-bellied, bombastic, and self-important, and became part of French popular mythology. This sonnet was the first poem of Verlaine's to appear in print (in *La Revue du progrès moral*, August 1863).

29 *He's the mother . . . Mayor*: freedoms in the translation are intended to accommodate Verlaine's pun 'maire/mère' (mayor/mother).

Savitri

A reference to the *Mahabharata*, the epic Sanskrit poem of India, reputedly the world's longest work of literature (100,000 verse couplets). Written over eight centuries, its earliest portion dates back to the fourth century BC. Vyasa is its supposed author. Verlaine sees Savitri's stoicism as a symbol of Parnassian impassivity.

Marco

Marco is the rapacious courtesan in *Filles de marbre*, a highly successful drama of 1853 by Théodore Barrière and Lambert Thiboust, now largely forgotten.

33 *Of that cruel . . . crime*: Robichez remarks in his notes to the Garnier *Œuvres poétiques* that he cannot understand this line. It is a fair point.

Epilogue

Another poem which seems to reaffirm Parnassian impassivity. It has echoes of Théophile Gautier's views on the workmanlike virtue of craft. The poet as artisan, perhaps, rather than artist. However, it is very possible that this credo of Verlaine's is ironical or insincere.

37 *Egeria*: goddess of fountains, also of childbirth. She had a sacred spring, from which the Vestals took water for their rituals.

Genius: in Roman religion, the spirit which was held to inhabit every individual. Verlaine misspells it.

Erato: one of the nine Muses of literature and the arts, daughter of Zeus and Mnemosyne, and Muse of the lyre.

Gabriel: the Archangel Gabriel, who announced to the Virgin Mary that she would bear Jesus Christ (Luke 1: 26 ff.).

Apollo: in Greek mythology, god of several things, including music, especially the lyre.

39 *Beatrice*: Beatrice Portinari, the young Florentine girl (1266–90) who haunted and inspired Dante, author of the *Divine Comedy*.

Faust: Verlaine is alluding to engravings which show Faust as the thinker and man of science who strikes his infamous bargain with the Devil by which he is granted temporary respite from death in exchange for his soul. Faust fascinated the Romantic generation in particular. See also the note above to 'Classic Walpurgis Night'.

Venus de Milo: the celebrated statue of an armless Venus, discovered in the Aegean island of Milos, and now on permanent display in the Louvre museum, Paris.

Paros: Greek island in the Aegean. Its marble was much used by the ancient Greek sculptors.

Memnon: in Greek mythology, son of Tithonus and Eos, killed at the siege of Troy by Achilles. The tradition grew that a statue in Thebes, and supposedly of Memnon, in reality of King Amenophis, gave out a musical sound when struck by the rays of the morning sun.

Fêtes galantes

On the grass

The influence of paintings by Watteau—pastoral scenes peopled by amorous and somewhat amoral characters some of whom are taken from the Italian *commedia dell'arte*—is felt in this and several other poems in *Fêtes galantes*, including all those chosen for this edition. Verlaine's favoured metre in *Fêtes galantes* is the eight-syllable line, though there is a handful of both shorter and longer patterns.

Weird as puppets

45 *Scaramouche*: figure from Italian *commedia dell'arte*; dressed from head to toe in black.

Pulchinella: also from *commedia dell'arte*; the lively and loud figure who is the origin of Mr Punch.

Boating

Note Verlaine's three-rhyme pattern.

47 *Atys*: name taken from Greek mythology; a beautiful youth who dies young.

Chloris: in Greek mythology, goddess of flowers.

Aglaia: in mythology, one of the three Graces; name conventionally given to a beautiful woman.

To Clymene

47 *Clymene*: in Greek mythology, she was the daughter of Minyas, beloved of the sun.

Songs without words: the title the composer Felix Mendelssohn gave to a series of pieces for solo piano. Verlaine later used the same phrase for what is arguably his finest single collection of poems.

Colombine

Note Verlaine's unusual combination of five-syllable and two-syllable lines.

49 *Colombine*: figure from *commedia dell'arte*; vivacious sweetheart of Harlequin and Pierrot.

Leander: figure from *commedia dell'arte*; the young suitor, eager but slightly ridiculous, and easily duped.

Pierrot: figure from *commedia dell'arte*; pasty-faced, moon-gazing dreamer out of whom has grown the classic sad clown.

Pantaloon: figure from *commedia dell'arte*; the old greybeard, credulous, stupid, and easily duped.

Harlequin: figure from *commedia dell'arte*; buffoon, dressed in diamond-patterned, multi-coloured costume and black mask.

Exchange of feelings

One of relatively few poems in *Fêtes galantes* to use ten-syllable lines, and in rhyming couplets. The subject of the poem might be seen as the ghostly remnants of what once had been gallant, or amorous, romps in the countryside.

Poèmes contemporains des 'Poèmes saturniens' et 'Fêtes galantes'

The burial

Could this be an allusion to the celebrated *Un enterrement à Ornans* (Burial at Ornans), the epoch-making realist painting by Gustave Courbet (1819–77), first exhibited in the 1850–1 Salon? Verlaine originally intended this poem to be included in *Poèmes saturniens*.

La Bonne Chanson

The landscape framed . . .

When written, this poem was remarkable for its description of a landscape as seen from a moving train. Railways were still a recent phenomenon in Verlaine's time, and were not always regarded as a fit subject for poetry.

One long fortnight . . .

A possible model for this poem may be found in Théophile Gautier's *Élégies*, XI.

I'm almost scared . . .

  65 *I love the All . . . you*: Verlaine's final line poses a difficult translation problem: how to render the difference between formal *vous* and familiar *tu*? I have attempted to suggest old *thee* for *tu* by placing *the* at the end of the penultimate line, where the pronunciation of its single vowel, itself followed by another vowel ('all'), will be more voiced than in an interior position.

Schoolgirl

This poem and the next ('On a naïve word from her') are examples of what might be termed Verlaine's sexually semi-explicit art. His most explicit poems are to be found in two collections: *Femmes* (1890) and *Hombres* (1904). Both have been expertly translated into English by Alistair Elliot.

Romances sans paroles

It's languor and ecstasy

  69 *Favart*: Charles-Simon Favart (1710–92), dramatist.

Falling tears . . .

This poem is one of Verlaine's most successful and most anthologized. The often-quoted opening two lines are good examples of pathetic fallacy, of which Verlaine made frequent and skilful use.

  69 *Soft rain . . . Rimbaud*: the line by Arthur Rimbaud (1854–91), sometime companion and lover of Verlaine, has not been found.

  71 *ennui*: the usual English translation of 'boredom' will not quite do. From Baudelaire onwards, 'ennui' meant more spiritual desolation, alienation of sensibility, than passing irritation. I have chosen, therefore, to leave it as 'ennui', here and in other poems. The French word is well understood in English.

You see, we have to be forgiven . . .

The 'couple' in question seems more likely to be Verlaine and Rimbaud than Verlaine and his wife.

The piano kissed . . .

73 *Borel*: Pétrus Borel (1809–59), poet and novelist.

Endless sameness

Note Verlaine's five-syllable line pattern, and the repetition of the first and second stanzas.

Tree-shadows . . .

77 *The nightingale . . . Cyrano de Bergerac*: From the *Œuvres comiques* by the poet Cyrano de Bergerac (1619–55).

Walcourt

This and 'Brussels: simple frescos I', 'II', 'Brussels: wooden horses', and 'Malines' are taken from the 'Paysages belges' (Belgian landscapes) section of *Romances sans paroles*. This section reflects the happiness Verlaine was enjoying in the company of Rimbaud.

Walcourt: a town some 25 kilometres south of Charleroi.

Brussels: simple frescos II

Note Verlaine's consistent use of the five-syllable line.

79 *Royers-Collards*: seemingly an allusion to members of a respected and respectable family, three of whom, in the nineteenth century, variously made glittering careers in politics, law, and medicine.

Brussels: wooden horses

81 *Hugo*: from the *Ballades* by Victor Hugo (1802–85), one of France's most revered poets, novelists, and dramatists.

Cambre woods: woods to the south of Brussels, and a fashionable venue for walkers and strollers.

Malines

83 *Malines*: a town situated roughly halfway between Brussels and Antwerp.

85 *Fénelon*: François de Salignac de la Mothe Fénelon (1651–1715), theologian, archbishop, writer. Verlaine's final line is probably a parody of a phrase in Fénelon's controversial *Télémaque* (1699).

Birds in the night

The subject is the hoped-for reconciliation in Brussels between Verlaine, in thrall to Rimbaud, and Mathilde, in thrall to her mother. The title may symbolize a brief meeting followed by a swift departure.

Green

89 *Take this fruit . . . leaves*: the first line may be a deliberate echo of Shakespeare. In *Hamlet*, one of Ophelia's speeches begins: 'There's rosemary, that's for remembrance; pray, love, remember; and there is pansies, that's for thoughts . . .' (*Hamlet* IV. v).

Spleen

91 *Spleen*: a noun used by Baudelaire for the 'Spleen et idéal' section of *Les Fleurs du mal*. Spleen was one of the four humours of medieval psychology. For Baudelaire, and perhaps for Verlaine, it has more to do with spiritual desolation and less with the physical commotion implied by English *splenetic*.

Streets I

Does Verlaine consider the jig, certainly very popular at the time, as the English dance *par excellence*?

Streets II

93 *A river in the street*: the allusion is no doubt to the Little Venice section of the Regent's Canal, in the Maida Vale area of north London.

Child wife

Title taken from Charles Dickens's *David Copperfield*, and denoting little Dora. The original title was 'The pretty one', echoing a popular song, 'The little pretty one'.

Beams

An enigmatic little poem about an encounter (imagined?) on the cross-Channel ferry with a beautiful female passenger. It has also been interpreted as a veiled allusion to Rimbaud.

Sagesse

Beauty of women . . .

The war of the sexes, in which women are soft and maternal, men coarse and brutal, is one to which Verlaine constantly returns. Note Verlaine's insistent, almost unvarying, pattern of rhymes in the first two stanzas.

Hear the soft . . .

One of Verlaine's best-known poems, which, in a drunken letter to a friend, he dismissed as a *musicaillerie* (neologism, meaning a treacly or hollow sound).

Voice of Pride . . .

This poem has some superficial affinities with Baudelaire's poem 'The Beacons' in *Les Fleurs du mal*.

The enemy . . .

The enemy, of course, is the Devil (cf. Matthew 13: 39). Note Verlaine's use of the imparisyllabic, nine-syllable line.

Peaceful eyes my only wealth

109 *Gaspard Hauser*: Gaspard Hauser, a youth of 15 or 16, was discovered in 1828 wandering the streets of Nuremberg. He knew nothing of his origins, and medical evidence suggested he had been imprisoned throughout all his childhood, and had become a virtual imbecile. He was adopted

and looked after, but an enemy or enemies unknown were after him. Twice he attempted suicide. Finally, he was murdered in Anspach in 1833. For the Romantics, Hauser was a hero of adverse fate.

A great dark sleep

Written, it seems, on the very day (8 August 1873) that Verlaine was sentenced to a two-year prison term, served in Brussels and Mons. Verlaine had planned to publish his poems about his prison life in a book which would have been entitled *Cellulairement*. This never appeared, but seven of the poems written from prison are contained in *Sagesse*. Others appear elsewhere. Verlaine's prose account of prison life is given in his *Mes Prisons*.

The sky above the roof . . .

A celebrated poem, about prison life. The last stanza can be compared to Rimbaud's poem 'Song from the highest tower'.

The sadness, the languor . . .

Note Verlaine's use of the imparisyllabic, eleven-syllable line.

Jadis et Naguère

Pierrot

119 *Pierrot*: see note to 'Colombine'.

Valade: Léon Valade (1841–84), poet.

Kaleidoscope

This poem is a dreamscape, not pinned down to any real city, though elements of Paris and London are here.

119 *Kaleidoscope*: the kaleidoscope, already a popular toy by Verlaine's time, was invented in England in 1815 by Sir David Brewster.

Nouveau: Germain Nouveau (1851–1920), poet.

Ten lines on 1830

This poem reveals the nostalgia felt by some writers of the late nineteenth century for the heyday of Romanticism, which was at its most colourful in 1830, the year of the famous 'Battle of *Hernani*'. When the play of that name, by the leading Romantic dramatist Victor Hugo, opened at the Comédie Française on 25 February, the supporters of Hugo's anti-classical principles fought with the upholders of tradition. The battle has passed into literary legend.

121 *Escorial*: a huge, imposing, and sombre castle to the north-west of Madrid, built by Philip II of Spain. Its construction took twenty-two years (1562–84).

Limping sonnet

The explanation of the title lies in Verlaine's choice of a highly unusual metre, the imparisyllabic, thirteen-syllable line. This in itself constitutes a kind of joke in that it inevitably calls to mind the regularity of the alexandrine, which it appears knowingly to deform. Hence *limping*. Note, too, the irregularity of rhyme in Verlaine's tercets.

123 *Delahaye*: Ernest Delahaye (1853–1930), teacher, friend of Verlaine, who in 1919 published a biography of Verlaine.

The art of poetry

This poem is one of Verlaine's most famous, but too much importance should not be attached to it. Written in 1874, that is, some ten years before the publication of *Jadis et Naguère*, its recommendations for good poetry—musicality, delicacy, nuance—were truly followed by Verlaine perhaps only in his relatively early work. 'The art of poetry' is not the expression of a consistently applied artistic credo.

123 *Morice*: Charles Morice (1861–1919), writer and friend of Verlaine.

Allegory

This poem can be compared to Leconte de Lisle's 'Midi'.

127 *Valadon*: Jules Valadon (1826–1900), painter.

Libellous lines

Note Verlaine's use of the imparisyllabic, eleven-syllable line.

127 *Vignier*: Charles Vignier (1863–1934), journalist and minor poet linked with the Decadent movement, and with one published work to his name: *Centon* (1886).

Lusts

The poem's theme no doubt concerns Verlaine's recent relationship with Rimbaud.

129 *Trézenik*: Léo Trézenik, real name Léon Épinette (1855–1902), poet and member of various eccentric literary movements, such as the Hydropathes (Haters of Water), the Hirsutes (Hairy), the Jeunes (Young), the Zutistes (Cursers), the Jemenfoutistes (Couldn't Give A Damn).

Harvests

129 *Rall*: Georges Rall was the eccentric editor of the short-lived literary review *Lutèce* (to which Verlaine contributed). He was associated with Léo Trézenik.

Languor

131 *Courteline*: Georges Courteline (1858–1929), comic writer and dramatist.

Empire: though the allusion is surely to the Roman Empire, perhaps others too, some of Verlaine's writing was done, of course, during the time of the Second Empire, the years between 1852 and 1870 when France was ruled by Napoleon III.

decadence: Verlaine's name has been linked with the Europe-wide artistic movement known as Decadence, whose occult leanings and taste for a rarefied vocabulary combined with a desire to regenerate art and language with new forms of expression.

Bathyllus: mediocre Latin poet who famously claimed as his own some lines by Virgil, but was unmasked.

Landscape

The poem is supposedly a pastiche of François Coppée.

133 *Saint-Denis*: originally a historic town just to the north of Paris, now an inner suburb of the capital.

   the Siege: reference to the Franco-Prussian War (1870–1). After the French Emperor Napoleon III was captured at Sedan on 2 September 1870, the Prussian army besieged Paris, causing major hardship and even starvation. The siege lasted until January 1871, when the war ended with France's capitulation. Verlaine himself served in the Garde Nationale (National Guard) during the siege.

The Poet and the Muse

133 *the Muse*: a personification of the Paris room (in the rue Campagne-Première) which Verlaine inhabited for a while with Rimbaud.

Crime of love

In a poem about the retribution of God and of society, Verlaine portrays his failed affair with Rimbaud (the 16-year-old bad angel) as loving, sincere, and glorious.

135 *Villiers de l'Isle-Adam*: Le Comte de Villiers de l'Isle-Adam (1840–99), novelist, dramatist, and major figure in Symbolism.

Amour

Written in 1875

Verlaine wrote this affectionate, non-ironical recollection of life in the Mons prison during his period as a French teacher at the Grammar School in Stickney.

143 *Lepelletier*: Edmond Lepelletier (1846–1913) was a close friend of Verlaine from their schooldays together. His biography of Verlaine was first published in 1907.

Bournemouth

This evocation of the English South Coast town was written when Verlaine taught for a short while in one of its schools, St Aloysius' College.

147 *Poictevin*: Francis Poictevin (1854–1904), writer.

A widower speaks

The influence of Tennyson, whom Verlaine was reading during his time in Bournemouth, is possibly felt in this poem.

Adieu

A poem apparently prompted by the remarriage of Mathilde, on 30 October 1886.

Parsifal

155 *Parsifal*: *Parsifal* was the last music-drama by Richard Wagner, and was inspired by the legends of the Holy Grail. It was first staged at Bayreuth in July 1882.

Tellier: Jules Tellier (1863–89), teacher, critic, poet.

And then . . . dome: the poem's last line is used (unchanged and in French) by T. S. Eliot in *The Waste Land*, part III: 'The Fire Sermon'.

Heroic sonnet

Without revealing it explicitly, this sonnet is about a statue of Léon Gambetta (1838–82), distinguished politician and government minister.

The Lucien Létinois poems

These are taken from a cycle of twenty-four poems about a young man Verlaine taught in Rethel, north-eastern France, and whom he 'adopted' as a surrogate son when Létinois was 19 years old, in 1879, until he died (of typhoid) in April 1883. Whether the relationship was ever physical is not certain. But Verlaine was seeking the intensity of emotion he had known with Rimbaud. A similarity has been pointed out between this cycle and Victor Hugo's poems on his daughter Léopoldine.

Lucien Létinois VIII

159 *deadly sin*: probably a peevish allusion to what appears to have been a physical relationship Létinois had with a woman in London in 1879 when Verlaine and he were teachers in England.

Lucien Létinois XVII

163 *This portrait*: the reference is to a portrait of Létinois painted in 1880 by Germain Nouveau, and in which certain of Létinois's characteristics were altered, notably his complexion, the colour of his hair, and the shape of his nose.

Lucien Létinois XVIII

165 *Auteuil*: when Verlaine was working in a school and living in Boulogne-sur-Seine, just to the west of Paris, Létinois would visit him there, taking the train to nearby Auteuil. The two would walk through the Bois de Boulogne, a huge wood and parkland. Létinois's short train journey began at La Chapelle, near the present Gare du Nord.

Batignolles

The subject of this poem is the Verlaine family vault in the Batignolles Cemetery, on the northern outskirts of Paris. Verlaine himself was buried there on 10 January 1896.

Parallélement

Boarders

The second in a sequence of homoerotic poems entitled 'Les Amies', which to an extent are reminiscent of Baudelaire's poems of lesbian love.

To Princess Roukhine

175 *Princess Roukhine*: the Princess in question seems to have been a prostitute called Marie Gambier, with whom Verlaine was involved during early 1886.

Fruit conserve: Verlaine's epigraph misspells *cabellos de ángel*, a Spanish sweetmeat.

Boucher: François Boucher (1703–70), painter and engraver.

177 *Delicious woman ... bed*: Verlaine's first line of the final stanza is a playful echo of the celebrated, obliquely erotic beginning of 'A sa maîtresse', one of the *Odes* by the sixteenth-century poet Pierre de Ronsard, and which runs 'Mignonne, allons voir si la rose'. See also note to 'Up in the air'.

That nightshade pillow: in French, 'sorcier' can mean sorcerer, full of wizardry, or enchanter's nightshade. I have used nightshade, in the hope that this word will encompass all these possibilities within the context of bed and bedroom.

Seguidilla

177 *Seguidilla*: a lively Spanish flamenco dance and the guitar music which accompanies it.

To Mademoiselle ***

181 *The little cattle-lad*: Verlaine is punning on the euphemistic use of 'le petit vacher' to mean penis.

False impression

The title might allude to a certain use of colour favoured by the Impressionist painters, and corresponding to the *méprise* of 'The art of poetry'; or it may indicate that any positive impression Verlaine might have had about imprisonment (the poem was written in the Brussels prison) was exaggerated.

Another

183 *care Flowers*: 'souci', of course, means both care and marigold.

un-Dalilahed Samsons: the biblical story of Samson, betrayed to the Philistines by Dalilah, is told in Judges 16.

Reversibilities

The poem's title had already been used by Baudelaire. The doctrine of revers-
ibility has to do with the dogma of the communion of saints. Verlaine seems to
be saying that prisoners, such as he was, are excluded from the communion of
prayer and grace.

185 *Everything lies in wickedness*: a biblical allusion to 1 John 5: 19.

Tantalized

In Greek mythology, Tantalus suffered the punishment of being set, hungry
and thirsty, in a pool of water which receded whenever he tried to drink, and
under fruit trees whose branches the wind blew out of reach whenever he tried
to pick their fruit.

Incredible but true

187 *Index*: the Catholic Church's list of proscribed books.

    Paul V: this refers to a dedication to Verlaine of a poem written by his
    friend Léon Valade.

In the manner of Paul Verlaine

A self-pastiche of indifferent skill. His styles in *Poèmes saturniens*, *Fêtes
galantes*, and *Sagesse* seem to be the major targets.

Limbo

Title earlier used by Baudelaire.

191 *Psyche II*: the poem opposes two aspects of poetic inspiration: first,
    Psyche I, who is Imagination in the guise of a butterfly; second, Psyche
    II, fast-moving mental agility and wit. In mythology, Psyche was the wife
    of Cupid or Love, and the personification of the soul.

Loins

This appears to be a declaration of Verlaine's homosexuality.

193 *Vouziers*: a small town in the Ardennes, where Verlaine was imprisoned
    for a month in 1885 for having drunkenly threatened his mother with a
    knife.

The last 'Fête galante'

195 *Sodom and Gomorrah*: the biblical story of the destruction of the cities of
    the plain is told in various chapters of Genesis, principally 19.

Guitar

195 *Duchatelet*: in this thinly veiled attack on Mathilde, the Duchatelet figure
    is an allusion to Verlaine's own autobiographical story entitled *Pierre
    Duchatelet*. It concerns a young government employee who serves in the
    National Guard during the Siege of Paris. While he is away on service,
    his wife abandons him. Duchatelet eventually winds up in London,
    where he dies of drink and of 'the idea of a woman'.

These passions . . .

A celebration of homosexuality.

199 *Be it the cup or the mouth or the vase*: the cup and the mouth might be seen as images of passivity, the vase as one of activity.

Footloose and fancy free

This poem is an account of Verlaine's and Rimbaud's great adventure of 1872–3.

> *Footloose and fancy free*: Verlaine is reworking Baudelaire's title 'Moesta et errabunda' (sorrowful and wandering).

205 *my great and radiant sin*: Verlaine's often-quoted description of Rimbaud.

Bad name ballad

205 *Lucullus*: Lucius Licinius Lucullus (*c*.114–57 BC) was a Roman nobleman who acquired great wealth, which he used to indulge his cultured tastes.

Trimalchio: an allusion to the Banquet of Trimalchio episode in Petronius' *Satyricon*. Trimalchio was wealthy and vulgar, the epitome of the nouveau riche, given to ostentatious displays of bad taste, as in the Banquet. But he was essentially a kind, simple, and good-natured man.

207 *Eros*: Greek god of love.

Bacchus: Roman version of Greek Dionysus, god of wine.

Marquis de Sade: the Marquis de Sade (1740–1814), the celebrated writer on sex, evil, pleasure, and pain—sadism—whose works such as *Justine* and *Les 120 jours de Sodome* were banned until relatively recent years.

Sappho ballad

209 *Sappho*: the celebrated Greek lesbian poet Sappho lived probably in the mid-seventh century BC.

Up in the air

211 *Delahaye*: see note to 'Limping sonnet'.

It's so good when you're lying: the adverb *supinément* is a neologism derived from English.

In the sweet post-prandial glow: the noun *aprication* is also a neologism; in English, the very rare *aprication* means *basking in the sun*.

213 *To write like Pindar*: the verb *pindariser* means *to write like Pindar* (521–441 BC), Greek lyric poet, born in Thebes.

Flow like Ronsard: *ronsardiser* is *to write like Ronsard*. Pierre de Ronsard (1524–85), the great Renaissance lyric poet, is closely associated with the region around the Loire river in western France.

Dédicaces

Manchester remembered

217 *Theodore C. London*: Theodore C. London was a young clergyman who was particularly welcoming to Verlaine when the latter addressed an audience in Manchester as part of a lecture tour of England.

Salford: Salford is a city which adjoins Manchester on its north-western side.

Than of a lofty seat of learning: the allusion is to Oxford University, where Verlaine gave a lecture during his tour.

Esther: one the last plays by the great seventeenth-century tragedian Jean Racine (1639–99). It was first performed in 1689.

Shakespeare: the title of Verlaine's paper, given on 1 December 1893, was *Racine et Shakespeare*.

To Arthur Rimbaud (On a sketch . . .)

Rimbaud died on 10 November 1891. His sister Isabelle sent a drawing she had made of him to Verlaine, who immediately wrote this little poem (on 30 January 1893).

To A. Duvigneaux

Given the nature of the phonetic humour in this poem, I have allowed myself considerable freedom in translating it, hoping the better to capture the joke.

219 *Duvigneaux*: it appears that nothing is known of Duvigneaux.

Bonheur

Life's harsh

Note Verlaine's use of the parisyllabic, six-syllable line, a relatively rare length.

Let's end it . . .

227 *Artois . . . Burgundy*: Artois was an old province of north-east France; Gascony, of the south-west; Champagne, of the east; Argonne is a region of the north-east; and Burgundy, an old province towards the south-east.

I said to that vain spirit . . .

This poem is perhaps a parody of the ideas Verlaine had put forward in 'The art of poetry'. Art, he now says, simply, lies in being absolutely oneself (l. 35). This rather untidy poem dwells less on technicalities than on the passion of poetry.

229 *Ilion*: another name for Troy, so-called after its legendary founder Ilus.

Zion: Mount Zion, outside Jerusalem, and by extension the holy city of Jerusalem itself.

Snow in the mist

Note Verlaine's use of the imparisyllabic, seven-syllable line.

You asked me for . . .

237 *Borély*: I have not been able to trace Monsieur Borély.

Poor Yorick: an allusion to the grave-digger scene in *Hamlet* (v. i).

Poor Lelian: 'pauvre Lélian', an anagram of his name, of course, was the title Verlaine gave to a short, critical piece he wrote about himself.

I imagine

239 *Meuse*: major river rising in north-eastern France, continuing through Belgium and Holland, merging with other rivers, and flowing into the North Sea to the south of Rotterdam.

Chansons pour Elle

Delectable companion

The companion of this and most of the poems in *Chansons pour Elle* is Eugénie Krantz.

Liturgies intimes

To Charles Baudelaire

This sonnet is the first poem in *Liturgies intimes*, a slim volume devoted to religious reflection, and first published in 1892. Although Verlaine concedes that there is an affinity between himself and his great predecessor—a troubled involvement in Christianity, a sense of sin—he seeks, perhaps surprisingly, to distance himself from Baudelaire, whose influence he had acknowledged in an article written in 1865. This poem originally was intended, more appropriately, for *Dédicaces*.

Odes en son honneur

And now, buttocks! . . .

The tenth poem (out of nineteen) of the *Odes en son honneur*, a collection of verse, sometimes erotic, whose subject principally is Philomène Boudin, one of the two women—the other was Eugénie Krantz—with whom Verlaine shared his last years.

Le Livre posthume

Last hope

The last poem in *Le Livre posthume*, although the first of that collection to have been written. Verlaine composed them in 1893, during one of his frequent sojourns in the Hôpital Broussais, in the 14th *arrondissement* of Paris.

Dans les limbes

Alas, you're no virgin

Taken from the short collection *Dans les limbes*, published in 1894 but conceived some time earlier, in the Broussais hospital. The limbo is the hospital itself, made bearable by the regular visits of Philomène Boudin. By 1893, Verlaine was quite seriously ill, and was dividing his time between squalid lodgings, hotels, and hospitals in Paris, a pattern which continued right up to his death.

Épigrammes

I admire the ambitions . . .

Taken from *Épigrammes* (1894), a collection of ironical and playfully parodic poems. Verlaine distances himself in this poem from free verse, whose newfound liberties were tempting a number of poets of his generation. For Verlaine, free verse was wrong to ignore the true strengths of established French prosody. Much of the best of Verlaine's early verse, typified by the short, imparisyllabic line, exemplifies a partial freedom of form, which has come to be known as *vers libéré* (liberated verse).

At the bottom of a sketch (The Siege of Paris)

The sketch in question is an ink drawing of Verlaine by the artist Félix Régamey (1844–1907), in which he depicts a semi-recumbent Verlaine in the Café du Gaz, rue de Rivoli. To preserve the epigrammatic wit, I have taken some liberties in the translation.

265 *Siege of Paris*: see note to 'Landscape'.

Chair

Assonantal compliments II

Taken from *Chair*, the first of Verlaine's collections to be published posthumously. Written in late 1893, 1894, and 1895, the poems in it are for Philomène Boudin, Eugénie Krantz, and perhaps others too. The main interest of this poem about Eugénie Krantz is that Verlaine eschews full rhyme in favour of assonance, something I have sought to mirror in the translation.

Fog!

269 *Leicester Square*: then a large, airy space in the heart of London; now a major shopping and entertainments centre.

Invectives

A madwoman . . .

Published posthumously in *Invectives*, an assortment of poems which date back to various stages of Verlaine's career, and which lash out in all directions at all kinds of target. This poem is about Eugénie Krantz.

To the only one

273 *Sainte-Beuve*: Charles Augustin Sainte-Beuve (1804–69), poet, novelist of debatable worth, but notable and influential literary critic. Also prominent political figure of the mid-nineteenth century.

Biblio-Sonnets

By the Seine

Taken from the collection *Biblio-Sonnets*, which was not published until 1913. The theme of the collection—the love of books—had been suggested to Verlaine in 1895 by Pierre Dauze, the editor of the *Revue biblio-iconographique*.

277 *bookanistes*: the famous Paris *bouquinistes* (second-hand booksellers) which line the Seine near the Île de la Cité, displaying their merchandise in rows of stalls and large wooden boxes along the riverside walls. Rather than lose the allusion to the *bouquinistes*, I have borrowed the neologism which the English writer Will Self created in his short story *Between the Conceits*.

Poèmes divers

To PH . . .

Written in the summer of 1893. Obviously, PH is Philomène Boudin.

Epilogue: in the 'farewell to first-person poetry' style

The farewell seems addressed not only to personal and confessional poetry (in favour of a more Parnassian kind), but also to life itself.

281 *Valhalla*: In Norse mythology, the celestial hall where the souls of slain heroes were taken by the Valkyries, and where they spent eternity in joy and feasting.

Feverish dreams

In Latin, the title means *dreams caused by sickness*. In the last years of his life, Verlaine suffered from an ever-worsening infectious erysipelas of the left leg.

INDEX OF TITLES

INDEX OF FIRST LINES

American Literature

British and Irish Literature

Children's Literature

Classics and Ancient Literature

Colonial Literature

Eastern Literature

European Literature

Gothic Literature

History

Medieval Literature

Oxford English Drama

Poetry

Philosophy

Politics

Religion

The Oxford Shakespeare

A complete list of Oxford World's Classics, including Authors in Context, Oxford English Drama, and the Oxford Shakespeare, is available in the UK from the Marketing Services Department, Oxford University Press, Great Clarendon Street, Oxford OX2 6DP, or visit the website at www.oup.com/uk/worldsclassics.

In the USA, visit www.oup.com/us/owc for a complete title list.

Oxford World's Classics are available from all good bookshops. In case of difficulty, customers in the UK should contact Oxford University Press Bookshop, 116 High Street, Oxford OX1 4BR.

SERGEI AKSAKOV	A Russian Gentleman
ANTON CHEKHOV	Early Stories
	Five Plays
	The Princess and Other Stories
	The Russian Master and Other Stories
	The Steppe and Other Stories
	Twelve Plays
	Ward Number Six and Other Stories
	A Woman's Kingdom and Other Stories
FYODOR DOSTOEVSKY	An Accidental Family
	Crime and Punishment
	Devils
	A Gentle Creature and Other Stories
	The Idiot
	The Karamazov Brothers
	Memoirs from the House of the Dead
	Notes from the Underground and The Gambler
NIKOLAI GOGOL	Village Evenings Near Dikanka and Mirgorod
	Plays and Petersburg
ALEXANDER HERZEN	Childhood, Youth, and Exile
MIKHAIL LERMONTOV	A Hero of our Time
ALEXANDER PUSHKIN	Eugene Onegin
	The Queen of Spades and Other Stories
LEO TOLSTOY	Anna Karenina
	The Kreutzer Sonata and Other Stories
	The Raid and Other Stories
	Resurrection
	War and Peace
IVAN TURGENEV	Fathers and Sons
	First Love and Other Stories
	A Month in the Country